ARMY EDUCATION CENTER
HQ 26TH GEN SPT GP
BLDG:

FAMILIES RUSH TO GREET THE RETURNING 513TH (Carl Pierce Photo)

513th Home From War

FULL CIRCLE

A North End Man's Odyssey
to Vietnam and Back

Ralph Masciulli

Trafford rev. 04/14/2023

Trafford
PUBLISHING®   www.trafford.com
North America & international
toll-free: 844-688-6899 (USA & Canada)
fax: 812 355 4082

Ó lá go lá, mo thuras,
an bealach fada romham.
Ó oíche go hoíche, mo thuras,
na scéalta nach mbeidh a choích.

From day to day, my journey,
The long pilgrimage before me.
From night to night, my journey,
The stories that will never be again.

-Author unknown

Dedication

To my wonderful wife Mary who faithfully wrote to me every day during my tour of duty in Vietnam, and to my boys, David and Michael, for tolerating my idiosyncrasies over the years.

Acknowledgments

A special thanks to my good friend Dennis DiGangi for his editing skills and attention to detail: and many thanks to Gerry Kaufman for his technical assistance, and to Carol Kaufman for her patience, tolerance and assistance in putting it all together, I can only say,

Grazie Tanto

Introduction

This is the story of one man's journey from one end of the world to the other. It's a journey that begins in the coldwater tenements of the North End of Boston, leapfrogs to the foothills of Phu Bai in Vietnam and comes full circle to the immured tenements of the North End.

Author Ralph Masciulli grew up in a close-knit, historical section of Boston. It was a close-knit neighborhood because it was comprised primarily of people of Italian extraction in the early part of the century. It was a milieu where everyone knew one another, everyone cooked Italian, and everyone spoke Italian. It is historical because two landmarks grace its landscape–the Old North Church from where the "One, if by land, and two, if by sea" signal lanterns were hung to warn of the British march from Boston on April 18, 1775, and the house in which Paul Revere lived a short distance away in North Square.

For the first two centuries Boston was home to the fashionable and elite Brahmins who were first to establish roots in the North End. Some of their mansions still grace the Boston landscape. After the Revolution there were changes that reshaped the North End. The Brahmins moved out to points south and west leaving behind a settlement in which the Irish were able to settle after the potato famine of 1842. The potato crop failure led to a great influx of Irish immigrants who set sail for anywhere–and landed in Boston. Many came from humble beginnings and established roots in the North End taking up residence in the homes vacated by the Brahmins. They worked menial jobs to gain upward mobility and their children enrolled in local schools. As they prospered they moved north to Charlestown and south to South Boston or Southie as it is called, allowing a new generation of immigrants–the Italians–to settle in the North End after the Civil War.

As the Italians moved in, the North End took on significant changes. The Jews were the last remaining group to exit leaving the North End comprised of residents primarily of Italian extraction. They brought their culture to the North End and made significant contributions to society in the field of education, science, politics, art, music, theater, and entertainment to mention a few. They used their entrepreneurial expertise to open businesses to provide services. Here is where Ralph Masciulli grew up: sampling his mother's meatballs and gravy before the usual Sunday pasta dinner, and then meeting in Coogie's coffee shop for the usual morning discourse with friends and the honing of his intellectual skills. He demonstrates his Italian ethos and lifestyle throughout the book: where he "hung out," the camaraderie he shared with his North End buddies and the servicemen in Vietnam who came from other parts of the country–and from diverse cultures.

The author draws on his intellectual acumen and Italian upbringing to deliver a journey that took him full circle–from the "caverns" of the North End to war-torn Vietnam and back.

This is Ralph Masciulli's story–one that delivers a unique account of his childhood, his upbringing and the activities he shared with his North End buddies; one that traces his activities and those of other servicemen in a heated war zone; one that truly comes full circle.

Dennis DiGangi
April 26, 2004

Contents

Preface

When I was a young boy I played the accordion. On Sundays my extended family would converge on a picnic area called Captain's Pond in southern New Hampshire for our summer outings. It was a beautiful place with a beach-front that gradually descended into the pond making it ideal for swimming. Leading to the beach was a plush grassy knoll where we set up our picnic site. Above the knoll was a parking area where Uncle Tom and Uncle Sam unloaded their cars and we would all help carry our belongings down by the beach. It was like the invasion of Normandy. We paid 25 cents a car to get in and most of the time we were the only ones there. We always had a wonderful time. Mom was crafty! She would always sneak the accordion for me to play and, when it seemed I was having the most fun with my cousins, she would take the accordion out of its case, lined in red velvet resembling a coffin, and would call, " Oh Ralph! Where's my Ralphie? I brought the accordion so he can play Santa Lucia for us." Obligingly, I would sit under the oak tree and play. No one seemed to pay much attention until I hit a discord, then everyone groaned and Mom would smile and say, "He needs a little more practice." No matter how hard I tried I always had the feeling I was trying to express myself through the accordion, but what I had to say wasn't coming out as it should. In junior high school I put the accordion away and like most normal young men entering adulthood I pursued other interests.

Turning forty, I dusted off my accordion, took it out of its red velvet case, and resumed lessons at Tosi's Music Store in the North End of Boston. Mom still loved to hear me play Santa Lucia and always encouraged me to practice. She still thought I had a future as an accordionist and had this vision of me playing on the Lawrence Welk program. When my two boys, ages four and six, were being pains, as punishment, I would sit them on the floor in front of me while I practiced. I can still see them sitting on the floor with their hands covering their ears jokingly saying, "Dad, please no more. No more. Enough! Enough!" Although I tried my hardest, what I was trying to express through my music still didn't come out. This was apparent when I heard my teacher Lou Bregoli play at Lombardo's in East Boston or when I listened to Lawrence Welk or Myron Florens and I would get sick at how they could make the accordion "talk." As my sons grew older they questioned my wanting to excel at the accordion and when they asked, "Dad why do you take accordion lessons?" I would simply smile and say, "Someday the accordion is coming back and, if I practice, I'm going to be ready." For lack of time to practice, I finally put the accordion away, knowing I would never play at the level I would like.

Now, my boys are grown and have left the nest. Mom and all of my 24 aunts and uncles have passed on and my 32 first cousins are spread far and wide. Rarely do I see them. This gives me more time, so occasionally I take my accordion out of its red velvet case, pour myself a glass of wine and play Santa Lucia. When I make a mistake I smile for it has a whole new meaning. I now find it much easier to laugh at the discords and find other ways to express myself.

Whenever my relatives were around they always made me feel good. I was happy in my own world and thought it would never change. But everything in life changes and with it we are forced to change. The 60s reflected this change and the Vietnam War with its stories and experiences was a catalyst for change. The experiences the men of the 513th Maintenance Battalion, an army reserve Unit out of Boston, incurred as a result of its activation and subsequent tour of duty in Vietnam is such a story. If there were any winners in Vietnam, I guess we were winners. With the exception of our first sergeant, who was medevaced, we supposedly all came home intact. We weathered fairly well with one other wounded and two attempted suicides. Of course, there was Packy Hughes who was exempt because of a family hardship, and unfortunately met with his own misfortune. During our tour we sustained twenty-six hits, two direct hits[1]. We were a support unit and although many had it much worse than us, many had it much better. Seeing the men come in from the field, with the infamous "thousand mile stare" or visiting one of the remote fire bases, always reminded me of how fortunate we were and yet, in contrast, being in Saigon was supposedly better duty. We were in Phu Bai, ten miles south of the Old Imperial Capital, Hue, not far from the Demilitarized Zone (DMZ). But we were a low priority army reserve unit and Vietnam wasn't supposed to happen. Neither was it supposed to happen for so many less fortunate. Every May 13th some of the men of the unit meet for a day of golf and a few brews and, of course, to exchange old stories.

This is a simple story that emphasizes the apprehension of going to war and the associated fear of the unknown recounted through the eyes of an idealistic individual who grew up in the North End of Boston. At one time I thought everyone was Italian and Catholic as those in Charlestown or Southie may have thought everyone was Irish and Catholic. In high school when the daily Irish invasion from Southie, Charlestown and Dorchester came to the North End to attend Christopher Columbus (CC) High School, I slowly became more understanding of other ethnic groups and began to see the good in all.

This story could easily be told through the eyes of any of the 256 members of the 513th Maintenance Battalion who left a little bit of their idealism in Phu Bai and moved on with their lives. Nonetheless, it's a story that should be told.

Chapter 1

Before the Reserves

One minute it was warm and sunny and the next it appeared we were in for a sneak winter storm. Living in Boston all my life, I should be accustomed to New England weather but I wasn't. It was May 13, but it didn't feel like May. It felt more like one of those March days when the wind is blowing making it feel cold even in the sun. It didn't know whether it should be spring or winter. As I looked out the window from my classroom, I saw two huge trash barrels rolling down Berkeley Street whipping up a dust storm as they rolled along. The heating system in Franklin Institute, where I was professor and chairman of the electronic and computer departments, was always turned off on May 1 to save on expenses. For no apparent reason, today I was feeling down. I rarely took any time off; however, today I decided to leave school early and go home.

Usually, when I arrive home, I work in the yard to unwind before dinner. I thought it was strange that I had a liking for yard work because growing up in the North End we didn't have any grass or trees to contend with. However, in true Italian tradition, we always had a couple of tomato plants on the roof. As a young boy it was my job to carry the soil up four flights of stairs to the roof for Dad. One time Dad had six tomato plants and in the process of helping him, I was being silly and managed to step on all six; only one was salvageable. Dad was so mad that he actually threw his shovel at me. I was grateful he missed. That year I gave Mom a plant for Mother's Day and three extra tomato plants for Dad. It turned out to be a banner year for roof-grown tomatoes.

Arriving home tired, I decided to retreat to my favorite easy chair in my bedroom and watch television. I tuned in one channel and the evacuation of the U.S. Embassy in Saigon caught my eye. I got a glimpse of those Vietnamese hanging onto that helicopter as it left the roof of the embassy. It was one of those moments in time, similar to when the planes crashed into the World Trade Center or the Japanese bombing Pearl Harbor. Two events that will always stay in my mind. Most of us have watched these scenes hundreds of times, and will always marvel at the dormant emotions they evoke. I changed the channel and the Tet Offensive was in full view. "What's this?" I thought. "Can't they leave it alone?" Then I remembered it had been more than twenty-five years since the fall of Saigon and more than thirty years since the Kent State debacle. In the recesses of my psyche I associated these events with something I wanted to forget. But how can one possibly forget? Like many of us, I tuck negative thoughts away in my mind because I want to forget. However, like a thief in the night, they unexpectedly have a way of sneaking up on me when I least expect it. Seeing these images made me retreat to my favorite place, a comfortable leather chair molded from many years of use. In the corner of my bedroom, this simple chair provided sanctuary, my special place where I felt safe. I sat in my easy chair and thought of the late sixties—a time when nothing was etched in stone. As a generation, we questioned the fabric of our nation. It was a time when the peace and civil rights movements were gearing up for what was

Photo © John Filo

coming. Columbia University was under siege by student protestors and every major university from Berkeley to Cambridge was involved in student uprisings. At Kent State National Guardsmen, bearing arms, shot into a crowd of student protesters killing four students and wounding many others. There was much controversy about the use of excessive force to quiet unrest at home.

In Southeast Asia things were also a mess. For many of us who graduated from high school in the late fifties and early sixties, we were the last remnants of the WW II era. Many of our parents had participated in WW II and for the preceding twenty years most of us truly lived through happy years. In the North End we certainly did, and I'm sure this was characteristic of other ethnic neighborhoods of Boston. The country focused on moving ahead both technically and socially and it was a great time to be in one's late teens. People in America felt good about themselves. The future was promising.

The transition from the fifties to the sixties was more than a transition of a few years. Considering the societal changes, it just as easily could have been one hundred years. It was a transition from the old to a new way of expressing ourselves. The civil rights and black power movements were in high gear. Feminism was coming into its own. Minority groups, springing up all over the country, wanted a level playing field to accommodate the disadvantaged and handicapped. The groundwork was being laid for special needs students to be main-streamed into regular classes resulting in subsequent legislation. It was a time of many counter-cultural, economic and artistic movements resulting in a way of thinking in which reasoning, understanding and compassion were the way to peace rather than force, violence and might. Through all of this emerged the unending conflict of the times between the hawks and the doves. Essentially, the hawks wanted us to escalate the Vietnam conflict and blow the hell out of North Vietnam; and the doves wanted us to pull out and come home. As I relaxed in my easy chair, my thoughts drifted back to a Sunday morning in 1966.

I was lying in bed half asleep when the aroma of meatballs simmering in spaghetti sauce awakened my senses. It was Sunday, and like many other Italian families in the North End, Mom was making sauce for the traditional Sunday afternoon dinner of pasta, ziti or rigatoni, with meatballs, broccioli and pork in the gravy followed by salad and dessert. Of course, there was always homemade wine from the cellar of Tony Di Pietro on North Bennet Street. My bed was along the wall adjacent to the kitchen. With my ear against the wall, I carefully listened and was always aware of what was going on in the family. To prevent the smell of food from getting in the bedrooms, Mom closed the doors when she cooked. Nevertheless, with my bed against the wall and the stove on the other side, the aroma penetrated the wall and always found its way in my direction. It didn't seem to bother me half as much as it did Mom, especially when she cooked fish. The smell lingered for days. I always enjoyed having my room close to all the action. However, now I was older with a decent occupation and in need of more privacy. It was difficult living in a small apartment with a large extended family. We always had a lot of company.

Meatballs were always my weakness. The aroma was overwhelming. I couldn't resist anymore. I quickly jumped out of bed in my shorts and tee shirt, and as Mom was taking the meatballs out of the frying pan and putting them in the sauce, I walked into the kitchen. My timing was perfect. Then, as she had done for the previous twenty-five years, she took two meatballs, placed them delicately on a small plate and covered them with the most delicious sauce in the world. She then placed two pieces of scali bread at the edge of the plate, making sure they didn't touch the sauce. As far back as I can remember we had this nonverbal communication manifesting itself in her performing this simple ritual whenever she made spaghetti sauce with meatballs. I sat at the kitchen table and savored every morsel. I had finished two meatballs and two pieces of scali bread when Mom asked, "You want another?" Easily, I could have sampled two more when I noticed the time. It was already 10:45 a.m.

"No thanks, Mom. They're great but it's late. You know I usually meet the guys on Sunday mornings in Coogie's at 10:30 a.m. and already I'm late." I quickly made myself presentable and as I left the apartment to descend the three flights of stairs to Hanover Street she yelled, "Don't forget dinner is at 2:00 o'clock sharp. Your sister and Aunt Marie are coming for dinner. Don't be late."

"Okay, okay," I responded, not knowing whether she heard me or not.

After several years of uncertainty and indecision, everything was finally beginning to fall into place. I had found the transition from high school to college extremely difficult. College was foreign to me. Like many North Enders of my generation, I was more comfortable in St. Anthony's playground than on a college campus. I never felt comfortable with the college crowd but realized I had to move forward. It took six years to get my degree. An electrical engineer by profession, my position was deemed critical to the defense initiative. As a result, every six months I was granted a critical industry deferment. Mary E. Lent, Director of the Draft Board in Boston, continuously checked on all eligible draftees. With trepidation, I would report to the draft board every six months with documentation from my employer in hand and I would have to defend my position as critical to the war effort. If I were fortunate, I would get deferred for another six months. As the Vietnam Conflict escalated, deferments were reduced to three-month periods. At the time I was traveling extensively and as a Technical Representative (Tech Rep), my travels brought me to several naval bases in the Far East. Once on assignment in Japan, I spent time at the Youkuska Naval Base, the departure point for many leaving for Vietnam. Everyone was talking about Vietnam and what it was like and what to expect. Some were anxious to go and were determined to get there and "kick ass" and others were simply petrified at the thought of being in a combat zone. On occasion, when out on the town in Japan with some of the GIs scheduled to leave for Vietnam, even the brave of heart would show their anxiety after a few "pops."

No matter how they tried to conceal it under their macho image their anxiety would eventually surface and manifest itself in verbal debate about Vietnam, sometimes even resulting in a barroom brawl. Then there were those who were drafted and at the mercy of Uncle Sam. One particular individual, a graduate of Dartmouth Law School and with whom I spent time in Tokyo, received his draft notice as soon as he finished law school. After he was drafted, Uncle Sam put him where he was needed. He was a grunt (infantry)—what a waste! All that time, effort and money to get through school to trudge through the rice paddies of South Vietnam. Perhaps a position in the Judge Advocate General (JAG) would have been more appropriate.

During the late 60s, stories like this were common in the military. Second lieutenants, point men, forward observers and helicopter gunners were military occupational specialties (MOSs) to avoid. They always had the highest casualty rates. No one was sacred, except of course the politically connected, those who fled to Canada, those who faked an illness and those who could afford to stay in college on the extended degree program—they were golden. The less fortunate who felt an obligation when called had no other alternative but to go. The high level of anxiety about the Vietnam Conflict was always present. No matter what, I always seemed to be around people or with people who were going to Vietnam.

In his postwar memoirs, "If I Die in a Combat Zone," Tim O' Brien assesses his dilemma when he tells us, "Like many men of draft age finishing college, I was worried about the draft. I had conflicting feelings about entering the military. I was convinced then as I am now convinced that the war was wrong. And since it was wrong and people were dying as a result of it, it was evil. Bad as the alternatives were—seeking exile abroad or resisting the draft at home and risking imprisonment—these clear and plausible options might be far more courageous and moral than to participate in a war that was evil?"

Like many of us, his doubts were fueled by a sense of obligation to his family, town and country. He had a happy and comfortable childhood and he felt he owed something to his country. He lived under its laws, accepted its education, eaten its food … and wallowed in its luxuries. He resented the form of service demanded of him and was incensed by the country's lethargic acceptance of the war and feared the consequences of resistance.[2]

Sunday mornings, Coogie's was always crowded. Coogie was close to eighty and his cronies would come around every Sunday for coffee and anisette. Most of them were from the province of Avellino, Italy. In one corner we had those with a high regard for Benito Mussolini, the leader of the fascists. In the opposing corner we had the followers of Garibaldi, the leader of the red shirts. This was the older generation and woe betide anyone who would dare discredit Mussolini. How can we forget! He made the trains run on time! Then we had some from the WW II and Korea generations, many of whom we identified with and looked up to, such as parents and uncles who made significant contributions during WW II. As I entered the doorway to Coogie's, I could hear Charlie yelling. Charlie always yelled. Maybe it's because his father George always yelled. His surname being Coppola, which means hat in Italian, his father was called "Georgie hats" and Charlie was appropriately called "Charlie hats." You could hear Charlie yelling halfway down Salem Street. "If you think I'm going halfway around the world to get my ass shot off in some damn rice paddy, you're soft! I'll go to Canada first." It didn't take much to get Charlie going, but today he was exceptionally wound up.

As kids, whenever we did anything, Charlie was always the mastermind. While hanging out on the corner of Salem and Sheafe Streets, where Marlen's Drug Store used to be, Charlie would always point at the drug store and say, "Right here! Right here! Some day I'm going to demolish this building and build a one-family ranch right

7

here." We would simply laugh and respond, "Okay, Charlie, don't forget to invite us over for dinner when it's finished."

I thought his ambition a bit odd but nonetheless a noble one for a teenager that made perfect sense at the time. Charlie boy always had everything under control. He always had a solution to all problems. He was omniscient. He was the schemer of schemers—the instigator, the wheeler-dealer "il magnifico." If there were a valid test to measure street smarts, Charlie would score off the Richter scale. At a party, if a guest was inept at social skills and one wanted to include that person in the group, all one had to do was introduce that person to Charlie. Not only would he give the guest his life history nonstop, he would also give the history of the North End and all its residents—and he would be very amusing with every detail. He knew it all—everything and everyone in the North End. He would often tell the same stories over and over and over again and we were always amused. He was especially good at entertaining the old ladies. Charlie had a heart of gold and an ego the size of the Grand Canyon. He always had a good deal for me. I can still hear him saying, "Hey, Ralphie! Come here. I have a good deal for you." As kids we always teased him about his good deals, for more often than not they resulted in disaster, even though he sincerely believed he was doing us a favor. Unfortunately, sometimes his good deeds had serious consequences. Like the time we were standing on the corner of North Bennet and Wiget Streets. Both streets are very narrow. If a car were not parked just right, that is, tucked in at the right angle to both streets when parked, making the corner onto Wiget Street could only be negotiated by one with expert driving experience in the narrow streets of the North End.

One hot summer evening we were hanging around when an attractive blond was having difficulty negotiating the turn. We couldn't help but notice her long slender legs because she was wearing a very short miniskirt. Then they started.

"Hey lady! Cut your wheels. Cut them to the right! That's right, to the right!" bellowed Johnnie.

"No! No! No! The other way! The other way!" yelled Vinny.

"Watch out! Watch out! You're going to hit the pole. Straighten them out," bellowed Emo. Charlie approached the young lady in a manner reminiscent of Errol Flynn—swordsman extraordinaire. He opened the door on the driver's side and leaned into the car and in a most seductive manner, as though he didn't want anyone to hear what he was saying whispered, "Slide over, lady, and give me the wheel!"

She was amazed by his overwhelming confidence. To her dismay, she readily complied. Charlie cut the wheels. Suddenly, his foot slipped off the brake and onto the gas pedal. The car jumped the curb and went into the lamppost putting a hole in the radiator. Fortunately no one got hurt.

"Hey Charlie! Good play. Keep up the good work," we immediately responded. Today Charlie was all wound up about Vietnam. He was taking on the WW I and the WW II generations. He continued, "Does anyone know why we're there and what we're doing there? Don't tell me it's to fight communism because that's bullshit. Those people don't give a damn about communism or democracy. All they want is what we want, a small piece of turf. They want to live in peace and grow some rice.

We, the benevolent Americans who can do no harm, have to impose our life style on them. Sure, they go along with us because whatever the final outcome, it has to be better than what they've been accustomed to since the beginning of time. Tell me, where are all the draft age sons of our patriotic leaders? I'll tell you where they are. They're hiding in some position that their wealthy connections secured for them. Probably deemed critical to the war effort. Either that or they're hiding in some Ivy League college that daddy serves on the board. Tell me who's fooling whom? Now they expect us to go halfway around the world to clean up this imbroglio. Tell them to go, I'll stay right here."

Joe who had spent time in the South Pacific during WW II commented, "If we don't stop them in Vietnam, they'll be at our doorstep."

Charlie quickly responded, "The propaganda campaign is working because that's exactly what they want the average American to think. As long as we continue to think that way, they'll keep shipping us home in body bags and all in the name of defending our country. Come on guys, let's rally round the flag boys. What a joke. It makes me want to barf. Why don't you talk to some of those guys who have been there? Yea, they're all screwed-up when they come home, but they tell it like it is. You name it, the black market, the lack of leadership, the preposterous rules of engagement. Can you imagine not firing unless they fire first, and if you kill someone and later find out that person had no weapon, you face a court martial? Can you imagine getting in a street fight and telling your opponent, I won't hit you unless you hit me first? You'd be dead. In WW II and Korea we knew where the line was drawn. In Vietnam there is no line. The rules are different each day. We should avoid it legally just like all the high "mucka, mucks" do. Morally we shouldn't be there. It's harder for guys like us because we're at the bottom of the totem pole."

To a degree Charlie made sense, and somewhat I agreed with him but, typical of his Italian heritage, he lost the substance of his message in his emotions. Finally he turned to me and asked, "What do you think? Would you go if you're called?" I didn't want to get dragged into a discussion that wasn't going anywhere. I deflected the question by answering, "I like to think we have enough street smarts to find a legal way to avoid what I consider a black mark on American history."

10

The conversation continued and as in most discussions, it escalated to a level that lacked common sense. It was well into the argumentative stage. Everyone was yelling at the same time and no one was listening. This is typical of Italians, especially when discussing an emotional issue. But then, in Coogie's, all issues were emotional. When the discussion got down to the level of personal attacks, I decided it was time to leave. It's amazing how much competitiveness can come out in individuals even in the silliest of conversations.

It was still early when I left. Leaving the smoke-filled coffee shop, the air felt good on my face, so I decided to take a walk down Salem Street to Cross Street and returned by Hanover Street all the while thinking about what was said in Coogie's. What would I do if I were asked to serve? Would I go? Violence never solved any problem and only in defense of one's self did I approve of violence. From what I read, this Vietnam War was different. It was total bullshit!

Chapter 2

Joining the 513th Maintenance Battalion

Each evening, with increasing anxiety, I watched the news on television only to become more concerned about being drafted. Like the "sword" of Damocles dangling by a single hair, the draft was a blade hanging over my head. I couldn't get on with my life. Just out of college, I wanted to make my way in the world. I was restricted to a position with limited travel to keep my pulse on the happenings in Vietnam. Even with limited travel, thinking of the resulting confusion if my deferment were rescinded while I was away, caused me to feel despondent. I had to find myself a more secure position in order to get on with my life. Sweating the draft every six months was no way to live. When I lived in the North End, I thought everyone ate lasagna and escarole soup with little meatballs at Thanksgiving. Growing up I thought everyone was Roman Catholic and Italian or at least wanted to be. I wanted no part of this conflict. I enjoyed the sense of security that came with being parochial. Suddenly, I felt as though I was being thrust into the chaos of the 60s and there was absolutely nothing I could do about it. I was helpless.

Whenever I returned home from one of my business trips, I visited the North End. One afternoon, while walking up Salem Street I recognized the familiar gait of the person in front of me. It was Charlie. "Hey Charlie! What's up?" I yelled. He responded. "Where're you going? Come on, take a ride with me, I won't be long. I'm on my way to the Hull Street garage to get my car. I'm going to the induction center at the South Boston Army Base to check out a newly formed Army reserve unit, the 513th Maintenance Battalion."

I decided to accompany him. We were both concerned about the Vietnam conflict and getting drafted certainly wasn't in the realm of things. Besides, the more I read about Vietnam, the more convinced I was about its futility. We picked up the car at the garage and drove to the army base. We parked on Summer Street and from there we walked to the guard house to ask for directions. We didn't know where we were going, but the guard told us to follow the people in front of us for they were going to the same place. We walked past some very old buildings that appeared ready for demolition. Finally, we arrived at Annex B and climbed three flights of stairs to this huge hall with about two hundred people all interested in joining the newly formed 513th Maintenance Battalion. It was then that I learned a little more about this newly formed unit.

The 513th Maintenance Battalion was a spin-off of the 245th from Roslindale. Approximately half of the members of the 245th were transferred to the 513th. Many were pleased with their new assignments because new units were placed at the bottom of the totem pole. We were classified as a low priority unit. High priority units had an increased number of drills per week in anticipation of being activated. They were referred to as being on stepped-up reserve forces (SRF).

It would take a low priority unit a very long time to prepare for an overseas tour of duty or so we thought. Who knows? By this time the conflict could be over. Since there were approximately 256 men in the battalion, this meant there were only 106 available slots since 150 slots were already taken. At the rate people were joining, it appeared all the slots would be filled by the end of the day. I can still remember Charlie's exact words, "Come on! It's a good deal. We can't lose. We'll join together."

After much deliberation, we decided to join the reserves together. We would go away for six months, and attend weekly reserve meetings.

This sounded like "snug harbor!" After speaking with some members of the 245th who were pleased to get into a low priority unit, we were convinced that the reserves were better than the regular army. Charlie and I filled out the necessary paperwork and were sworn in pending a physical exam, a mere formality for we were both in excellent health. All indications pointed to it being a good deal. As Charlie said, "We can't lose."

The next week we reported for our physicals. The Medical Unit was swarming with draftees, most of whom looked impoverished. The individual in front of me held his court papers. His hair was long and greasy and his jeans were covered with grease. He had on a tattered tee shirt with the inscription on the back that read, "Born to Raise Hell" which he openly flaunted inciting the judge to give him a choice: six months up the river or the army. At the time he was not much older than many of the students I had in my classes. Most of the inductees were from the inner city. I didn't see many preppies, which made me think about the whole process. It was scary.

> From 1964 to 1973, from the Gulf of Tonkin resolution to the final withdrawal of U. S. troops from Vietnam, 27 million men became of draft age. Sixty percent were not drafted due to college, professional, medical or National Guard deferments. Forty percent were drafted and saw military service. A small minority, 2.5 million men (about 10 percent of those eligible for the draft) were sent to Vietnam.[3]

> This small minority was almost entirely working class or rural youth. The average age was 19. Eighty-five percent of the troops were enlisted men; fifteen percent were officers. The enlisted men were drawn from 80 percent of the armed forces with a high school education or less. At the time, a college education was universal in the middle classes and making strong inroads in the better off sections of the

working class. Yet in 1965-1966, college graduates were only 2 percent of the hundreds of thousands of draftees.[4]

In the elite colleges, the class discrepancy was even more glaring. The upper class did none of the fighting. Of the 1,200 Harvard graduates in 1970, only 2 went to Vietnam, while working class high schools routinely sent 20 to 30 percent of their graduates and even more to Vietnam.[5]

When college deferments expired, joining the National Guard or Army Reserves was a favorite way of getting out of serving in Vietnam. During the war 80 percent of the Guard members described themselves as joining to avoid the draft. You needed connections to get in which was no problem for Dan Quayle, George W. Bush and other ruling-class draft evaders. In 1968 the Guard had a waiting list of more than 100,000. It had triple the percentage of college graduates than the army did. Blacks made up less than 1.5 percent of the National Guard. In Mississippi blacks were 42 percent of the population, but only one black man served in a guard of more than 10,000.[6]

Charlie's last name and my last name began with letters from opposite ends of the alphabet, resulting in us being separated and brought into different examining rooms. Draftees were doing whatever they could to flunk the physical. One particular individual decided he was going to submit his fiancee's urine in place of his because she had sugar diabetes, which would disqualify him. When the medic came out of the lab and called, "Henry Jones? Henry Jones? Is there a Henry Jones here?"

Henry Jones excitedly jumped up and bellowed, "That's me! That's me!"

The medic repeated, "Henry Jones. Are you sure you're Henry Jones?"

"Yes! Yes! I'm sure I'm Henry Jones." He pulled out his wallet and said, "See, here's my ID card."

The medic laughed and said out loud for everyone to hear, "Well, Henry Jones, I've got news for you—you're pregnant." The room broke out in laughter. Although everyone laughed—and there is a certain amount of humor in such situations I could not help but feel sympathetic for Henry Jones knowing that he'd been drafted and now his fiancee was pregnant.

After passing my physical I waited downstairs for Charlie. About an hour passed when Charlie finally came running down the platform at the rear of the army base.

"Guess what? Guess what?" Before I could respond he yelled, "I flunked the physical! I flunked my physical!"

Ironically, my good friend Charlie flunked the physical and I passed. The ride back to the North End left me with a bittersweet feeling. I was glad for Charlie, but I was sort of upset that I would be going it alone. As we parted on Hanover Street that spring morning, I sensed it would be awhile before I saw Charlie again. Since high school our lives were drifting apart and now with this latest development we were destined to drift even further apart. Up till now I was happy in my own cocoon. Nothing in my background had prepared me for what lay ahead.

Chapter 3

Reserve Meetings

Once I was sworn in, I attended reserve meetings every Tuesday evening and one weekend per month. These meetings were boring and uneventful. As a new unit and my being a newcomer in the unit, I attributed this to growing pains. However, it was imperative that we be on time for all meetings and in attendance for the 7:00 p.m. roll call. Once we checked in we would disperse and find a place to hide or nap until 10:00 p.m. dismissal. Many of us would go out to eat or hang out at the local bar until it was time for the final formation. At 10:00 p.m. we would all mysteriously reappear out of nowhere ready to answer the final roll call and head home. However, there were always a few missing.

One particular meeting during final roll call, the first sergeant summoned PFC Thompson, "Where is Thompson? I know he was here earlier." A barely audible voice coming from the center of formation whispered, "He's sacked out in locker number 32 Sarge." The first sergeant responded, "Who said that? Who said that?" After no response, the first sergeant ordered, "Open locker number 32." We opened wall locker number 32, and to our amazement there he was sleeping like a baby in a standing position with his head propped up to the right on a makeshift pillow. Unfortunately we had to wake him.

Missing more than two meetings without justifiable cause could result in being activated. It was important to attend all reserve meetings and to be on time. On weekend drills we checked in at 8:00 a.m. and hid until lunch. After lunch we would hide until 4:00 p.m. and reappear for final formation. Some even went home and came back. Sundays were a little better. We attended Mass in the morning, which took up a fair amount of time. After Mass we hid until lunch and then hid again until the final 4:00 p.m. roll call. On occasion, we would receive training for fear that some day we might need it. Some of the older sergeants attempted to involve us in training activities. Usually it was poorly organized and not functional.

My first weekend on bivouac we left the South Boston Army Base by convoy at 6:00 a.m. destined for Ft. Devens in Ayer, Massachusetts. There were three sections to our convoy: the advanced party which left first; the second and larger of the three groups, the main convoy, left at the regularly scheduled departure time; and the Battalion Commander's mini convoy which left last. At best, Ft. Devens is a couple of hours from Boston. When the Battalion Commander arrived at Ft. Devens, the rest of the Battalion was nowhere to be found. After several hours of waiting the state police were summoned to search for the convoy. It seemed the advanced party broke down on Route 2 and were waiting for the Army wreckers to tow them back to Boston. At the same time the regular convoy got its orders messed up and were halfway to Camp Drum in Watertown, New York before it realized it should be going to Ft. Devens in Ayer, Massachusetts. It was Sunday before the entire unit reassembled; just about time to pack up and go back to Boston. Unfortunately, most of our reserve training escapades were usually poorly organized and were truly a waste of time. Many of the men would take reading material or office work and sneak off to a remote area to do personal work. As long as we played the game and gave them no trouble, we could remain anonymous. Subsequently, we learned we always looked great on paper.

Every summer our unit would spend two weeks training at Camp Drum in Watertown, New York. Our new unit went there twice before it was activated. At the risk of offending the many good people who live in Watertown, the best description I can give of it is "depressing."

It takes eight hours to get to that God-forsaken place and when one finally arrives, there is nothing there but Alexandria Bay. Just at the height of depression in the middle of two weeks of training we would get a two-day pass to Alexandria Bay. Each weekend thousands of reservists would converge on Alexandria Bay as though it provided the rite of entry into manhood. Everyone looked the same. We all had the same haircuts, shaved around the ears, and with an army cap on our heads, our hair appeared shortly cropped, conforming to army regulations.

I was always amazed at how fast the "sleaze factor" developed around military installations. We would call these little towns where one could buy everything and anything, and catch anything and everything, "Boomtowns." Such a place was Alexandria Bay.

You may ask, "What in the world is there to do in Alexandria Bay?"

"Absolutely nothing," I would have to answer. We would walk the streets, thousands of reservists, looking at each other and eventually winding up in some sleazy overpriced bar drinking cheap warm, draft beer and playing pool. Eventually we would drink ourselves to sleep and find an overpriced third-rate motel in which to sack out. It was then that I first experienced the ability of many GIs to consume enormous amounts of alcoholic beverages. At the time drugs were just arriving on the scene and were not as prevalent as alcohol. The beer brewed for consumption in the military contained 3.2% alcohol, instead of 5% alcohol. The only good scenario was the bond developing within the unit. This bond would further develop as time went on. I wish I could say Alexandria Bay improved the experience, but unfortunately, it made it worse. This was the highlight of our summer camp experience.

After my first two weeks of summer training, I received orders to report to Fort Jackson, South Carolina, for basic training. I packed and went home to pick up an official copy of my orders and left on a troop train from South Station. It was August 22, and it was extremely hot. The trip down to Fort Jackson took twenty-five hours. I had a sleeper car in which I refused to sleep because of the disgusting condition of the mattress and lack of ventilation in our compartment. I tried covering the mattress but still felt very uncomfortable. I knew some type of infestation was happily nesting therein. I thought it best to let them be and not join them.

When the train pulled into Ft. Jackson, South Carolina, the Ft. Jackson Army band greeted us with "The Stars and Stripes Forever." Filing off the train we saw a lean, impeccably dressed, first sergeant who stood on the platform bellowing out orders.

It was close to ninety-five degrees. I looked closely at his shirt and couldn't see any perspiration stains on his neatly starched shirt. He stood erect, wearing a chrome helmet and reflective sunglasses. The glare of the sun from his helmet was blinding and from a distance he appeared cool despite the ninety-five degree temperature.

He then yelled to the guy on my left, "You, get that butt out of your mouth and put it in your pocket. To the guy on my right he bellowed, "Take that hat off and fall in over here." He had an order for every individual as they stepped off the train. While standing in formation I looked in front of me and about fifty feet ahead I saw ten neatly arranged garbage barrels behind the mess hall, five to the left of two swinging rear doors and five to the right. The five barrels to the left had edible written across the front and the five to the right had non-edible written on them. It took a few minutes before this city boy realized that all edible garbage would be sent off to the pig farmers and was not for human consumption.

The training at Ft. Jackson, although rigorous and intense, was meaningful. It gave me a lot of personal satisfaction to get back into shape and hopefully to stay that way. We trained with many who were destined for Vietnam. Our drill instructors were aware that many would go off to war so the training was purposely more intense than normal. When I left basic, I was proud of the shape I was in and felt good about the skills I had acquired. After basic training I was off to Aberdeen Proving Grounds in Maryland for advanced individual training as a Field Artillery Repairman, MOS 45C20. Here we learned the intricacies of the 105mm and the 155mm howitzers. I received good training at Aberdeen and left there lean, fit and confident in what I learned. When I returned to my reserve unit, I hoped it would be different. Many of the men now trained, I anticipated we would function as a unit. Unfortunately, it was worse than ever.

For the next two years I never saw a howitzer, never qualified on the rifle range or fired any weapon, never received any training with flares, mines, booby traps, M79 grenade launchers or crew served weapons in spite of the Quarterly Reports and Annual Unit History specifying we were trained in these areas.

Chapter 4

Summer Camp

I first met Butch while we were at Camp Drum. He was the other field artillery repairman in our unit with whom I soon became acquainted. We always seemed to share the same pup tent together. As part of Army issue each one of us received a shelter half with either snaps or buttons. To set up a tent one had to join the buttons and snaps together. If your shelter half had buttons, the object of the game was to bunk down with someone who had snaps and visa-versa. When we arrived on location we would empty our duffle bag and lay out our equipment. Then the fun would begin. We would search for the soul mate with a compatible shelter half. If there were not an even number of halves then some slept under the stars and hoped for a dry evening. No less than three times during my military experience did I have the unique pleasure of sharing quarters with Butch. Each occasion was a test of patience, tolerance, and above all, self-control. The virtues of humility and brotherly love, which the Franciscans so diligently tried to instill in me in grade school and high school, now took on added meaning. Until now, I always took a certain amount of pride in getting along with difficult people, but Butch was the ultimate challenge. It was as though the idiosyncrasy I disliked most was purposely set upon me so I could grow spiritually. Either that or the devil purposely put Butch in my path so I could choke him to death, which, on two occasions, almost came to fruition. Butch was an absolute slob.

The second year we went back to Camp Drum for summer training again I had the pleasure of tenting with Butch. It seemed that he always gravitated in my direction. At first, I was reluctant to say no at the risk of offending him. But then it became expected that I share my tent with him. This time he came running up to me with his half a tent in hand. He thought it would be a good idea if we bunked together since we had the same Military Occupational Speciality (MOS). After all he had the snaps and I had the buttons, how could I refuse? This time I wasn't as patient with him as I had been the first time and found it more difficult to be understanding of his habits. He was a decent person but our life-styles were very different. I kept telling myself that almost anything was tolerable for two or three nights at a time. Anything longer became increasingly testy. Pup tents are very small by design; therefore, it's important to be neat and organized at the risk of living in damp and dirty quarters for the duration of the field exercise, which could last up to a week. Let's take army boots for example. Army boots have a tendency to accumulate mud in the corrugated soles. If one enters the tent with boots on, then the tent, sleeping bags and duffle bags will be covered with mud. Sleeping with boots on made everything filthy. I was always concerned about a reasonable semblance of order and Butch could have cared less. Each time I spent one or two nights with him; this was bearable. However, it was when we went back to Aberdeen Proving Grounds for a crash course on howitzer repair, before we went to Vietnam, that things got worse. We spent three weeks supposedly coming up to speed on the 105mm and 155mm howitzers. It wasn't until we spent three weeks together and shared the same room that I got the full flavor of my soul mate.

We were both assigned to the 4th Enlisted Men's Training Center (4th ETC). The barracks were hot and stuffy. It was mid-July and Butch was up to his old tricks. Maybe it was the heat of the summer and the room was unbearably hot. Perhaps because the class was full, making it difficult to get any hands-on experience. Half the time we didn't attend classes; we were never on the roster and never got called on the carpet for absenteeism. Maybe it was because we were auditing the course and the instructor didn't give a shit and teased us, referring to us as the reservists who got screwed. I suppose it was mostly because this was another charade and we knew we were going to Vietnam and were concerned. Whatever the reason, we got on each other's nerves. Butch's dirty clothes were all over the room. He had left a partially consumed ham sandwich to the right of his footlocker for two days. It was difficult to sleep because of the heat and Butch would lie in bed, covered with two heavy wool army blankets in ninety-five degree temperatures, reading hot rod magazines while simulating the sound of his favorite hot rod. Periodically, he would blurt out something extremely profound such as, "Hey look at this V-8 with overhead cams and dual exhaust able to go from 0 to 60 in 6.9 seconds. Broom, brooom, brooom." This scenario would play itself out night after night. However, little did I know I was developing a level of tolerance that would later prove beneficial. After three weeks of his bullshit, one day in desperation, I took a piece of duct tape and ran it down the center of the room. I then collected all his belongings including half eaten apples; banana peels, and rotten ham sandwich and several empty coke bottles and placed them on his side of the room. I politely informed him that if he so much as stepped across the tape or placed anything on my side of the room, I would beat the shit out of him.

Chapter 5

Greetings from Uncle Sam

Two years after I had been through basic training, I was teaching in a technical school. I found teaching to be more rewarding than working in industry. It was my first year teaching and I was convinced education would be my life ambition. I liked what I was doing. My life seemed to be focused for the first time in a long time.

It was Friday, May 13, 1968, a day the men of the 513th Maintenance Battalion will never forget. I was in front of a high school class on this warm spring afternoon teaching a lesson on power amplifiers. Not a terribly interesting subject for a warm Friday afternoon, or any other afternoon, when unexpectedly, ten minutes before the 2:30 p.m. dismissal bell, there was a knock at my classroom door. I thought it was a little late in the day for someone to be horsing around. I asked myself, "Perhaps a teacher let class out early and some joker is banging at the door? It wasn't a slight knock but a knock that had some force behind it indicating the bearer meant business."

Knock! Knock! Knock!

I opened the door and found a somber looking individual — a messenger from Western Union standing outside with a telegram in hand.

"Mr. Masciulli?" he asked.

"Yes, I'm Mr. Masciulli," I responded. He then handed me the telegram.

"What's this?" I asked apprehensively. A personally delivered telegram in the middle of the day gave me ample reason to be concerned. The messenger peeked in the classroom and shook his head. My initial reaction was he was being critical of my class, but the sad expression on his face led me to believe he was being sympathetic and knew what the message was all about. It was as though he recognized that the timing couldn't have been worse. My initial reaction was that someone close to me died; but why a telegram? Some family member would surely call if that were the case. I signed for the telegram and sent the messenger on his way. Classes were to be dismissed in ten minutes. Students were restlessly waiting for the bell to signal the end the school day and begin the weekend. I also had plans for the weekend. It was spring and my future wife, Mary, and I were planning a June wedding. We had much to do. We were actively looking for a house in Norwood, Massachusetts. The evening before we had seen a house we liked but wanted to see it one more time before we made a final decision. Anxiously, I opened the telegram and started reading. One of the students sitting in the far left front row, Larry MacIsaac, whom I will never forget, looked up and with the facial expression only a 9th grader can display in times of distress asked, "Mr. Masciulli, are you all right? You look sick! What's wrong?" I was too involved in my own thoughts to answer him. Again, I read the telegram to myself. It read:

Headquarters
513th Maintenance Battalion (DS)
Army Base, Boston, Massachusetts 02210

LETTER ORDER 5-01 1 May 1968
SUBJECT: Order to Active Duty
TO: Assigned Members

Announcement is made that by direction of the President this unit and assigned members thereof, as indicated in Annex A to this order, are ordered to active duty.

Effective date: 13 May 1968

Period: Twenty-four months unless sooner relieved or extended.

Place of entry on active duty: Army Base
                                Boston, Massachusetts

Authority: General Order Number 77, Headquarters, First United States
                Army, 18 April 1968.

DISTRIBUTION: EUGENE MARTINEZ
2-Unit file   LTC OD USAR
1-201 file reservist concerned   Commanding
2-Reservist concerned

I tried to maintain my composure and deal with a class anxious to be dismissed. Surely this had to be a mistake. Yes, today was Friday the 13th of May and our unit was called the 513th Maintenance Battalion. This had to be a joke. The bell finally rang and I dismissed the class. A couple of students realizing I was upset remained behind. Larry, who also stayed behind once again asked, "Mr. Masciulli, are you okay? Is there something we can do?"

"No thanks, Larry. It says in the telegram that my Army Reserve unit has been activated. This has to be a mistake. We're a new unit and a low priority unit — not even two years old — and we're certainly not combat ready. Other units have been on stepped-up reserve status for some time and rumor has it they're ready to go. They've been preparing for this. The Army is always messing up. I'm sure there's a logical reason for the mix-up. I'll go home and straighten it out and everything will be fine on Monday. You'll see. Have a good weekend."

When I left my class that day, it would be the last time I would see many of these students for some were seniors and would be gone in a year. Some would also be on their way to Vietnam. In 1968, every able-bodied male I knew of draft age was concerned about the draft.

Chapter 6

Why Our Unit

As a result of a string of defeats by the South Vietnamese, the 1968 decision to activate the army reserves came three years after Secretary of Defense Robert McNamara first presented the idea to President Johnson. In 1965 upon returning to Washington after a fact finding mission, McNamara recommended the number of U.S. personnel in Vietnam be increased from 75,000 to 275,000 with a large part of this increase coming from the Army Reserves. In examining all his options President Johnson later acknowledged, "I realize what a major undertaking it would be. The call up of a large number of reservists was part of the package. This would require a great deal of money and huge sacrifice for the American people."[7]

At this time President Johnson made a political decision not to call up the reserves. At a meeting with his top advisors Johnson concluded, "We would get the required appropriations in the new budget, and we would not boast about what we are doing. We would not make threatening noises to the Chinese or Russians by calling up reserves in large numbers."[8] In a subsequent press conference Johnson went on to say that he was increasing the number of troops in Vietnam from 75,000 to 125,000 and that this would be done by increasing the monthly draft from 17,000 to 35,000 and concluded that it "was not essential to order Reserve units into service now. If that necessity should later be indicated,

I will give the matter most careful consideration and I will give the country, you, an adequate notice before taking such action, but only after full preparations." [9] Johnson rejected the notion of calling up the reserves because he had to declare a national emergency to do so. Lyndon Johnson was gradually involving the U.S. in a land war and disguising his every move for political reasons. There was "general satisfaction" in the Congress not to call up the reserves. "Reservists and guardsmen were better connected, better educated, more affluent, and whiter than their peers in the active forces, and the administration feared that mobilizing them would heighten public opposition to the war."[10]

Under the Armed Forces Reserve Act of 1952, a presidential declaration of emergency was required in order to call the reserves to active duty. In 1967 the Russell Amendment was passed which gave the president until June 30, 1968 to activate any unit of the Ready Reserves of an armed force for a period of no more than 24 months.

Although the Tet Offensive of 1968 was a military defeat for the North Vietnamese, it was also a psychological defeat for the United States, coming as it did when the US officials had been proclaiming the North Vietnamese and the Viet Cong were on the verge of military collapse.[11] After the Tet Offensive, it was General Westmoreland's perception that with additional strength and removal of the old restrictive policies we could deal telling blows—physically and psychologically—well within the time frame of the reservist's one-year tour. The time had come to prepare and commit the reserves."[12]

Initially seventy-six Army reserve units were called up totaling 20,034 personnel. In this relatively small call-up forty-two units were mobilized. Most of the members of these units first learned of the call-up through the media, rather than through official Army notification channels. According to the after action report of the Army, the Department of Defense had prohibited the Department of the Army from following the procedures developed and described after the 1961 mobilization. This led to the confusion that followed and contributed to a general feeling of consternation among veterans. Supposedly the final selection of types of reserve units was based on specific requirements set forth by the U.S. Commander in Vietnam with consideration given to the need for these troops in case of civil disturbance. This had a greater bearing on activated National Guard units than on reserve units. The initial goal was to select 31.9% from the Army Reserves and 68.1% from the National Guard. In reality the breakdown was 40% Army Reserves to 60% National Guard. Units were spread geographically as much as possible; the final troop list representing 34 states. Every attempt was supposedly made by the Department of the Army to select the most operational ready units of each type required, but a lack of up-to-date information hindered the effort.

Of the seventy-six Army Reserve units in the final call-up list, fifty-nine were current or former members of the Selected Reserve Forces (SRF). Two units, one of which was the 513[h,] *had no SRF counterpart.* Few of the Army Reserve units had 100% of their authorized strength, so the Department of the Army had to find filler personnel for them. Since there had been no national emergency declared there were few options available within the reserve system. One primary source of fillers for the mobilized units was among the 4,132 Individual Ready Reservists (IRR) who had enlisted for a six-year hitch and after completing basic training were fair game. On May 13, 1968, 5,000 Army Reservists reported for duty.

Army Reserve units, even those in Stepped-Up Reserve Force (SRF) status, had never received all of the equipment required by its Table of

Organization and Equipment (TOE) and the forty-two mobilized units were no exception. However by July 12, all these units supposedly received equipment to bring them up to readiness conditions.

After receiving a telegram informing me to report for active duty, I immediately returned home. I could hear the phone ringing as I ran up the front stairs to answer it, "Hello." A voice at the other end answered, "Hello Ralph? It's Nick!" Nick was a friend from the North End whom I've known all my life. He sounded nervous as he continued, "Ralph, your unit has been activated. It's in the afternoon newspaper and on the midday news. I don't understand. The 513th is classified as a low priority unit. My unit, on the other hand, has been on stepped-up reserve force (SRF) and I've been sweating it. Ralph, it's pretty tough in Vietnam, you know. This is terrible. There must be some mistake. I'm sorry about the bad news. Let me know if there's anything I can do. Let me know what you find out. You know the Army. It's always screwing up. I have to go. Talk to you later."

After speaking to Nick, I felt as though I was dealt a death sentence and he had called to express his condolences. I turned on TV to hear Jack Heinz, a local news commentator, verify the news and tell all members of the 513th to report to the army base. I left immediately.

While driving to the army base I was still convinced this was a stupid mistake and it would soon be remedied. As I approached the guard at the gate he waved me through without checking my I.D. I then drove down to Annex B where we usually had our drills and illegally parked next to many other illegally parked cars. I ran up four flights of stairs to the assembly area only to find it swarming with people: sons, daughters, wives, parents, friends, you name it, they were all eager to find out what was going on. No one knew what was happening. Several times, the first sergeant made a feeble attempt to address the unit. If he called out attention once, he called it out at least a couple of dozen times. No one paid any attention to the first sergeant. It was at this time when I seriously started to question the ability of our officers to lead. We were now in a crisis mode and no one was paying any attention to him. What would the future hold? Finally, a small group of enlisted men joined together and asked one of the officers to brief us on the current situation. When the unit managed to quiet down, one of the first lieutenants addressed the group with a few words, "We've been activated. From now on, report to the army base at 0700 hours daily until we get further orders." The look on the faces of the men when we first assembled at the army base after being activated said it all. Panic had set in.

It was about 11:45 p.m. when I cornered the first sergeant. I mentioned I was teaching at a technical school and that I would like a few days to take care of business before I reported for duty.

"Masciulli, you're not the President of the United States. You'll report here tomorrow morning at 0700 hours like everyone else."

Those were his parting words as he stepped on the freight elevator for the ride to the rear parking lot where his car was parked. As he descended in the elevator all I could focus on were his parting words which reverberated back and forth in my head. Walking down the stairs to the parking lot, I felt extremely nauseous. By the time I approached my car I couldn't control myself any longer and barfed on a white corvette parked next to my car. I then left in a hurry. It was now 12:45 a.m. I should go home and get some rest but I couldn't. Seven a.m. would soon be here. I didn't want to go home and I didn't want to stay out. I drove through the North End and was fortunate enough to find a parking space. I must have walked through every street in the North End focusing on the past and thinking about the future.

Up until this time I had been privileged. I was the oldest male offspring of a large extended Italian family, mostly females. I had twelve aunts and eighteen female cousins who always doted over me. I was fair-haired with light complexion and blue eyes. In an Italian neighborhood where most of the females were olive skinned with dark eyes, I never wanted for lack of attention and I was pampered. Life was good. As a child I was well liked and usually got my way. In grammar school and high school I would usually get one of the girls to assist me with lengthy assignments. While employed at MIT Lincoln Labs and working toward my degree, I would always manage to get one of the secretaries to do my typing and assist with detailed assignments. It was the same in graduate school. I was very comfortable in my own small universe in the North End and I wanted it to last forever. Sadly, I knew this was all about to change.

For the next several weeks we attended reserve meetings on a daily basis. We were preparing to go to Ft. Meade, Maryland via convoy. Each day was more depressing than the preceding. Morale was low and no one seemed to know what was happening. Each day a new rumor came down from headquarters. One day we were going to Vietnam and the next day we were not. Confusion reigned. We looked to our officers for leadership, but it was apparent many of the enlisted men knew more about our situation and, in fact, were more knowledgeable about military policies and procedures than the officers. Many of the men in the unit were educated and well read about our involvement in Vietnam. The concept of preserving liberty was a cynical notion among the men. Some were convinced our leaders were naive and the truth never reached them or they weren't interested in the truth. The average enlisted man in the unit had a college degree and several had advanced degrees. Many had more education than the officers. Consequently, the little respect the officers had was eroding and slowly the enlisted men began to form an alliance against the leadership. Preserving liberty could not have been further from the truth.

In other wars, it was different. If one can find justification in any war, comparatively speaking, one can make a valid argument for the justification of our involvement in WW II, Korea, the Gulf Conflict, the most recent war against terrorism, and the war in Iraq. Vietnam was different for many reasons. For years we have listened to the arguments opposing our involvement in Vietnam. No need to reiterate what was said time and time again. In comparison to other wars, if one can declare war unjust, then Vietnam was an unjust war. History has proven this to be true.

In 1998, Robert McNamara, Secretary of Defense during the Vietnam Conflict, published his memoirs about Vietnam. In his book he gives us eleven very eloquent reasons why we lost in Vietnam. After all these years his perception still has an inherent intellectual arrogance. His perception remains that of an armchair politician who spent little time if any in the trenches. Above all, he was ignorant to the ways and cultures of not just the Vietnamese but of the peasant class in general, be it Vietnamese or otherwise. Ultimately, this was his ruination. If he truly wanted to find the truth, it was there among the Vietnamese people.

Growing up in the North End in the 1940s and 1950s gave me a reference point that I believe is fundamental to all ethnic groups. During this time the North End was mostly comprised of poor immigrants, a class from which most North Enders emerged. My grandparents and parents and those of many of my peers with minimal means had to turn inward and rely on each other to survive. Rarely were the authorities called when trouble arose. It was the common perception that the authorities made matters worse and they often did. As North Enders formed a bond to keep outsiders at bay, the Irish in South Boston did the same, and the Vietnamese formed an impenetrable bond with each other, characteristic of many ethnic neighborhoods in Boston. We saw this in the Italian Mafia, the Irish Mafia and the Russian Mafia, to name a few. At one time anyone of non-Italian descent living in the North End was suspect. The same applied to the non-Irish in South Boston. The Vietnamese were no different in what they wanted. We were never needed in Vietnam and the Vietnam people did not want us there. They resented us. However, what they did want was the economic stimulation brought to the country. They would be fools not to. As a result many small businesses flourished.

In order for us to win such a conflict, we needed the Vietnam people on our side. Many GIs coming to this realization harbored resentment at a government that put us in this situation. Eventually this resentment was directed inward and would occasionally explode and manifest itself into acts of aggression, sometimes toward each other but mostly against the Vietnamese. We attempted to dehumanize them, by calling them "gooks," "zipper heads" or "slop heads" in an attempt to make it easier for us to abuse them. We didn't want to be there and the Vietnamese did not want us there. How could we possibly win? It truly was a catch 22 situation. As much support and enthusiasm the American people exhibited in joining forces to fight the war on terrorism, a comparable amount of negativism and dislike was directed against the government and ultimately the American soldier took the brunt of this negativism for fighting the Vietnam War. When going on leave from Ft. Meade, Maryland, we had to leave the base in military uniform. Once we arrived at Friendship Airport for the flight to Boston we would all rush to the men's room where we would change into civilian clothes. In uniform, we were treated poorly and looked upon with disdain.

The weekend before we left for Vietnam, Joe and I each purchased two first class plane tickets to ensure our return trip to Ft. Meade. Joe was a quiet unassuming guy who always avoided confrontation. Flying standby, as we normally did, was too risky and being AWOL wasn't in our best interest, especially for a troop movement. Our families bid us farewell at the boarding dock and were waiting impatiently for the plane to leave. Earlier that day I had spoken to Mary, my fiancee, about the uncertainty of the future and that I didn't expect her to sit home waiting for me. Nevertheless she promised to wait and write every day while I was in Vietnam, and to continue to make wedding arrangements. She had faith that everything would work out and I was glad we were finally leaving for I always found saying good-bye to be difficult. I embraced Mary and my parents and boarded the plane. At last Joe and I were comfortably seated in military uniform when the first class attendant walked over to us and ordered, "You two, come with me." She brought us to the gate and escorted two businessmen to our seats. The attendant assumed we were flying standby and bumped us for two individuals with regular tickets. We were infuriated. This meant we would miss our morning troop movement. As we watched the plane taxi to the runway Joe became incensed. Normally a quiet passive individual, I was somewhat surprised to see such a volatile reaction, but not that surprised, for I shared his frustration. The more he tried to explain to the ticket agent that we should have been on the plane, the more adamant the ticket agent became and refused to acknowledge the error. Immediately, I realized the situation was going nowhere. Finally, Joe's parents spoke up, but to no avail. In the meantime, several bystanders noticing the commotion, called security and the military police arrived on the scene. We were apprehended and brought to a waiting room where we were reamed out for being disrespectful in uniform. When they finally realized we had paid for bona fide first class tickets, they were less than apologetic but assured us we would get back to base to make our troop movement. Subsequently, we waited at the airport for six hours and left on a 2 a.m. flight. I was hoping my family would leave but they insisted on waiting. This made for a very long six hours. Finally, we went through all our ritualistic good-byes for a second time and caught the 2 a.m. flight arriving at Ft. Meade at 5 a.m. for a 6 a.m. roll call. Later Joe and I both wrote letters of disapproval to Northeast Airlines and each of us received a letter of apology that was very nice, but tantamount to nothing.

Chapter 7

Welcome to Fort Meade

It is my opinion that many high ranking officials secretly opposed our involvement in Vietnam, but it was too late. What does one do in the middle of a stream when it's equally as dangerous to go forward as it is to retreat and by retreating one's career is finished? The decision then becomes personal. It takes a strong person to admit to a mistake in the middle of battle. Secretary of Defense Robert McNamara, in his recently published book, *In Retrospect*, admits:

> "...the danger of Vietnam's loss and through falling dominoes, the loss of all Southeast Asia made it seem reasonable to consider expanding the U. S. effort in Vietnam. None of this made me anything close to an East Asian expert, however I had never visited Indochina, nor did I understand or appreciate its history, language culture or values. The same must be said to varying degrees about President Kennedy, Secretary of State, Dean Rusk, National Security Advisor, McGeorge Bundy, military advisor Maxwell Taylor, and many others. When it came to Vietnam we found ourselves setting policy for a region that was terra incognito. Worse our government lacked experts for us to consult to compensate for our ignorance." [13]

In 1998 McNamara visited Harvard University to promote his book. He admitted he lacked knowledge and experience about Vietnam. His visit was tantamount to a confession of guilt with the expectation the American public would forgive and absolve him. As he had failed in the past, relative to his expectations about the Vietnamese, once again, his knowledge about the American people was also limited. Although many Vietnam veterans try not to harbor animosity, some cannot help resent the fact that 58,000 American lives were lost and over 250,000 were disabled and approximately 100,000 suicides were linked to the conflict. To those who survived, there was guilt because they made it and to the millions of Vietnamese who fought and died, they were human beings too, caught up in a mess as we were. These facts can never be dismissed as a simple mistake. The price we paid was too dear. Ultimately, was it not the responsibility and obligation of Secretary of Defense Robert McNamara to fully understand this issue or at least surround himself with those who knew something about the Vietnamese culture and its people? As portrayed by his intellectual arrogance, he lacked education and experience for the position. But it seems we must have been impressed with his background. After all how could he fail? He was a Harvard boy held in high esteem with the rest of the dream team. He was one of the so-called "whiz kids."

After several weeks of preparation we left Boston via convoy for Ft. Meade, Maryland. The adjustment to Ft. Meade was difficult. We were reservists and although supposedly activated to fill a need, we were considered "less than" by the regular army. This added to my sense of insecurity about our readiness. Although some of the high-ranking sergeants and officers tried to provide us with training, they were less than enthusiastic about our mission; i.e., if we truly had a mission. They revealed to us that they were just as concerned as we were, if not more so, about our preparedness. On paper, however, we always looked great.

As we passed the gate at Ft. Meade, Maryland, I could not help but feel this was a real army base and I wondered what they were going to do with us. On paper it appeared we could fight and win the war single handed. In reality I knew we were ill prepared. I looked for a comfortable slot that would give me a sense of belonging but this was difficult to find. Instead I found myself performing many details. In a very short period of time it became evident to me we had no real mission or, if we did have one it was a big mystery. It also became obvious we would fill vacancies depending upon where they could find busy work for us. Arbitrarily, we were put into slots without training. I perceived performing details on a daily basis as putting me in even greater danger for I had no specific duties. What would happen when I got to Vietnam? Thus, I was looking for a comfortable slot where I could ride out the storm.

When I first got to Ft. Meade with no equipment to work on, I was assigned to barracks fireman with two other reservists. It was our job to keep the furnace going to make sure the troops always had hot water for washing. We used coal and wood for fuel to heat the boiler. Shoveling coal in the old round pot bellied furnace made me laugh for beside the boiler was a large promotion poster that read, "For Fun, Travel and Adventure join the Modern Action Army." Being a fireman was a good job unless I got lax and failed to keep the home-fires burning. Once I let the fire burn out. At the cost of having 257 angry men yelling, screaming and threatening a possible lynching, it didn't happen again. There were three firemen assigned to each barracks when one with an IQ of 50 could have managed quite nicely. That person would probably enjoy having the men depend on him for hot water; a true example of the law of diminishing returns. In the morning we would fill the stove with coal or wood, depending on availability, and at the risk of the fire going out a second time, one of us would always stay in the company area and watch the fire. The other two would find a place to hide. On occasion we would head for Washington or Baltimore. However, there was truly no place to hide. I kept thinking of Vietnam and what I was going to do when I got there. The anxiety was unbearable. Was I not wasting valuable time goofing off when I should be training for what could be the most important chapter in my life? The most difficult thing for me to do was to pretend to be busy. If I didn't pretend to be busy stoking the fire, God only knows what my assignment would be.

Chapter 8

513th Organizes

We had already been through fifteen first sergeants and we were still stateside. It was obvious they couldn't control the unit. The men knew enough about Army regulations to walk a very thin line and stay within the law. It came as no surprise when many old timers who had been with the unit the longest started to bail out. Several senior ranking Non-Commissioned Officers (NCOs) expressed concern about the readiness of the unit and jumped at the opportunity to go elsewhere. I can't say I blamed them. It was difficult for many first sergeants, especially those with limited education to maintain discipline. Many wanted no part of the 513th Maintenance Battalion.

As a result of the efforts of a nucleus of about five individuals, the situation escalated. It started with the two Delany brothers, William and Robert, both from Jamaica Plain in Boston. Army regulations prevented both brothers from going overseas at the same time. It was undecided who was going. The Delany brothers teamed up with Jim McLaughlin and Bill Freedman. Jim, a confirmed conscientious objector, was an intellectual's intellectual. He was a laid back, quiet guy who was sincere in his objection to all wars and said from the beginning he was not going to Vietnam, no matter what the cost. I believed him, for later he stood his ground. Jim's demeanor was so mild, it was difficult imagining him in a physical confrontation. He was not athletic, somewhat awkward, gross and fine motor skills were certainly not his best assets and physical activities presented problems for him. Looking at him you could tell he would avoid confrontation at any cost. He was less concerned with practical matters and more concerned about lofty ideals. He would always be reading while puffing on his meerschaum pipe. Jim was friendly with Bill Freedman, a graduate of Merrimack College. Bill was naturally more aggressive and, at the time the unit had been called up, he was a pharmaceutical salesman.

The Delanys transferred from the 245th out of Roslindale to the 513th Maintenance Battalion. Like everyone else in the unit they felt we were getting the shaft and decided to work within the law to express our concerns. Together they organized an alliance and immediately received support from sixteen others in the unit. One weekend, when many of the men were home on leave, we received a departure date for late September. An emergency meeting was called at the local inn in downtown Baltimore. The meeting was well attended with more than half the unit present. I sat in the back of the hall and listened … we were reliving the debate on Vietnam. A debate that had torn apart the country and had continued for several years. The hawks and the doves were at it again; only this time we were the pawns. I was never so confused.

On one hand we had the idealists who claimed, "There wouldn't be a war if no one went." The average Vietnamese was less interested in politics and simply wanted to farm a section of land; perhaps have a simple hut for their families and, above all, to be left alone and live in peace. They were not interested in wall-to-wall carpeting and flush toilets which Americans have an infinite capacity to impose on less developed countries. As is the case with all wars, the supposed 'do gooders' convince the people that war is the only alternative for the betterment of the country and future generations. No matter what side of the fence they're on, they have the innate ability to always make things worse under the guise of making things better for the common people.

Howard Zinn of Boston University may have been right in his

43

assessment of the truth when he said, *"There wouldn't be a war if no one went,"* but he couldn't have been further from the truth in its application. Unfortunately, we do not live in a society that realizes the senselessness of war. Dr. Zabin of MIT in his series *On Life Beyond the Stars* says that man is a level five civilization out of a possible ten. Perhaps some day if we are fortunate to survive beyond this point, we will look back with disbelief at waging war to solve our problems. Since the Industrial Revolution we have continued to make tremendous strides in technology. No doubt technology has made our life easier. Electricity, central heat, cars, dishwashers, automatic garage door openers, computers and micro processors have made life easier but they have also complicated our lives. We panic when these technological marvels malfunction. It is important to recognize the level of technology required to simplify our lives. Anything beyond this critical point makes matters worse. This applies to nations as well as individuals.

Further complicating the issue is that the growth we have experienced in technology is at least one thousand times greater than the growth we have seen in the social sciences. This means that socially we are still at a primal level when we want to pick up sticks and stones and kill each other. The difference is that today, technology of war is no longer sticks and stones but weapons of mass destruction. The concept is the same but the toys are bigger. Should weapons of technology continue to develop at this rate and our social development continues to fall behind, the inevitable will be at hand. History has proven this as a fundamental truth. From 1942 to 2002, a period of sixty years, the U. S. has engaged in at least five wars; namely, WW II, Korea, Vietnam, Desert Storm and Operation Enduring Freedom. This is an average of one war every 12 years. Look at the technological advances we have made since 1942 as compared to the progress we have made in the social sciences in the same period of time. However, what other alternative do we have but to defend ourselves against aggressors? To emerge victorious is sweet but short lived. In the long run it usually makes matters worse. It harbors resentment among the vanquished. They exaggerate this resentment and pass it on to the younger generation. In many cultures revenge is the rite of entry into adulthood. For what other reason would a nineteen-year-old Muslim woman strap herself with explosives and detonate herself in the midst of a crowd of Israelis?

Vietnam was different. We were sucked in, and then at the cost of continuously losing more lives we kept trying to save face as a country and further increased our involvement. It was fought by those who had little clout and, for the most part, minimal education. Eventually, they also realized it was futile. But they were not empowered to do anything to remedy the situation. The war effort was a self-perpetuating machine. The economy of South Vietnam was flourishing and many influential Americans and Vietnamese were getting wealthy as a result. Needed or not, mistake or not, ready or not, after our meeting I was now convinced we would be going to Vietnam.

Our level of awareness about living in harmony with nature and our fellow man is still at a primitive level. It has to be if we resort to force to prove a point. The Pope, the Dalai-lama, Mother Theresa and Mahatma Ghandi are a few who have achieved a level of awareness and self actualization, easily recognized for their rare qualities.

Technology is a double-edge sword. No doubt advances in technology have given us a standard of living unparalleled since the ascent of man. Microprocessors and the use of Global Positioning Systems (GPS) enable us to drop bombs with pinpoint accuracy from a distance of thousands of miles. We store such weapons in ammo depots just waiting to be used. In Vietnam many generals had a prime playing field to try out some new toys. Puff the Magic Dragon, a helicopter capable of firing 600 rounds per second, was a sight to see; literally raining bullets.

No doubt technology in general raises our standard of living.

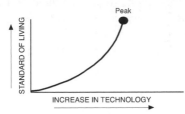

We have now peaked and any further increase in technology results in a decrease in our standard of living.

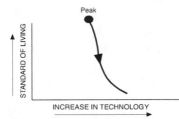

We also experience this concept on a personal basis — washing machines, dryers, dishwashers, central vacuum systems, automatic garage door openers, cars, lawn mowers, computers. These items are all great unless they malfunction. Ugh! Therefore, we should utilize that level of technology which is most convenient for us and to know the point at which any further technology simply complicates matters.

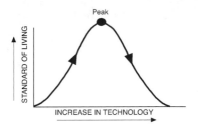

Chapter 9

513ᵗʰ Retrains

Knowing the men in the unit, I was also convinced there would be repercussions. Rumor had it that some would refuse to go and others openly spoke of violence against the officers, especially the battalion commander, Colonel Eugene Martinez. When the unit met at a downtown Baltimore inn to discuss our next move the battalion commander Colonel Martinez, hearing rumors of what was coming, summoned several men into his office. LTC Eugene Martinez (OD) commanded the Battalion since its inception in 1966. He was a veteran reserve officer with more than 28 years of military experience at the time of activation. Martinez entered the active Army in January 1941 and was commissioned as an Artillery Officer in June 1942. During WW II, he was promoted to captain while commanding a tank company in France. After the war he returned to civilian life but was active in the early phases of the Army Reserve program and was promoted to major in the reserves in 1947. In 1951, because of his civilian maintenance experience, LTC Martinez was transferred to the Ordinance branch. He has served in the reserves with the 94ᵗʰ Reserve Division in various capacities. He was promoted to lieutenant colonel in 1959 and assumed command of the 513ᵗʰ Maintenance Battalion upon its formation.[14]

One of the clerks kept us well informed. He revealed to some of the men that he had reviewed some personnel records and many of the records appeared to have been falsified. In many instances they indicated we had qualified in training exercises when we did not.

Most importantly and of gravest concern was they indicated we qualified on the rifle range when many had not fired their weapons in two or even three years. Finally, one of the "lawyers" in the unit addressed the men and recommended we establish a legal fund to pursue the issues of record falsification and lack of training. Although Senator Kennedy's office offered its support we decided to consult a lawyer, Peter Sherman, from Washington D. C., who worked through legal channels to have a judge hear our plea. I came away from our meeting convinced the men of the 513th were intelligent enough to recognize that one cannot function at a level of expectation unless one has had some experience and has received at least a minimum amount of training in that area. To do this in a combat zone was foolish. Subsequently, a complaint had been filed with the Inspector General's Office.

Like everyone else who went to Vietnam we were afraid of what to expect but our concerns went beyond the normal level of anxiety because we lacked training to function in our Military Occupational Specialties. Our officers and sergeants actually admitted this to the enlisted men and some secretly supported our cause. We had received a deployment date for October 15, 1968. As a result, an action was brought against the military (1) for a judgment that the men in the 513th Maintenance Battalion had the right to receive adequate training as required by Army Regulations before deployment to overseas duty, (2) a preliminary and permanent injunction against such deployment until they have received adequate and required training, and (3) a writ of mandamus ordering defendants to correct the appropriate military records to reflect the training actually received by the members of the 513th. An injunction was prepared and Chief Justice Douglas who was always opposed to U.S. involvement in Vietnam signed the injunction without hesitation. As a result we were to remain stateside pending an investigation into the readiness of the unit. Initially the army adamantly refuted the charges and incited the wrath of the inspector general. The media began paying more attention to our cause and gave us news coverage. In the meantime we were assured that no one would be deployed without proper training. Finally, in a *Boston Globe* article dated October 10, 1968, a spokesman for Secretary of Defense of the Army, Harold Resor, admitted that, *"...a continuing investigation into the training received by the 513*[th] *Maintenance Battalion at Fort Meade, Maryland had shown some of that training to be incomplete."*

The irony was that after all the confusion, and revision and consideration of the proper mix to support our efforts in Vietnam, the total seventy units mobilized was finally decided by financial considerations. The criteria for activation were supposedly based on need for a specific mission. It was also revealed that in February of the same year, a readiness report submitted by Colonel Martinez depicted the unit as being combat ready. Subsequently, the army decided to infuse us into other units, assuring us that no more than 25% of the units tour of duty would end at the same time. This was to add stability to the unit and its mission.

This leads me to believe that we were activated, not necessarily because they needed us but, as time went on, it became obvious that it was a political decision made easier by the February 1968 readiness report submitted by Colonel Martinez in which he stated we were ready. Also, certain political groups opposed to Senator Kennedy's dovish position had no remorse when a reserve unit from his state was activated.

One of the greatest strengths of the Army Reserves in Vietnam was that the men in the unit knew each other well. Although the 513th was only two years old, many of the men had been through basic and advanced training and had been together for two years, resulting in a unique bond. The infusion program implemented when we got to Vietnam was a means of breaking up the unit to distribute individuals with key skills thus preventing them from leaving Vietnam, compromising the mission of the unit. It was also a safeguard against casualties of men from the same towns.

Four brave men who do not know each other will not dare attack a lion. Four less brave, knowing each other well, sure of their reliability and of mutual aid, will attack with vengeance. This is the science of organizational armies in a nutshell.

If we were activated as a unit, in order to perform a mission as a unit, we should serve as unit.

In reviewing one of quarterly reports of the 513th Maintenance Battalion, I learned the mission of the unit was:

- To provide direct maintenance to all U.S. Army non-divisional units located north of the Hai-Van Pass including Camp Edwards in the Republic of Vietnam

- To provide general maintenance support for signal and light engineering equipment to all U.S. Army Divisional units in I Corps

- To provide backup support to all U.S. Divisional units located in their area of responsibility, including Camps Gia Le, Eagle and Evans.[15]

The army later admitted in a letter to Senator Kennedy that consideration for activation had been given to the geographical location of the unit and its need in a time of unrest. Assigned unit strength and individual qualification data were of utmost consideration in the report. When the Army realized that maintaining discipline in the unit would be a problem, it was then that the idea of infusion surfaced. It was better to break us up. It was also speculated that Colonel Martinez would be in line for a promotion if he volunteered our unit.

In Vietnam the officer corps was drawn from the 7 percent of troops who were college graduates, or 13 percent who had one to three years of college. They were middle class in composition and managerial in outlook. College was to officer as high school was to enlisted man. Ruling-class military families were heavily represented in its higher ranks.[16]

In the Second World War, officers were 7 percent of the armed forces, a figure normal for most armies. The officer corps used the postwar arms economy and a bloated arms budget as its vehicle for self-expansion. By the time of Vietnam, the officer corps was 15 percent of the armed forces, which meant one officer for every six plus men.[17]

In 1953 the Korean War ended, opportunity for combat commands was minimal. As the old army song goes, "There's no promotion/this side of the ocean." In 1960, it took 33 years to move from second lieutenant to colonel. Many of the "lifers," professional officers and noncommissioned officers (NCOs), welcomed Vietnam as the opportunity to reinvigorate their careers. They were not disappointed. By 1970, the wait to move up the ladder from second lieutenant to colonel had been reduced to 13 years. Over 99 percent of the second lieutenants became first lieutenants, 95 percent of the first lieutenants became captains, 93 percent of the qualified captains became majors, 77 percent of the qualified majors became lieutenant colonels and half of the lieutenant colonels became colonels.[18]

The road to military advancement was a combat command. However there were too many officers of high rank producing competition for combat commands. There were 2,500 lieutenant colonels for command of only 100 to 130 battalions; 6,000 colonels, 2,000 for 75 brigade commands; and 200 major generals for the 13 division commands in the Army.

General Westmoreland, commander of the armed forces in Vietnam, accommodated the officers by creating excessive support units, of which the 513th was one, and rapidly rotating combat commands. In Vietnam, support and service units grew to an incredible 86 percent of the military manpower. Only 14 percent of the troops were actually assigned to combat. Extravagant support services were the basis for the military bureaucracy. The armed forces created "…numerous logistical commands, each to be headed by a general who would have to have high-ranking staffs to aid each of them." It was possible for 64 army generals to serve simultaneously in Vietnam, with the requisite compliment of support staff.[19]

These superfluous officers lived far removed from danger in rear base camps and in luxurious conditions. A few miles away, combat soldiers experienced a nightmarish hell. The contrast in living conditions was too great to foster confidence — in both the officers and the war — to survive unscathed.

Westmoreland's solution to the scarcity of combat command added fuel to the fire. He ordered a one-year tour of duty for enlisted men in Vietnam, but only six months for officers. The combat troops hated class discrimination that put them at twice the risk of their commanders. They were contemptuous of officers, whom they saw as raw and dangerously inexperienced.

A majority of officers considered Westmoreland's tour as unethical. Yet they were forced to use short tours to prove themselves for promotion. They were in situations in which their whole careers depended on what they could accomplish in a brief period, even if it meant taking shortcuts and risks at the expense of the safety of their men — a temptation many could not resist.

The outer limit of six-month commands was often shortened due to promotions, relief, injury or other reasons. The outcome resembled a series of "revolving-door" commands. As a Vietnam veteran recalled,

"During my year in-country I had five second-lieutenant platoon leaders and four company commanders. One CO was okay ... All the rest were stupid."[20]

This was a common occurrence. Battalion commanders had a 30 to 50 percent chance of being relieved of command. Search-and-destroy missions produced enormous casualties for the infantry and many officers corrupted by career ambitions would ignore this and draw on the never-ending supply of replacements from the monthly draft quota.[21]

No doubt the good Colonel Eugene Martinez volunteered the unit to advance his career, hopefully resulting in his retiring as a full bird colonel. His plan backfired when he was relieved of his command shortly after we arrived in Vietnam. Perhaps this was partly due to the high degree of revolving officers, but perhaps, more importantly, because he never gained the respect and control of his men. We also went through at least five company commanders and about 21 first sergeants.

The validity of the reports resulting in activation of our unit was of concern to the men. Ninety-two men signed affidavits supporting a lawsuit in Baltimore Federal District Court alleging we had not received the training credited to us on Army records specifically in physical training, chemical warfare and rifle training. Some of the sergeants also admitted this to the troops and were later questioned by authorities about falsifying records indicating men were in attendance in classes when they were not.

Colonel Eugene Martinez, who was known as the skunk because the top of his hair was jet black and the sides white, was often seen patrolling the company area with a swagger stick in his right hand. He would periodically strike the swagger stick on the right side of his thigh as an assertion of his new found authority. In civilian life he was a supervisor in the machine shop at the Coast Guard Base in Boston. Coincidentally, as a young boy, I spent many hours sitting at my grandmother's window overlooking Commercial Street and the Coast Guard Base. The machine shop was across the street, a distance of approximately one hundred feet, literally a stone's throw from her window.

The colonel who was becoming increasingly aware of the difficulty and unrest among the troops invited several of the men to speak with him. Three representatives of the unit were requested to report to the Colonel's office. Upon approaching the outer office the company clerk phoned the Colonel to inform them of their presence. Immediately Colonel Martinez invited them into his office and requested that they be seated in front of his desk. The colonel gave them a pep talk about patriotism and concluded by telling them he knew we were not qualified in our Military Occupational Specialties (MOSs). He knew they had not received training but would receive it in Vietnam. To date we hadn't received it and there was no reason to believe we would receive it in Vietnam.

> The Annual Historical Supplement for Headquarters and main support company states, "The 513th Maintenance Battalion (DS) conducts range firing on a monthly basis. The purpose is to allow all replacement personnel to fire their assigned weapons as soon as possible after arrival. This also allows all personnel in the company to fire their assigned weapon (M16A1 Rifles), the M-79 Grenade launcher, and the M-60 Machine Gun at least once every three months. Integrated with the range firing are classes on mines, flares, and booby traps. Personnel who serve on perimeter defense are given weekly classes on weapons training by the sector commander and his staff. Also included as part of weapons training are weekly classes on weapons safety, integrated into the weekly safety classes."[22]

I have yet to find anyone who acknowledges receiving training to this degree. Other than Basic Training and Advanced Individual Training (AIT), this had been the last time many had fired weapons. Training on mines, flares and booby traps, to the best of my knowledge, did not occur.

Other high-ranking officers admitted it would be nine months in Vietnam before we could perform a mission. I suppose in civilian life Colonel Martinez probably was an okay guy; however, like everyone else, he was caught up in the frenzy of the times. In the meantime, tensions continued to increase and morale continued to get worse. However, we continued legal recourse.

We retained a lawyer and filed for an injunction. Two of the men in the unit hand carried the injunction to Chief Justice Douglas. We chose him because in speaking with his aides we learned he too was concerned about our plight and would support us. Senator Kennedy's office was also very supportive of our concerns. To our dismay Senator Brooke's office was far from supportive and gave us the impression we were avoiding Vietnam at any cost. In the meantime the Army launched its own investigation and in a subsequent report sent to Senator Kennedy's office and to the Battalion Commander, Colonel Martinez, the training we previously received was found to be "incomplete." The next question was, "What do you do with 256 men, many of whom lack training, before you send them to Vietnam?" The answer is simple. You train them. That's exactly what happened. This gave us more time stateside. In desperation, a month or two before our departure, the army realized the gravity of the situation and made an attempt to give us a crash course in training by sending the men out to different units to train.

First the entire unit went through a modified basic training program. It was quickly put together and, like the training we had received in the reserves, it was poorly organized. It was obvious that it was done to keep the men quiet and to harass us for it turned into another farce. In one attempt at Ft. Meade we simulated taking equipment and troops to a designated location on Highway Route 1. This represented the main highway along the coast of Vietnam similar to our U.S. Route 1. Along the way we were confronted with a simulated V.C. attack. By the time we finally got organized and set up a perimeter defense, we had supposedly suffered 100 percent causalities and 85 percent of our equipment had been destroyed. When we finally settled down, Colonel Brian further "encouraged us" when he told us, "In all my years in the military this is the sloppiest unit I've commanded. Now, get out there and do it again."

It was a month before we were sent to Vietnam that Butch and I were sent to Aberdeen Proving Grounds for a refresher course on Howitzer repair. We spent three weeks supposedly improving our skills on the 105mm and 155mm howitzers.We were auditing the course and the instructor didn't care, sometimes teasing us and referring to us as the reservists who got screwed. The classes were full, making it difficult to get any hands-on experience. We were never on any roster and never got called on the carpet for not attending classes. To us it was another charade and we knew we were going to Vietnam. The training was an absolute farce.

It had been at least two years since basic training when I last participated in war games, and for some of the senior men it had been even longer. Some of the older sergeants were grossly overweight and couldn't function. Many of them had the time and the grade to retire, and they soon did. Others managed to get transferred to other units where they would be safe until they could retire. It seemed that before they left they all took a crack at being first sergeant. It was good on their record and would help them advance. By now we had been through 15 first sergeants, one worse than the other. Colonel Brian of the regular Army at Ft. Meade participated in war games once or twice before he joined the ranks of those who left the unit for better opportunities. Other high-ranking sergeants and officers had time and grade and more influence in the system and pulled strings to get transferred which further increased our anxiety and destroyed our confidence in our leadership.

The regular Army at Ft. Meade, Aberdeen Proving Grounds, and subsequently, in Vietnam did not want to deal with reservists as a unit. The 513th Maintenance Battalion was activated because our unit was supposedly needed for the war effort. It became obvious they did not need us nor did they want us. We were infused with existing training programs to develop skills in our MOSs. This was devastating for at 26 years of age I trained with men in their late teens who were ready to "kick ass."

During our training two of the men were sent to Vietnam by advanced convoy. It just happened to be two of the "rabble rousers." Then things started to get nasty. It started when we were coming back from a field exercise earlier in the day. The chosen two had been informed that they were leaving the next day on advanced convoy to Vietnam. Was it just a coincidence that these individuals were instrumental in getting the injunction against the Army? This was perceived as more harassment and an attempt to quiet those who had the most to say. Half the battalion was out on field maneuvers and everyone was pissed off at everything. A long flat bed trailer, called a cattle car because it resembled the trucks used to transport cattle, was sent to pick up the men. Specialist Fowler, with whom I would later spend some memorable time on R&R, was driving. Fowler was known not to take any shit from anyone. Earlier in the day two of the men were raking sand in the company area and decided to rake two large peace symbols into the sand in front of the Colonel's office. Both men were threatened with a court martial. This further upset the men. Fowler decided to drive by the company area to see the two peace symbols. The truck was pulled off the road in front of Battalion Headquarters with more than 100 men simulating the sound of cattle. Then, as though everyone had the same idea at the same time, it was decided to give the Colonel a H Y M N. Fowler orchestrated, as he was inclined to do, and, while standing on the hood of the truck he bellowed, "Okay, guys, on three let's give the good Colonel a H Y M N."

On three Fowler directed the chorus as we chimed in "Him ..., Him ..., F--- Him ...." The entire battalion was now restricted to the company area pending a court martial.

Ted Pleads for Boston Reservists

SENATOR KENNEDY

By MILTON R. BENJAMIN
Herald Traveler Washington Bureau Chief
Copyright 1968 Boston Herald Traveler Corp.

WASHINGTON—Sen. Edward M. Kennedy yesterday asked the Army to postpone temporarily shipment of the 513th Maintenance Battalion to Vietnam pending a "full investigation" after 67 more Greater Boston reservists charged they had not received all their mandatory training.

A Pentagon spokesman informed the Herald Traveler shortly before Kennedy's action that the Army had investigated "as far as they're going to and as far as they are concerned, it's a closed case." The men are scheduled to be shipped out to Vietnam Sunday.

Kennedy, in a letter to Army Secretary Stanley R. Resor, asked him to "conduct a full and prompt investigation" of the reservists' claim they haven't been adequately trained and to "keep this unit available until an appropriate inquiry is satisfactorily completed."

"I don't question, nor do these men question, their obligation as reservists on active duty," Kennedy said. "They only question their preparedness to fulfill their reserve obligation."

An additional 67 members of the unit, who had been home in the Boston area on leave, signed affidavits yesterday on their return to Ft. Meade, Md., backing their 18 fellow reservists who filed suit last Thursday charging they had not received all their mandatory training.

A total of 51 of the 156 Greater Boston reservists in the 513th unit now have signed affidavits contending

(Continued on Page Fourteen)

See appendix for full text of articles

See appendix for full text of articles

Chapter 10

Unit Rebels

Each day, tensions rose. Many of the men who had nothing to do with the latest incident were upset at being confined to the company area with the rest of the battalion. This exacerbated the situation. When you're grounded at the age fifteen or sixteen, that's your parents prerogative. But men, many in their mid-twenties ready to go into hell, present a more serious problem. On a hot fall evening at Ft. Meade many of the men had been up drinking until the early morning hours, rehashing the events of the previous day. Before we knew it, it was 6 a.m. and time for the morning formation. No one knew what to expect. I was glad the entire company was not in the stockade. The company commander (CO) addressed the unit. He was of average height, approximately 5 feet 9 inches and wore smoked framed military issue glasses and baggy fatigues. His pants were tucked in unpolished boots. It was customary to use blousing garters which were a lot cooler than tucking pants inside boots. He may have been in a hurry because the bottom of his pants were sticking out of his boots. His nerdy appearance was more characteristic of an engineering major in college. All he needed was a slide rule strapped to the side of his pistol belt instead of the 45 caliber handgun many officers wore. Unaware of his nerdy looks, his facial expression tightened. His voice was high pitched, more conducive to leading a church choir than 257 men through one of the most crucial, if not the most crucial period, of their lives.

He was far from merciful in his character assassination of the men. At first it appeared no one was paying any attention to him but when he referred to us as a bunch of yellow-bellied cowards, several of the men cringed. Out of the corner of my right eye I saw private Johnson clench his teeth. I looked straight ahead for I knew there were going to be repercussions. At an early age I learned to let derogatory comments wash over me and not to take them personally, a survival technique I developed growing up in the North End and used extensively in Vietnam. Nothing was personal there and the sooner one detached from the insanity at hand, the greater the probability of surviving both emotionally and physically.

Johnson was quiet and unassuming and that's why it appeared totally out of character when he bellowed, "Sir! Private Johnson requests permission to speak, sir!"

Without thinking the Company Commander (CO) responded, "Permission granted."

If the Captain had any indication of what was coming, I'm sure he would have denied Johnson the opportunity to express himself. There was silence in the company area. The men knew something was about to happen. Then to everyone's astonishment Johnson bellowed, "Sir! If you're man enough to take those bars off and accompany me behind the Dempsy Dumpster, we'll see who's the yellow bellied coward." The silence was deafening for the Captain put himself in a corner. He looked straight ahead as if to ignore the statement. I saw the tenseness in his body followed by a look of embarrassment. He didn't know what to do. He glanced around at the men standing at attention and kept looking from left to right, searching for something, anything, to deflect attention away from him. Then unexpectedly Private Voss, standing to the right of Johnson, blurted out, "Sir! Private Voss also requests permission to speak, sir." Perhaps the Captain thought Voss was going to placate the situation or say something to change the subject, for without hesitating he made a second fatal mistake when he turned to Voss and said, "What is it, Voss?"

"Sir, I also challenge you. Perhaps you would like to take me on instead of Johnson?" bellowed Voss.

The Company Commander was flabbergasted. Then someone from the rear of the company yelled, "Sir, we'll pick ten of our wimpiest men and you can choose any one of them to take behind the dumpster and that will prove who the yellow bellied coward is." I couldn't believe what I was hearing. I don't know what the Captain should have done but he did the wrong thing by doing nothing. There was heavy silence as the men slowly started breaking ranks and whispered among themselves. A blanket of sadness hung on us. The sun was finally coming up as we walked along the long narrow road to the mess hall.

Walking down Ernie Pyle Road to breakfast, the topic of conversation was the previous encounter. As a teacher in civilian life, I realized control was paramount especially under these life and death circumstances. Once a leader gives his subordinates the perception he is weak, regaining control is impossible. On one hand, I felt compassion for the CO but then he deserved what he got. Had he treated us with the slightest amount of dignity and respect, he would have been okay, but he treated us like shit because he truly thought we were shit.

The following week morale declined even further. A don't-give-a-damn attitude prevailed. The men were volatile and would react at the slightest provocation. Each night after duty they would meet in a bar called Rappaport's just outside the gate at Ft. Meade on Pulaski Highway. The highway was named after General Pulaski, a famous Polish hero of the American Revolution. There we would drink into the early hours of the morning. Several drank excessively and smoked pot. Drugs were slowly creeping in. Until now it had been rare to see someone smoking pot.

We had received our final orders and were preparing to leave within the week. Again the men had been up drinking all night. At least two-thirds of the unit was intoxicated. Then things started to get out of control.

It was a Sunday evening and the order for dinner was usually lunch meat sandwiches. This particular evening the lunch meat was exceptionally gross. It was olive loaf but by the time we got in the mess hall it had discolored because it had been sitting there for some time. Naturally, some of the men construed this as a conspiracy against us by the regular army. The men were milling around complaining about the evening meal when it was decided that army chow was unfit for human consumption and no one should have to eat in a regular army mess hall. Every time we went through the chow line we were reminded that we were the reservists going to Nam, and the regular army personnel would scoff at us. I wasn't prepared for what came next. It was decided to burn down the mess hall. The perimeter of the mess hall was doused with gasoline and torched. Next, it was decided to blow up two five-ton trucks parked at the rear of the mess hall. This was accomplished by igniting two gasoline soaked rags protruding from the gas tanks of each truck.

From my bunk I could hear the sirens. The base was on full alert. The men came running into the barracks and jumped in bed as the MPs cordoned off the area and started to search. If the Army decided to have a full investigation, which would have occurred under normal circumstances, it would further delay our departure and make matters worse. The company area was secured by MPs and further policing and security were the responsibility of Colonel Martinez and ultimately us. Now the fox was in charge of the hen house. A further internal investigation during the evening revealed nothing.

When the MPs finally left, I had hoped to get at least a one hour rest before 6 a.m. formation when, after fifteen minutes, I was again awakened by the sound of a chain saw. I was shocked to find the support columns in the center of the barracks sawed in half. The barracks were two stories high. When the men came running down from the top floor it increased the stress on the bottom timbers, now slightly off center, causing the barracks to sway. The barracks were now unsafe. Any heavy movement was dangerous, so the barracks were placed off limits. A similar scenario played itself out in two other barracks occupied by the unit. Only a few men at a time were allowed back into the barracks to gather their belongings in preparation for our troop movement.

Six o'clock came quickly and the company area was buzzing with activity. The men were lined up waiting for the trucks to take us to the airport. Jim McLaughlin insisted he was not going. Finally he was ordered to fall in with the rest of the unit. Jim ran into the barracks and handcuffed himself to his bunk. All along, Jim insisted he would not go, and now he refused to go. The MPs were called; they shackled him and carted him off to the stockade. That was the last time I saw Jim McLaughlin. However, some time later in Vietnam we heard he had been placed in the stockade for a period of time and then placed in garrison until he was granted a hearing. Supposedly, he was eventually granted the status of conscientious objector. Butch and I stayed behind with additional equipment waiting for the last trucks to arrive.

While waiting for the trucks, I walked around the barracks looking in every window as I went along. Only a few hours earlier everything was abuzz. Now there was silence. A feeling of despair came over me. I thought about Jim McLaughlin. Did he do the right thing? I thought about the time he had taken me and several GIs to Georgetown University for a seminar about defecting to Canada. At the time, Jim was undecided whether he should defect or apply for conscientious objector status. The room was packed with GIs. Several GIs defected that evening and never went back to the base. I also gave it some thought and spoke with a counselor. However, my father and many of my uncles fought in WW II. My father and his brother Joe served in the South Pacific where my uncle Joe was wounded and received several commendations. I was proud when Dad and I would see him march in the Veterans Day parade and after the parade we would go into the legion hall and Uncle Joe would introduce us to all his army buddies. I had several other uncles who also served in WW II. One uncle stayed in the service after the war, served for twenty-five years, and retired as sergeant major. My future father-in-law was a WW I veteran and was very active in the American Legion. He was a member of the *Forty and Eight Regiment* and would never let me forget it. I was extremely proud of him when at seventy-eight, and serving as post commander of the American Legion, he denounced the Vietnam War from the podium at a time when it was very unpopular to do so. He later resigned as post commander because none of the other officers would go along with his official denunciation. I was close with my relatives, and I was concerned about what they would think if I went to Canada. I decided Canada was not an option.

Ruling on Mass. Reservists Today

Court Ruling Sends
Reserves to Viet

OK on Training
Reserves
Will Get
'Go' Order

Hub Reservists Lose Viet Bid

It's 'Go'
For the
513th

Reservists Viet-Bound
After High Court Acts

Hub Reservists
Lose Bid to
Stay Viet Duty

513th Starts for Viet Today
250 Reservists
On Viet Plane

By BERTRAM WATERS
Globe Washington Bureau

The 250 men of the 513th Maintenance Battalion,

See appendix for full text of articles

67

Chapter 11

Leaving for Vietnam

On a late summer morning thirty army trucks rolled into Andrews Air Force Base in Maryland. We were leaving for Vietnam. When we arrived at the base several protesters confronted us, attempting to block the entrance to the base. Butch and I were riding in one of the first trucks of the convoy when the order was given for the men in the first few trucks to fall out and assist the military police in pushing the crowd away from the main gate. Immediately, we complied. As we pushed forward, I noticed a woman a short distance away. Her hair was long and greasy and her appearance was unkempt. She had that drawn appearance of not having slept in a while. She had on a pair of old torn dungarees covered with peace symbols. She was the beatnik looking college student of the 60s we always poked fun at while hanging out in front of Carlo's Pool Room. Suddenly, I made eye contact with this young lady. Her eyes were piercing. The look in her eyes and the forlorn look on her face told me she was upset. Unexpectedly, she threw a coke bottle in my direction. It struck the ground and shattered into many pieces causing the contents to splatter over several other soldiers and myself. Immediately, we apprehended her and she was taken away by the military police. Later we learned the bottle contained urine.

When I finally boarded the plane, I looked outside at the demonstrators. In the distance the military police were apprehending several other protestors. I started thinking about this young woman and what she had done, and thought about her violating my dignity and I started feeling sorry for myself. My self-pity turned inward and I felt I was losing control and became visibly upset. "What's wrong?" Butch asked. I dismissed it as something I ate and slumped in my seat hoping no one would notice. Here I am, I thought, supposedly a street-smart kid from the North End caught up in this mess. I should have had more brains and avoided the military. There I was, wallowing in depression as I asked myself over and over, what was I doing here and how had I gotten involved in this? I knew it was going to be a difficult year. I worried about the future and was petrified at what tomorrow would bring. I was afraid and sat down and tried to control myself. If I lost control now, what would happen when I got to Vietnam? I was considerably older than the average GI. I was twenty-six and the average GI was about nineteen. They were young, well trained and eager. Most of all they believed in the war effort and I did not.

I pulled the window shade down, sat back in my seat and my thoughts drifted to happier times in the North End. I thought about grammar school and high school and all the fun we had at the CYO dances. I thought about all that stuff the nuns and Franciscan Friars constantly drilled in our heads about faith and religion. Was it all true, I asked myself? Or was it just a crutch we use to cope with adversity? Feeling totally dejected, I prayed and asked God to give me strength.

The flight from Andrews AFB to Vietnam was extremely uncomfortable. Anyone who has traveled by military transport knows they are functionally built and not comfortable. We were all given malaria pills as we boarded the plane, and as a result many of the men became ill with dysentery. With one tiny rest room, this presented a few problems. I waited in line to use the men's room and when I finally got there, the holding tank of raw sewerage was overflowing and sloshed back and forth over the toilet seat. Fortunately I was able to control myself until we stopped at Alpendorf Air Force Base for refueling. It was there I called my wife to be, Mary, to tell her we were finally on our way. Since the 513th was activated in May of 1968 and we were to be married in June of that year, it was especially difficult for her because we had to put our marriage plans on hold. I tried to catch some rest, but my anxiety level was too high. After twenty-two hours we were hovering above DaNang airfield.

Chapter 12

Welcome to Vietnam

As we approached DaNang, from the windows of the plane we could see the rounds striking the perimeter of the airfield. We taxied on the runway and waited for the all-clear signal. When the all clear was sounded we filed off the plane and reassembled in one of the hangers to await reassignment. Butch and I were put on separate details; it would be a long time before

we would see each other again. The sergeant in charge led me and two other GIs to a makeshift commode at the far end of the runway. He brought us to an open shed and showed us a piece of plywood upon which to sit. It measured approximately 3 feet by 8 feet with three equidistant holes about twelve inches in diameter. Beneath each hole was a fifty-five gallon drum sawed in half. A handle with a three-foot rope was fastened to the side of each drum. We pulled the barrels out a safe distance from the shed, poured kerosene over the contents and ignited them. Thus, my first detail in Vietnam was none other than Shit Burner Extraordinaire. We sat on our duffle bags observing the plumes of smoke as they faded into the gray sky. It was the beginning of the monsoon and a damp, dank smell, unique to Vietnam, permeated the air. At first I thought the odor was a result of our burnt offerings, but the odor was much too concentrated to be caused by us. I then turned to my left and looked diagonally across the runway and saw several body bags lined up on the runway. They blended in with the gray background. My imagination was running wild. Now the smell was overwhelming. A C130A cargo plane transport taxied to the end of the runway. The bodies were loaded in the belly of the plane and taken away. Welcome to Vietnam.

We finished our detail and waited to be picked up. After waiting awhile we decided to walk back to the hanger, hoping we would meet our ride on the way back. The airfield was bustling with activity. Planes were everywhere: cargo planes, jet planes, Chinooks, Cobras—you name it. We were exhausted. With our duffle bags over our shoulders we walked along the edge of the runway toward the hanger in disbelief. I wanted to go home. The hanger was on the other side of the airfield and was at least a half hour walk. Along the way we encountered a GI off to the left of the runway supposedly guarding the perimeter of the airfield. At least that's what he told us. Strangely enough he wasn't dressed like he was on guard duty because he had on a green rain outfit with heavy green rubber boots. It looked as though he was prepared for a fishing expedition. He was nervous, pacing back and forth and pointing to the hills in the background. He couldn't stay in one place. First I thought he was on drugs, and maybe he was, but later I came to realize he exhibited a level of anxiety very common in Vietnam. As we approached him he commented, "You'll see them there hills over there? Charlie's there and comes out every once in a while." In the meantime two helicopters were hovering back and forth trying to smoke him out. We then double-timed back to the hanger.

When we got to the hanger we had started in-country processing. The first sergeant took me by surprise when he asked, "Where do you want your remains sent in case of death?" Once again I prayed and asked for strength. Suddenly an unusual calm came over me. I was convinced that someday I would be going home. However, I was going to have to rely on all my skills and abilities to get through the next year. I purposely avoided the question and hoped he wouldn't ask again but he did.

"Well, where do you want your remains sent in case of death?"

"Nowhere. I intend to go home in one piece," I bellowed.

He looked at me giving me that far away look that I would come to recognize so often in Vietnam and replied, "Yea, we're all going home, some day, one way or another." Now I was reminded of that same look on the faces of many homeless veterans I see on my way to work in Boston, and they prepare for another day on the streets after spending the night in a shelter. It's the same look I see on the faces of the many disappointed veterans tucked away in some remote corner of a VA hospital. So different, I said to myself, yet we have so much in common. "Hey you!" The first sergeant called me again, this time with more determination, "Hey you! Where do you want your remains sent in case of death?" This time I blurted out my home address.

We left DaNang and travelled north by convoy along the famous Highway 1 on the east coast which runs along the coast similar to our Route #1 in the Northeast. Helicopters escorted us along the way to Phu Bai. This was the first time I rode through the Hai Van pass. The road conditions were very poor, slowing our progress to the top of the pass. At the top I looked down in amazement and a feeling of anxiety came over me as we passed through the clouds. Looking ahead at the dangerous bends in the road increased my anxiety. I never adjusted to high places. The pass is 21 kilometers long and winds back and forth to a height of 1500 meters. The peak of the mountains reaches the clouds and its base stretches to the sea below. I kept thinking of how beautiful it looked but I sensed underneath the dense foliage, to the left and right of the pass, there was a lot happening of which I was

unaware. As we continued we saw many areas that still had a faint semblance of beauty but were now devastated. We all commented on the odor that permeated the air. It was a pungent, stale, funky odor that was everywhere. Some GIs eventually adjusted to it. I could never. Finally we arrived in Phu Bai. By the time we checked in, it was so dark I couldn't see much of the landscape and had absolutely no idea where we were.

There was another reservist from the 513th I recognized on our trip up to Phu Bai, his name was Johnnie. When our unit was activated, Johnnie was a senior at Boston College. I didn't know too much about him except that he was quiet, unassuming, liked to drink and sleep. The sergeant in charge brought us to hooch Number 7. I could not help but see the sign in front of the hooch which read "Semper Fi," the abbreviation for Semper Fidelis (Always Faithful), the Marine Corps motto. I looked at Johnnie in disbelief and whispered, "This is a Marine Corps hooch." Johnnie looked at me and responded in desperation, "I don't give a shit. I'm exhausted. All I want to do is go to bed." We stood in front of the only bunk in the hooch, double bunk, and argued about who would take the bottom and who would take the top.

I always felt more secure in the bottom bunk for several reasons. First, it was lower to the ground in case I fell out of bed. Secondly, if we were abruptly awakened, I might just forget I was in the top bunk and fall to the floor. Also, from the bottom bunk I could exit the hooch quicker. Johnnie once again insisted he wanted the bottom bunk. A couple of the men heard us bickering and yelled, "Keep the damn noise down. Tomorrow comes quick." At the risk of further repercussions I threw my duffle bag on the top bunk to use as a pillow, jumped up and tried and get some rest. I was more concerned about resting than getting the bottom bunk.

At about two in the morning I finally dozed off. There were 12 men in my first hooch. My bunk was on the left hand side at the far end near the rear exit. Unfortunately the bunker was at the other end near the entrance to the hooch. Since we were the new kids on the block, and I was the oldest by almost six years, this still didn't give us much clout in our choice of accommodations. The space beside my bunk was extremely limited. The inside of a two tiered orange crate served as a shelf for underwear and socks and the top was used as a night table and desktop to write letters home. Behind the orange crate was a two-by-four piece of wood supporting the corner of the hooch. I noticed that the two-by-four had notches on all four sides. Each side represented a different GI and each notch represented a day in the life of the GI previously occupying my bunk. Starting from bottom up, there were three hundred and sixty notches carved on three sides of the two-by-four. At the top written in pencil were the words "going home!" The fourth side caught my eye because nothing was inscribed at the top. I looked down and noticed that the notches stopped at two hundred. This meant his tour was cut short. "What happened to this poor bastard?" I wondered. The more I pondered his fate the more depressed I became. Nothing was written on top of the fourth side of the two-by-four.

No sooner had I dozed off when the lights went on. It was 5 a.m. A faint voice in the background, barely audible said, "Fall out." I listened with much trepidation. I was still half asleep. In the meantime

I could hear the men running around, "getting their shit together," as they say in the Corps. We were inclined as reservists never to accept anything at face value but we would soon learn. Johnnie bellowed, "Blow it out of your asshole." Suddenly, the entire bunk and all our gear began to move toward the entrance with me on the top bunk and Johnnie on the bottom. Evidently the troops had been through this exercise a number of times because they positioned the beds at just the correct angle to squeeze them through the entrance. The beds, mattresses, all our gear, including Johnnie and me, were thrown into a mud pit in front of the hooch. Our duffle bags were then emptied. The men started laughing. As we lay there in the midst of this imbroglio a black gunnery sergeant at least 6 feet 4 inches tall and about 250 pounds stood over us. He was built like Mohamed Ali and had a face like Mike Tyson. He stood above me with his hands on his hips and at the top of his lungs bellowed, "The next time I tell you to fall out, you will fall out and on the double. Do you understand?" From a reclining position I looked up and responded, "Yes, sir!" His immediate response was, "Don't you call me, sir. I am not an officer. I am Gunnery Sgt. Jones." I then responded, "Yes, Gunnery Sgt. Jones!" Everyone continued laughing until the gunnery sergeant turned and yelled, "What's so funny? Knock it off or I'll have you guys for breakfast." The men immediately quieted down. He continued, "I'm only going to say this once, so get your head out of your asshole and listen. Do you understand?"

"Yes, Sergeant," we both responded. "You're with a marine unit, MAG 36, and you will do things the Marine Corps way and no other way. Get it?" Again we responded, "Yes Sergeant." "Where did you guys come from anyway?" the gunnery sergeant asked. Johnnie replied, "Boston, Massachusetts, Sergeant." The gunnery then asked, "Both of you from the same place? You join on the buddy system?" Johnnie responded, "We're with an army reserve unit, the 513th Maintenance Battalion from Boston. We were activated and sent here." Everyone chuckled. The gunnery laughed, "You got screwed." He pointed to the men in formation and said, "These shit heads asked for this fucking bullshit but you guys got fucked, royally! You guys going to win the war for us? If not, what the hell are you doing here? You better come up to speed in a hurry 'cause this ain't no Boy Scout camp and we have enough problems without worrying about you two jokers."

This was exactly what we wanted to hear, more words of encouragement! "Now get yourselves cleaned up and report back to me on the double. I'll give you ten minutes." We gathered up our belongings as quickly as we could and brought them into the hooch. At least they were out of the rain. In this dampness it would be awhile before they completely dried. That was the least of my concerns. While taking our gear back to the hooch I turned to Johnnie and whispered, "Look, do exactly what he tells us to do and keep your damn mouth shut. We're new kids on the block and eventually he'll back off only if he thinks we'll comply. If we fight him, we're dead." Fortunately, we had slept in our fatigues and kept our boots on, which was of some help rather than sleeping in shorts and a tee shirt which would offer no protection. We cleaned ourselves off and reported to the gunnery sergeant.

Chapter 13

My First Assignment

As ordered, we reported in ten minutes and were both sent on separate details. Johnnie was sent off to help reinforce a bunker on the perimeter of the camp. Beside each hooch was a bunker made of sandbags with corrugated steel supported by wood posts to support the additional weight on the roof. When the weather was good, we would also use the roof as a sun deck. The walls and roof were layered with sandbags four to five feet deep. The more sandbags the better. There was no limit except that the crevices between the sandbags provided very nice nesting accommodations for rats. Many of the rats did not scare easily which made me think they were either rabid or perhaps a highly domesticated strain of rodent.

I remember an encounter one of the marines had with one of our unwelcomed vermin. I had been in-country two months when there was some talk that I would replace a supply clerk who frequently drove from Phu Bai to Camp Eagle among several other firebases. The night before he left to go home he was ecstatic. He had been counting the days and each day he would let us know his status. Thus, he would always give us the number of days he had left in-country and the number of wake-ups. He was a short-timer and like all short-timers he was held in high esteem for he was going home in one day and a wake-up. During his last night in-country he was in another hooch drinking and raising hell in honor of his departure. He was going home in the morning. He returned to our hooch at about nine and wanted to retire early because he had a 4 a.m. wake-up call for his trip to DaNang. He was lying on his bunk, with his arm above his head, contemplating life in the real world when an exceptionally large rodent appeared at the entrance to the hooch. I was lying on my bunk in my shorts and as I turned I saw the rat positioned in the doorway. I lifted my mosquito net and winged my book at it. To my dismay I missed it by three feet and, even more surprisingly, it did not seem to be bothered. The vermin casually walked down the center of the hooch and stood between our bunks. I always slept with my mosquito net tucked underneath my mattress and now it gave me a slight feeling of security for I knew the rat could not get through the net without some difficulty. On the other hand, "the short timer" was lying on his bunk in his shorts with no net to cover him. The rat jumped on his bunk and bit him on his big toe! He was scheduled to go home in seven hours and now this. He had to undergo a series of rabies shots. His time in Vietnam went from one day and a wake-up to sixty days and a wake-up in a heartbeat!

Officers were more fortunate. They had special bunkers. Much of our equipment would be transported via Connex container, a heavy steel metal container approximately five feet by twelve feet with one opening in front. It was difficult for rodents to get inside a Connex container because they were sealed to protect the contents against the weather which made them great during the monsoon season. Many officers used them for their personal hooches and would have the men constantly working on surrounding the container with multiple layers of sand bags. Many even had a small door with a lock in front. Some had personal generators outside the bunker to supply power to an air conditioner, which cooled the inside of their glorified hooches. Then they wondered why the men lost respect for them!

After we drove Johnnie to his detail, the gunnery sergeant led me to the rear of the compound to the stockade. The stockade was exposed to the weather and framed with two-by-fours wrapped with several layers of concertina wire separated by a moat surrounded by a layer of barbed wire. In the corner sat a prisoner. Another GI who had been guarding him perked up when he saw us. The gunnery sergeant turned and snapped at me, "I want you to guard this prisoner. If you're lucky, I'll find someone to relieve you and I'll put you on something else. In the meantime, if you talk to him, you join him. Get it?"

"Yes, Gunnery Sergeant," I responded. I guarded the prisoner for two days. At night someone would relieve me. We were isolated at the rear of the compound and with the exception of helicopters coming and going, it was boring. That's what Vietnam was all about, long periods of boredom followed by periods of intense anxiety. Charlie kept it that way, always keeping us off guard and then he would strike just when we lulled ourselves into complacency.

The prisoner sat in the corner staring at the foothills in the distance. His head was shaved and he was placed on rations of bread and water. I was afraid to make eye contact for fear that any compassion I showed would be misinterpreted. Standing there all day I was tempted to ask the reason for his dilemma but I kept thinking of what the gunnery sergeant said. The thought of being in the stockade, stripped of human dignity, fed bread and water, and given a pot in a corner to relieve myself was too much to bear. I stared away from him and pretended I wasn't watching when I observed his every movement. Periodically, he would walk over to his ration of bread, break off a piece, dip it in water and take a bite. Then he would go back to his spot and stare into space. He was no older than eighteen but looked like an old man. I wondered what offense warranted such treatment and how could such treatment be justified.

The fact is it could not be justified. At least that's what Fr. Francis always preached in religion class. Where was Fr. Francis when I needed him? Nonetheless, I was sure he was with me in spirit. Later I found out that the prisoner confiscated the company jeep and drove to an off-limits brothel in Hue, eight miles up Highway 1. While intoxicated and on drugs he assaulted one of the patrons. On the way back he wrecked the company jeep. He was screwed!

In the meantime I still didn't feel comfortable without a permanent niche. I had to find a better arrangement.

It was 7:00 p.m. and I had just finished duty. Still exhausted from the events of the past week, I was hoping to get some rest. I cleaned my gear the best I could and at 9:00 p.m., after the sun went down, I dozed off. It was shortly after midnight when the all alert was sounded. Everyone yelled, "Hurry up! Hurry up! Everyone, in the bunker." We ran to the bunker and waited. An hour passed without incident and the all clear was finally sounded. I got back to bed and started to doze off when the all alert sounded again, this time with more trepidation. We ran back into the bunker. There was a long lull. Johnnie and I stared at each other, not knowing what to expect when the GI beside us said, "That Charlie, he's fucking with our brain. That's what he does best." Again about an hour passed and the all clear was sounded. Back to the hooch! I lay on my bunk, staring at the night sky that seemed unusually clear and after thirty minutes, I thought, what the hell! I have to get some rest. I'm no good to myself and a greater risk to everyone if I'm exhausted. The thought of dying while I was asleep didn't bother me as much as the thought of waking up wounded and continuing on with life half-baked. I thought, "Que Sera, Sera" and dozed off a third time. Again, just as I hit the feathers, the all alert was sounded! This time the men seemed more upset. As we ran toward the bunker the GI in front of me yelled, "Move! Move! Move! This time it's for real. That Charlie, he just loves to break our balls." We crouched down in the bunker and waited. A tall lanky GI from South Carolina looked at me and said, "Listen! Listen, you can hear them!" "Hear what?" I asked.

"The mortars as they come in — it's in-coming!" If you can hear them whistling and then walking, then you're okay. They'll get louder and louder, which means they are coming closer. Then the sound will fade away. No sooner did he finish telling us what to expect when we heard a whistling sound followed by "Whomp! Whomp! Whomp…Whomp! Whomp! Whomp!…Whomp! Whomp! Whomp…." Two struck in front of us and one to the rear. Next we heard the sound of rockets as they whistled in. This sound was much higher in frequency and when it hit it made a piercing crackling sound that always seemed closer than it was. No bunker could withstand such destructive power, no matter how many sand bags surrounded it. The destruction it caused was more devastating than that of a mortar and the sound of the impact was so deafening it always seemed much closer than it was. This was the first time I experienced such horror. I knew it was going to be a long year. During the first six months in Vietnam, we seemed to get hit two, maybe three times a week.

Chapter 14

My First Visit to Camp Eagle

I moved often during my tour of duty. I counted thirteen different hooches where I spent time. Each one different in its own special way. I preferred to be in a remote area, somewhat isolated, because Charlie would always strike where it was more densely populated. My first hooch was the most interesting. Perhaps it was my first reality check because I found myself living with marines. My hooch mates were between 18 and 19 years of age. I was 26. They believed in the war, apple pie, motherhood and flag waving whereas I lacked enthusiasm. They had trained to fight and they wanted to fight. They often reminded me that they were lean mean fighting machines. If they didn't fight the VC or the North Vietnamese regulars, they fought among themselves. They were ticking time bombs and the slightest thing would set them off. They sincerely wanted to make an impact but couldn't.

To kill the pain, many turned to hard drugs and alcohol. They would grow pot in the hooch, harvest it and hang it to dry on the hooch frame. Once dried they would roll it in toilet paper and smoke away. In the center of our hooch they had a statue of Buddha. Each night they would burn incense in front of the statue, play hard rock music, usually Steppenwolf, do drugs and consume enormous quantities of alcohol. Each time they would walk past the statue of Buddha and rub his penis as though this had some special significance and would bring them good luck. Eventually the bronze wore off, giving it a unique appearance. I watched this scenario play itself out night after night only to ask myself, where had we gone wrong? I saw what it was doing to them but I was helpless. It was consuming them. Night after night I lay on my bunk with my arm over my forehead pretending to be asleep, anxiously anticipating each moment.

Still not having a specific assignment, I reluctantly filled in whenever they needed an additional body. I dreaded morning formation for I never knew what lay ahead. On occasion we would bring supplies and materials to Camp Eagle, Headquarters for the 101st Airborne Division which was north of Phu Bai and to landing zone Sally, another firebase up by the DMZ. If we arrived at these locations late in the day we would stay overnight and leave at daybreak. However, we planned most of our trips so that we left early in the morning and returned before sunset. Staying at these bases wasn't a wise move for at night they were often under attack. I was always concerned when traveling to these locations because a wrong turn or a wrong road could be disastrous. If I were not on a mission most likely I wound up on KP, guard duty or filling sandbags. Guard duty wasn't bad, depending on what I guarded and where I was located. Sometimes in a remote area it could get lonely and if we were under attack I preferred to be with someone.

It was my forth day in Vietnam when, one morning in formation, the Gunnery Sergeant called out to me, "Hey Mas-cu-lee-lee, what did you say your MOS was?"

"45C20, Field artillery repairman, Sergeant."

"Good. This morning you can help rebuild the bunker at Post #2. This afternoon we have six men leaving for Camp Eagle. You can join them. There's a 155mm howitzer in need of repair. The tube needs to be replaced. The new tube should already be on sight. Make sure you're back here by dusk. That should give you plenty of time."

That morning I kept filling sandbags and after awhile each sandbag looked alike but they were all different. As boring as it was, I was happy to be bored considering the alternatives.

I had a lot of questions and concerns about our trip to Camp Eagle and about changing the tube under such conditions. I never did this before and knew it required a substantial amount of heavy moving equipment which I didn't see in Phu Bai nor in a remote area such as Camp Eagle, but I decided to go along with the flow.

At 3 p.m. we arrived at our destination. The howitzer was located in a crow's nest on top of a peak. The new tube was not yet there and I couldn't conceive of removing the old tube and replacing it with a new one before dark. The sergeant in charge decided to wait because the tube was coming directly from DaNang. We waited and waited in a huge pit behind the howitzer but nothing arrived. With dusk approaching, we decided to stay where we were for the evening and head back to Phu Bai in the morning.

It was about midnight when we got hit. There was nowhere to go but to remain in the pit. When in-coming subsided the pit crew decided to fire up the resident howitzer, "Big Bertha." Some of us didn't have earplugs and the constant sound was deafening. I sat in the corner with my hands covering my ears until dawn. All the while I was thinking, if I get through tonight, I *will* find a more comfortable niche to ride out the storm. Not having a slot to fill made me available to the gunnery sergeant's whims, and worrying from day to day about my next assignment was a situation I had to change.

I tried desperately to avoid the gunnery sergeant for making contact with him would bring me to his attention, thus resulting in some unpleasant assignment. The more I got to know the gunnery sergeant, the more I disliked him. He truly had a mean streak in him and seemed to get pleasure in other people's misery. It was through him that I got to know Clarence.

Clarence was a Vietnamese woman in her early thirties but looked at least mid fifties. She was short and hunched over. It was a Vietnamese custom to chew beetle nut once a female took a husband. Constant chewing caused the dye in the beetle nut to turn one's teeth black. As a result Clarence's front teeth were blackened. This purposely made her appearance unappealing, so other men would not show any interest in her. However, her husband had died in the war and her teeth remained black. Unfortunately, Clarence was also cross-eyed. The GIs in the hooch named her Clarence because she resembled Clarence the cross-eyed lion, the star of a popular sit-com in the sixties. Her main claim to fame was she was the best hooch mouse in Vietnam. She took personal pride in keeping the hooch swept out and always made sure we had an extra pair of fatigues to take with us in case we needed them. Because of the French influence in Vietnam, she spoke fluent French and was a devout Catholic. The men would often belittle her, call her names and degrade her sexuality. I could sense the animosity she harbored. Unfortunately, she was never shown much respect. It could have been any Vietnamese woman in the same position and it would have been the same. She also worked in the chapel helping out Father Anderson, the chaplain. If she was good enough for the chaplain she was good enough to be our hooch mouse. I tried to show Clarence my appreciation by being nice to her in simple ways. We paid her a pittance to keep our hooch and do our laundry so when I went to the PX, I usually bought her something she needed. After all she was the best hooch mouse in Vietnam.

Chapter 15

Colco Island

I continued to pull guard duty on a regular basis, fill sandbags and pick up supplies when necessary. No matter how hard I tried to avoid the gunnery sergeant, he would always seek me out when he needed someone for a detail. One morning while in formation I was thinking about my assignment for the day when the gunnery sergeant asked, "Hey, Mas-cu-lee-lee, you want to work in the mess hall?" I hesitated, not knowing what to expect, and before I could answer he continued, "I knew you'd agree. You can help pick up food supplies. By the way can you cook? Well, if you don't you can learn. From now on you're assigned to the mess hall." I figured I could hide out in the mess hall until something better came along and at least I knew what my daily assignment would be. After all, Clarence was in the mess hall and many of the men in my original unit were working in the area. Also, it gave me access to the mess hall truck for transportation purposes since I would also be picking up supplies. I was hoping I could get out of guard duty but I wasn't that fortunate. I must admit I felt a sense of relief knowing I had a steady assignment.

Being assigned to the mess hall wasn't bad at all. It gave me time to look around and possibly find a more comfortable arrangement. Clarence knew the ropes here and was very helpful. It gave me an opportunity to see other reservists during meal times. I had learned to appreciate Clarence. She had lost her husband and two children in the war and she wasn't as imposing as many other Vietnamese. Although her parents were alive, their village had been destroyed and they lived in a refugee camp on the coast of South China Sea called Colco Island.

Home Sweet Home

Clarence was living in a small hut outside the base camp along Highway 1. At the end of each day I would see her rummaging through the barrels behind the mess hall for leftover food to take to her village. Realizing we usually had leftovers I approached the gunnery sergeant and asked, " Hey, Sarge, how about giving the leftovers to Clarence to take home?"

He responded, "Let her take the scraps from the garbage. It's against regulations to give her any leftover food."

"Well, what do you want us to do with it?" I asked.

"Pour kerosene over it and burn it!"

I learned that it was customary to pour kerosene over perfectly good leftovers and burn them. For an Italian from the North End this was sacrilegious. At first I complied, but after three weeks of this nonsense I decided I wasn't going to do this anymore and somehow I would find a way to break this custom.

Of course, the Gunnery Sergeant laughed and thought the whole idea of burning food instead of giving it to the Vietnamese was hilarious. The next time I was on mess duty and we had leftovers, I insisted on taking care of the situation. I took the edible leftovers and neatly place them in several clean plastic bags we used for rubbish and sealed the bags. I then took a larger plastic bag, opened it, placed it in a barrel and covered the bottom with garbage. I then placed the sealed bag with edible food on top of the rubbish and covered it with additional rubbish. Thus, it appeared to be all garbage. If for any unforeseen reason the gunnery sergeant had to check out the rubbish barrels, he would probably rely on one of his subordinates and if someone else discovered the food, I was confident I could handle the situation. It didn't take long for Clarence to realize what was going on even though we never spoke about it. Since then, Clarence became very helpful. She told me when to expect in-coming (rocket and mortar fire) and where to be and where not to be and who amongst the Vietnamese to watch out for. Many of the Vietnamese would work in the compound by day and join the Viet Cong at night fighting against us. Often we would see Vietnamese pacing off the company area to determine coordinates. Clarence always warned us what to expect. One time she told us about ground-up glass that was put in the mashed potatoes by one of the Vietnamese. I insisted she tell the gunnery sergeant. At first she was reluctant. However, with some prodding I accompanied her when she spoke with him. He was forever grateful and promised to let me take the jeep to Colco Island to help her find her parents. I knew she was playing both sides against the middle, but she had a level of sincerity I respected. I trusted Clarence and she trusted me.

It was a Saturday morning a week before Christmas when the gunnery sergeant asked me if I wanted to take the mess hall jeep and drop some supplies off just outside Hue. I felt good that he actually asked politely instead of barking out an order as he usually did. I asked, "What's in Hue, Sarge?" He paused a moment and for the first time since I had been assigned to his hooch he showed some compassion when he said, "You know the Marines are heavily involved in the 'Toys for Tots' program and each Christmas we gather toys for the homeless and the needy. There's a Maryknoll orphanage in Hue where I'd like you to drop off these toys. Christmas Eve we'll get some guys together and spend some time at the orphanage opening presents and playing with the kids. You can take Clarence with you if you like. Take your time. Take the day, but make sure you're back before sunset." I then realized he was giving me the unofficial okay to take Clarence to Colco Island.

We left Phu Bai early in the morning and drove up the coast to Hue along the "Perfume River." It was called the "Perfume River" because it supposedly gave off a fragrance. I found the fragrance far from pleasant. We briefly stopped at the orphanage and dropped off the Christmas gifts. One of the Maryknoll nuns came to the courtyard where we unloaded the jeep. She insisted that we stay for tea and normally I would have enjoyed the visit. However, we convinced her that we should be on our way and would come back another time.

I always considered Hue similar in size and character to Lowell, Massachusetts. They both appeared to be the same in size, both had large rivers running through the center of each city and both had large Catholic populations. Also, there was a strong French influence in Hue as there was in Lowell. Hue was the old imperial capital of Vietnam and during the TET offensive of 1968 Hue was decimated. It went back and forth and finally we regained it and kept it. Now there was talk about a counter offensive.

It was approaching 9 a.m. and the heat of the sun warmed the air causing the dust from the rubble to rise creating a surreal atmosphere. As we approached a fork in the road leading to the city, sitting on a triangular tract of land were the remnants of a Catholic church. The only portion of the church intact was the front.

On the walkway leading to the front doors was a large statue of the Blessed Mother with her arms extended as though to welcome us. I thought it odd that the front portion of the church was the only part to remain standing. It was more than one hundred feet high, completely intact with no roof, no sides and no back. It defied the laws of gravity. Looking closer I noticed what appeared to be rings of light shining through the brick facade. I then noticed the entire structure was riddled with bullet holes no less than one inch apart. Probably the result of one of our most advanced weapons of the time called, "puff the magic dragon." It was capable of firing 600 rounds a second over the surface area of a football field. The holes in the brick appeared to be clean as though each one had been individually drilled. The rays of sunshine reflected off the dust giving a prism effect as the sunlight exited each hole. We paused a moment, said a prayer, and continued on our way.

We drove along Highway 1. To our left and right the Vietnamese were working in the rice paddies with their pants rolled up. In the far distance to my right I could see a platoon was coming up from the beach. The humidity was unbearable so we decided to stop at the first location that provided shade. On the other side of the highway a Vietnamese approached us. He seemed unaffected by the heat and was toting two honey buckets. They appeared to be heavy but that didn't seem to affect him. His gait and rhythm, as he bounced up and down, was akin to a highly efficient machine. His barefoot wife who appeared to be in her third trimester of pregnancy followed suit. At first I was concerned at their sudden appearance but when the men in the platoon favorably acknowledged them I realized they knew them and my concerns went away. The woman then ran in front of her husband and yelled, "Hey, GI, you want Coca-Cola. I have iced cold Coca-Cola. Two dalla." With both hands on the top of her stomach, she continued, "Baby son, come soon. Need milk for baby. Coca-Cola good. You take two. Four dalla." We purchased one each and so did the men on patrol. Clarence and I sat under a tree when I noticed our Coke cans were stamped "Not for sale." "Look Clarence it reads not

for sale." We both laughed. One of the GIs picked up on it and responded, "You're lucky today it's cold. Most days it's warm." It appeared as though this was a daily ritual between mama-son, papa-son and the GIs. The men then spread out on the side of the road as though they were happy to be alone, if only for a moment. They didn't speak and appeared to be preoccupied.

I had been in-country for four months and the thousand-mile stare I so often saw on the faces of many GIs now seemed more intense. Until now I had remained distant. Only now I realized it was starting to bother me as it bothered everyone else. I couldn't fight it anymore. I gazed off in the distance and felt comfort in tuning everything out. I enjoyed the feeling of numbness. If only for a brief period, it brought some peace.

Corruption ran rampant. "The stench of corruption rose to unprecedented levels during William C. Westmoreland's command." It was rumored that the CIA protected the poppy fields of Vietnamese officials and flew their heroin out of the country on Air America planes. A major who flew the U.S. ambassador's private jet was caught smuggling 8 million dollars worth of heroin on the plane.[23]

Army stores (PXs) were importing French perfumes and other luxury goods to sell on the black market. But the black market extended far beyond luxury goods: The Viet Cong received a large percentage of their supplies from the United States via the underground routes of the black market. Supplies such as kerosene, sheet metal, oil, gasoline engines, claymore mines, hand grenades, rifles, bags of cement were publicly sold at open, outdoor black markets.[24]

By this time we were disillusioned with a war in which American-made military material was being used against us. And then there were endless scandals: PX scandals, NCO-club scandals, sergeant-major scandals, M-16 jamming scandals. In interviews, when Vietnam veterans were asked what stood out about their experience, a repeated answer was "the corruption."[25]

The ethics of many servicemen imitated those of the business elite they served. They were corrupted by the system. Many officers placed career advancement at the welfare of their troops. Through black market profiteering many lived in luxury while other low ranking troops had difficulty in getting basic supplies. The corruption of many officers, combined with the combat plan that avoided many officer casualties while guaranteeing men of lesser rank to be put in harm's way, produced explosive results.

We continued north along the coast until we came to an area that appeared to have been a very nice beach. It was now strewn with concertina and barbed wire with beer cans attached filled with pebbles to alert the guards of any infiltration. There was a path in the middle of the beach leading down to the edge of the water where passengers and vehicles could board an LST for transportation to Colco Island. To the left and right of the path were signs forbidding entry. No doubt the area was mined. Far removed off the mainland was a huge island. At first I thought this to be Colco Island but I was politely informed and felt silly when one of the guards told me it belonged to China. The reason for all the security became clear. The LST was used for transportation to the far side of the island. We could have taken the jeep across in the LST but this seemed too precarious so we decided to drive.

The access road was long and narrow with marsh grass on both sides of the road. Encountering a vehicle coming in the opposite direction did not leave much room for both to pass. Already several vehicles had driven off the road and it wasn't yet noon. I now knew why many chose to take the LST and not drive. As we continued on our way we approached a guard house. The guard, a young marine, came out and asked me to state my business. He was less than supportive when I told him why we were there. He tried to discourage us but finally relented when we told him how far we had come and our purpose in being there. After some persuasion, he let us enter.

We approached a section of the island that looked like a storage area for huge discarded drainpipes. Closer observation revealed the drainpipes to be shelters for the homeless. I drove very slowly, all the while observing the living conditions. We brought candy and some packaged rations, which we foolishly thought we could share. As soon as I passed out a piece of candy to a young boy who had followed the jeep since we entered the compound, Vietnamese came from everywhere looking for food. Many were severely deformed without arms or legs; others had more gruesome deformities, the likes of which I had never seen. Amazingly with makeshift prosthetic devices, made out of discarded crates and supplies strewn about, they were able to keep up with the jeep. With everyone crowding the jeep, the situation was quickly getting out of control. Clarence started crying and screaming. In haste, we emptied out two bags of candy bars and sped away. We drove down to the MP station at the end of the island to ponder our next move. I turned and looked back only to see the Vietnamese scrambling for the few pieces of candy left on the ground. Clarence was determined to continue on this quest. I wanted to go back to Phu Bai. The MP at the station knowing our dilemma offered to escort us about. I reluctantly agreed to give it another shot. He brought us to someone who appeared to be the matriarch of Colco Island. Clarence spoke to her for a few minutes and when I saw the sadness in her expression I knew something was wrong. She revealed to Clarence that both her parents had been killed leaving Hue during the Tet Offensive. Clarence was now alone.

We left the island disappointed and drove south down Highway 1 toward Hue. Every now and then I would glance across at Clarence only to see her staring out into the rice paddies holding back the emotions she probably learned to hold back since childhood. We drove for a while until I found a shady spot underneath a tree where I pulled over. It was now early afternoon and the sun was at its zenith. In the distance you could still see the Vietnamese with their pants rolled up working in the rice paddies. While sitting under the tree engrossed in my thoughts, again I glanced at Clarence. I felt sorry for her. Even amongst the Vietnamese she seemed to have been short-changed.

She was only twenty-eight but she looked much older and appeared to be borderline retarded. By comparison my grandmother was in her seventies and Clarence looked at least that. She was hunched over as though she had premature osteoporosis and now she realized her last hope of reuniting with her parents was gone. She had no education, no family and her only source of income was the pittance she made in the mess hall and the little she made as our hooch mouse. She worked in the chapel helping Father Anderson but this was "gratis." She didn't have much going for her. In spite of it all, she relished the little she had and rarely complained. There was nothing I could say or do. I felt awkward. For that brief moment the agony and pain inflicted on the many who were affected by Vietnam seemed to weigh on the shoulders of this simple Vietnamese woman. The pain of the fathers who never got to see their children and the pain of the many wives who waited in vain for their loved ones to come home. The pain of the mothers who sent their eighteen-year-old sons off to fight a war they believed in. The pain of the mothers of those MIAs who naively cling to the hope their sons will walk up the front steps with duffle bag over their shoulders just in time for Christmas dinner—all this pain I saw in the burrows so clearly distinguishable on the face of this frail individual. I waited with anticipation hoping she would say something. We sat staring at the rice paddies when she reached into the small bag that held her candy and pulled her hand out of the bag and turned in my direction. She covered her face with her hands and cried uncontrollably. In the palm of my hand she then placed a pair of rosary beads. She carved a small crucifix out of wood and made small knots out of rope for the Hail Marys and larger, more distinguishable knots, for the Our Fathers. I was touched by her humility and her unwavering faith, and I was embarrassed when she turned and said, "You Number 1 GI."

It wasn't long after we started up again and were stopped by MPs at a security checkpoint. I looked across the highway down into a gully off the side of the road and saw several GIs from the 101st Airborne. All the traffic had been stopped on Highway 1. I asked Clarence to stay in the jeep while I walked across the highway and approached the gully. I was hoping to make it back before evening meal and I wanted to see Fr. Anderson. I was concerned about being delayed for any length of time. In the bottom of the gully was a tree. I thought it unusual that everyone was looking up from beneath the tree. Several had their shirts over their mouths and noses. I walked within 50 feet of the tree and ran into this God-awful stench the likes of which I will never forget. We had been in this area just 8 hours earlier and everything appeared normal. As I approached the tree I saw a GI from our compound hanging from a limb. He was last seen at an off-limits brothel in Hue. He was hanging upside down, his penis severed and stuffed in his mouth. The stench and the sight of this young GI, certainly no more than 20 years old, dying in such a humiliating way is what war is all about. The horrific stench of a decaying body has a sobering effect and makes the strongest of atheists cling to something more than the present. It awakens the senses to realize there must be more to this existence than eventually rotting into nothingness. It makes the strongest of hawks want to find an alternative to war. I felt nauseous and at the same time thanked God for keeping me well.

It was almost 3 p.m. and we still had a one hour ride. The drive back to Phu Bai was horrible. Not one word was spoken. When we arrived at Phu Bai I thanked Clarence for the rosary, which I always kept with me and treasured. I brought her to Father Anderson, the chaplain, with the hope he could be of some assistance. Father Anderson was just returning from headquarters. It bothered me that he was laughing and joking with one of the Vietnamese workers outside the chapel. Guess what, he was quick to tell us, "I just made full bird colonel." I was saddened that he was feeling so up beat and all I could do was to ask him, "Well, now that you made full bird colonel, Father Anderson, the question is, do you feel any closer to God?"

That evening I had difficulty sleeping. I kept going over the events of the day. After lying in bed a few hours with no luck, something told me to get dressed and go over to 24th Corps and try calling home. Traveling north along Highway 1 the Phu Bai Compound was on the right and across the highway to the left was 24th Corps Headquarters. There was a ham radio shack at 24th Corps and occasionally I would try to contact a radio operator in the vicinity of Massachusetts. During my first few months in-country, I made several unsuccessful attempts to call home. I wandered over to 24th Corps and was fortunate for there was no waiting in line to get on the air. After several attempts I was lucky enough to contact a radio operator from New Jersey and from there he telephoned my home. Theoretically, I should have been able to speak to my parents from Phu Bai through the microphone if the ham operator in New Jersey had placed his phone close to the mike. Of course, the only difficulty I had was that we had one-way communication; that is, after each transmission the speaker had to release the call button on the mike after concluding the transmission with the word "over." The person at the other end would then press the call button and speak and also conclude with the word "over." This presented some difficulty for many including my mother. Not being able to hear and speak on the telephone at the same time can be difficult. The ham operator assured me that my mother was fully aware of the protocols and was anxious to speak with me. Once everything was in order I brought myself close to the mike and tried to enunciate distinctly as I said, "Hello Mom, Hello Mom, this is Ralph, over." Then there was a 30 second delay and the ham operator came over the radio and said, "Ralph, your Mother is having difficulty with one way communications, over."

"Let's give it another try. Over."

"Okay, Ralph, give me a second to reconnect the phone to the mike.

Over."

"Hello Mom, this is Ralph. Make sure you say the word "over" at the end of your transmission so the ham operator can release the talk button. Okay? Over."

Finally, "Hi Ralph, this is Mom. Where are you? Over."

"I'm still in Vietnam, Mom. Where do you think I am? Over."

" How's the food there? Are you eating well? Over."

" Please, just keep sending those packages with pepperoni and artichoke hearts. Over"

"You must have heard about your father? Over."

"What? What about Dad? Over."

"Didn't Mary tell you? He had a stroke. Over."

"Is he okay? Over"

"Well now he's…."

At that moment we lost contact. I didn't want to over react, but under these circumstances one always thinks of the worst possible scenario. I had no idea of the seriousness of the stroke and to what extent he was incapacitated. All I knew is that he needed me and I couldn't be there. I wanted to be with him in his time of need. I felt helpless. I slowly walked back to my hooch feeling totally beside myself. All the while I asked God to help out Dad and to help me get through the year. With the help of God I knew I could cope with anything that came my way.

When I got back to the hooch, I climbed on my bunk and didn't bother to take my clothes off. I could see a faint tinge of red in the sky that meant morning would be coming soon. I was driving myself crazy trying to complete the sentence my mother had started, "Well now he's…. he's what? I kept repeating in my mind." Just then the siren went off. I was at an advantage. I was already dressed. Immediately I hit the bunker and sat in the far corner. I had grown numb to the sound of mortar. I had the feeling that if my name was on one, there was nothing in my power that could prevent it. When the all clear was sounded I stayed in the corner for a period of time and tried to pull myself together. I was at my breaking point.

Several days had passed with no mail. Finally on the 4th day I received three letters from Mary and two from my mother. Dad had a stroke and was hospitalized for a while and he was now in rehabilitation. Although he had lost partial mobility they were optimistic they could improve his condition and increase his mobility. Like most of us, Mom had trouble dealing with adversity. I felt I should be there to help them but I had no alternative but to care for myself. Without taking care of myself I would be of little use to anyone.

Chapter 16

More Shit

As the U.S. Marines were slowly leaving Phu Bai and being replaced by the U. S. Army, I moved back to a hooch with some reservists and regular army members. Although I had a new hooch commander, I was still assigned to the gunnery sergeant on the duty roster. In all I moved thirteen times. It was 2 a.m. when the hooch commander came running into the hooch yelling, "Hurry up! Hurry up! Everyone, get dressed. I just received an S-2 intelligence report expecting in-coming followed by a ground attack. Get dressed and out to the perimeter on the double!" When I finished dressing, one of the GIs in our hooch asked me to secure the clasp on his backpack. He was tall and lean and lacked coordination. He must have been a newcomer. I didn't recognize him. I kept thinking: if we ever have a ground attack he'd never make it, but then, so what if he's uncoordinated? Who's to say I'll make it? Anyway, what determines whether one makes it or not? Is it fate, skill, Providence, or is it just plain luck? We went out to assigned locations and hunkered down. We received in-coming. The sound was deafening. As soon as it subsided, I looked at my watch and noticed it was 3 a.m. We still had three and one-half hours before sunrise. If we made it to sunrise we would be temporarily out of the woods but three and one-half hours was a long time. We positioned ourselves behind sandbags and waited. No one spoke. There was absolute silence. The thought of death and dying came to mind and whether or not it mattered how I died. The question is if you're dead, do you know how you died, and if not, it didn't matter because you don't know? Maybe it matters to you before you die and to those you leave behind. They're the ones who live with your legacy, good or bad. I suppose if there's a higher being we all report to, then it matters, and if not we're all in deep shit.

If how we die doesn't matter, then the old cliche, "I'd rather slip on a banana peel and hit my head on a curbstone than die in Vietnam" might apply. If one died helping out an old lady in distress, it would matter to a Supreme Honcho, but what about war. Is war not inherently evil and does it not oppose the teachings of the Church? Would my Maker think less of me if I died fighting for this Godforsaken country as opposed to helping out the lady in need? I thought about a GI from the North End named "Sterite" who was one of the first casualties in Vietnam. What did it get him?" Big deal, they named a playground after him. Three a.m. came and nothing happened. Still there was silence. I knew from experience that as soon as we lulled ourselves into complacency that's when Charlie would strike. I thought of Dad and Uncle Joe in WW II and I wondered if they ever felt as cowardly as I did. I wanted to be home hanging around in the North End having Coogie's lousy coffee and joking with my friends. If I had a choice at that very moment I would have chosen to go home and to hell with the consequences. Then what about all those men who have given their lives? Their lives have to be worth something, but what?

My thoughts wandered to one of our summer picnics at Captains Pond. I convinced my father to bring my Red Ryder BB gun for target practice and took my first shot at a chipmunk in a tree above the picnic site. It was a long shot but I hit it and it fell to its death in the middle of our picnic area just missing the table. I was grounded for two weeks and could not go in the water all afternoon. It was of no consolation that one of my cousins and I gave the chipmunk a decent burial.

It was now 4 a.m. and we still waited in fear. I discretely placed my right hand in my pocket and tightly held onto the rosaries Clarence made for me and Fr. Anderson blessed. Quietly, I tried to say the rosary. Still no one said much. I suppose we were all thinking the same thoughts of home and loved ones and good times past and hoping we could get back home to enjoy the freedom we were supposedly fighting to protect. The anxiety was visible on everyone's face. What quirk of fate had brought me from a street corner in the North End to a bunker in Vietnam scared to death?

Finally 5 a.m. came and the red tinge of sunlight came over the foothills. Seeing the sunlight get brighter and brighter made me want to cry but I couldn't. When the all-clear was sounded we all slowly dragged our asses back to the hooch exhausted but eternally grateful. Still no one spoke. I felt old in a young man's body and thanked God for another day.

No sooner did we return to our hootch when one of the original members of the 513th came running into the hooch yelling, "Did you hear the news? Did you hear the news? Packy Hughes got shot! He got shot in the head! He's dead!" A young GI from the regular army not knowing the history of the unit and that Packy Hughes was once a member of the unit asked, "Where was he when he got shot?" Jim looked at him knowing that he expected to hear he got shot somewhere in Vietnam when he responded, "He got shot in Mission Hill, Roxbury!" Danny, one of the original members of the 513th cynically commented, "Are you shit'n. He was the only one of us that got out of going to Nam and he got shot in Boston. How ironic."

Packy Hughes' family owned the Hughes Drug Store on Tremont Street in Mission Hill. Hughes was 27 at the time, married with a baby boy and a wife who was pregnant when the 513th was activated. His family status undoubtedly aided his receiving a hardship deferment and he was released from the Army, thus remaining at home. At the time he was the envy of the unit. No one wanted to go and I must admit I was somewhat envious that Packy was staying behind. I don't think there was anyone in the 513th who would not have traded places with Packy. As it turned out had Packy known what fate was in store for him, I'm sure he would have taken his chances in Vietnam. Packy Hughes was employed with the city housing department and was attending law school. Four nights before Christmas he was at the pharmacy covering for his father who was home ill. Hughes was at the cash register when in walked three young adults looking for drugs and money. When they asked for cash and drugs Packy responded with a wet mop hitting one of them in the face. The assailant responded by pulling out a .22 caliber rifle and firing only to hit Hughes in the head. His uncle Patrick came to his rescue only to be hit by another round. Patrick now fell dying on top of Packy who was already dead. Ironically Packy was taken to Brigham's Hospital where Nancy Buckley the wife of John Buckley, also a member of the 513th and Suzette Desrosiers who subsequently married Kevin Sullivan, also a member of the 513th were nurses in the emergency room when both victims were admitted. Packy was declared dead on arrival and his Uncle Patrick lasted two days before succumbing. A very pregnant Nancy Buckley, from Jamaica Plain who knew the assailant, also from Jamaica Plain, greeted a very pregnant Mrs.Huges at the door to the emergency room knowing her husband had just died.

Many years later the grandmother of the Hughes' son, now a young adult and Nancy Buckley again crossed paths at a ceramics class in Stoughton, Massachusetts. At the time the assailant was up for parole. Nancy Buckley unknowingly sat across from Packey Hughes' mother-in-law and overheard her expressing concern about her son-in-law's assailant being set free. It was then acknowledged that each of them, together unknowingly, shared one of the same most important moments in each of their lives.

Some of the other men with the original 513th were also in the same compound infused with the 26th General Support Group. The youngest individual in the original 513th was Danny, a baby faced eighteen-year-old from Somerville, Massachusetts. He had joined the reserves right out of high school. Considering that many of the men in the unit were in their mid-twenties, Danny was not as mature as most. He always seemed to want to prove himself and would get extremely upset when the hooch commander would have him sweep out the hooch or impose some similar menial task on him. Danny thought we always picked on him. He thought everything was grossly unjust and was always complaining. Danny worked at the front gate where he checked out trucks entering and leaving the compound. As a result he managed to confiscate his own personal Connex container and placed it not far from the main gate. Traveling north we were located to the right of Highway 1 and to the left of the highway was the 24th Corps Headquarters. Danny worked very diligently, although in secret, to fix up his Connex container with the hope of some day having his own personal hooch. After all, if it was good enough for the officers it was certainly good enough for Danny. Each day he would add additional sandbags around the container to make it safer and when he would confiscate something useful, he would add it to his personal belongings. One day he proudly showed me his new hooch to be. I was impressed and even envied him. We never knew where or when Charlie would strike. It seemed reasonable to assume that the remote location of Danny's hooch was in a more secure place than where we presently were because Charlie always wanted to get the biggest bang for his buck. Granted, the rockets used in Vietnam didn't have internal guidance systems one-quarter as accurate as we have today. Nevertheless, I would bet on a rocket aimed in the middle of the compound than on the perimeter where his new hooch was located.

When the hootch was finished he requested permission to move to the new location but his supposed friend, Sergeant Conway, denied his request. As Danny was inclined to do, he pestered Sergeant Conway about moving to his new hooch. The issue came to a head when they were both sitting around one evening having a few brews. That evening tempers flared when Danny yelled at Conway, "I don't give a rat's ass who you are. I put all that time and effort to have a little peace and quiet and tonight I'm sleeping in my new hooch." Sergeant Conway rebutted, "I told you all along, you could fix it up but I would never let you live there. You're a part of this unit and you'll sleep where you belong and that's right here." They went back and forth for a while until Sergeant Conway, visibly upset, insisted, "Look, I'm your superior and you report to me. I've known you a long time and you're a friend. However, in front of all these guys, I promise you if you leave this hooch against my orders you will be court-martialed." Danny hemmed and hawed, moaned and groaned, and pouted and moped, but still insisted on moving into his new hooch. Of course he was eighteen years old and his macho instinct had a lot to do with his behavior. We finally convinced him to stay in his old hooch with the promise we would ask Conway to reconsider at a more appropriate time. He grudgingly complied and complained all night.

When we finally got to bed the all-alert sounded. "Hurry! Hurry! Hurry! On the double! It's in-coming. In the bunkers." We ran to the bunker and waited in a crouched position. As the rockets entered the compound, we heard the high-pitched whistling sound. Next you could hear them striking. We waited a long while in a crouched position. This time it was close. It was always too close. While listening to the whistling sound before they hit the target, the thought of a direct hit was ever present. Everyone would have the same look in his eyes. It's the look you see in the eyes of someone who is gravely ill and doesn't know what evil misfortune may lie ahead. Nothing survives a direct hit. It was close. When the sun finally came up, we decided to take a look at the damage. Danny and I walked out to the entrance to the compound. From the distance we could see an area cordoned off. In the middle of this area was Danny's hooch to be, now a mass of twisted metal. It had received a direct hit. I turned to Danny only to see his face turn pale gray. His bunk, in which he never slept, resembled a piece of Swiss cheese. He turned to me and said, "I almost slept there!" Then he was quiet for the longest period of time.

After this incident Danny quieted down and was less willing to complain. Danny had grown up. He had been in the right place at the right time. Unfortunately, many were in the wrong place at the wrong time. We never knew from moment to moment what to expect. That's what Vietnam was all about!

Chapter 17

First Sergeants, First Sergeants and More First Sergeants

First sergeants, first sergeants and more first sergeants! Although I remember about five first sergeants, other members of the 513th have reminded me that we had no fewer than twenty-one first sergeants. Perhaps that's because early in the game I learned to tune things out. At morning formation I remember seeing a different face addressing the troops just about every other week and hearing the same old routine about how this sergeant was going to kick butt. Each sergeant was destined to bring the wrath of God upon the unit and "whip us into action" but this too always passed.

Sergeant Caruso, one of the original first sergeants, had been with the 513th when it was activated. Although overweight and one whose leadership abilities were questionable, he was well liked. He had been in the reserves for many years and had become friendly with many of the men. As a matter of fact he became so close to the men that his ability to function in a leadership capacity was clouded. It was obvious he lacked the physical and mental demands of a first sergeant and although he functioned well in a reserve environment, Vietnam was another story. Caruso led from his heart and not his head. Shortly after we were activated, he left the reserves and did not accompany the unit to Vietnam.

Then there was fat Sully of the 245th in Roslindale who joined the unit. Sully was one of the boys and knew all the men in the unit. After duty hours he would often join the men at Rappaport's bar on Pulaski

Highway at the entrance to Ft. Meade where we would meet every evening, have a few brews and discuss our fate. Fat Sully stays in my mind because I remember looking up one morning in formation and noticing he had lost at least 60 pounds. I guess he was concerned about his physical condition had he gone to Vietnam. He too had time and grade and either transferred out of the unit or retired from the reserves. It seemed there was always someone new in front of us dressing us down and telling us our butts would be in a sling if we didn't shape up. Rarely did they have a kind word to say about the 513th Maintenance Battalion. The officer corps had even less success in maintaining discipline.

If an officer attempted to impose disciplinary punishment upon a soldier, the power did not exist to get it executed. With the falling away of their disciplinary power, the political bankruptcy of the staff of officers was laid bare.[26] The sacrificial refusal of an order to advance into combat is an act of mutiny. In time of war, it is the gravest crime in the military code, punishable by death. In Vietnam, mutiny was rampant, the power to punish withered and discipline collapsed as search and destroy was revoked from below.

Until 1967, open defiance in the military was rare and harshly repressed, with sentences of two to ten years for minor infractions. Hostility to search-and-destroy missions took the form of covert combat avoidance, called "sandbagging" by the grunts. A platoon sent out to "hump the boonies" might look for a safe cover from which to file fabricated reports of imaginary activity.[27]

But after Tet, there was a massive shift from combat avoidance to mutiny. One Pentagon official reflected that "mutiny became so common that the army was forced to disguise its frequency by talking instead of 'combat refusal.'" Combat refusal, one commentator observed, "resembled a strike and occurred when GIs refused, disobeyed, or negotiated an order into combat."[28]

Acts of mutiny took place on a scale previously only encountered in revolutions. The first mutinies in 1968 were unit and platoon-level rejections of the order to fight. The army recorded 68 such mutinies that year. By 1970, in the 1st Air Cavalry Division alone, there were 35 acts of combat refusal.[29] One military study concluded that combat refusal was "unlike mutinous outbreaks of the past, which were usually sporadic, short-lived events. The progressive unwillingness of American soldiers to fight to the point of open disobedience took place over a four-year period between 1968 — 71."[30]

The 1968 combat refusals of individual units expanded to involve whole companies by the next year. The first reported mass mutiny was in the 196th Light Brigade in August 1969. Company A of the 3rd Battalion, down to 60 men from its original 150, had been pushing through Song Hang Valley under heavy fire for five days when it refused an order to advance down a perilous mountain slope. Word of the mutiny spread rapidly. The *New York Daily News* ran a banner headline, "Sir, My Men Refuse To Go."[31] The GI paper, *The Bond*, accurately noted, "It was an organized strike.... A shaken brass relieved the company commander...but they did not charge the guys with anything. The Brass surrendered to the strength of the organized men."

This precedent—no court-martial for refusing to obey the order to fight, but the line officer relieved of his command—was the pattern for the rest of the war. Mass insubordination was not punished by an officer corps that lived in fear of its own men. Even the threat of punishment often backfired. In one famous incident, B Company of the 1st Battalion of the 12th Infantry refused an order to proceed into NLF-held territory. When they were threatened with court-martials, other platoons rallied to their support and refused orders to advance until the army backed down.[32]

As the fear of punishment faded, mutinies mushroomed. There were at least ten reported major mutinies, and hundreds of smaller ones. Hanoi's Vietnam Courier documented 15 important GI rebellions in 1969. At Cu Chi, troops from the 2nd Battalion of the 27th Infantry refused battle orders. The "CBS Evening News" broadcast live a patrol from the 7th Cavalry telling their captain that his order for direct advance against the NLF was nonsense, that it would threaten casualties, and that they would not obey it. Another CBS broadcast televised the mutiny of a rifle company of the 1st Air Cavalry Division.[33]

When Cambodia was invaded in 1970, soldiers from Fire Base Washington conducted a sit-in. They told, *Up Against the Bulkhead*, "We have no business there... we just sat down. Then they promised us we wouldn't have to go to Cambodia." Within a week, there were two additional mutinies, as men from the 4th and 8th infantry refused to board helicopters to Cambodia. [34]

In the invasion of Laos in March 1971, two platoons refused to advance. To prevent the mutiny from spreading, the entire squadron was pulled out of the Laos operation. The captain was relieved of his command, but there was no discipline against the men. When a lieutenant from the 501st Infantry refused his battalion commander's order to advance his troops, he merely received a suspended sentence.[35]

The decision not to punish men defying the most sacrosanct article of the military code, the disobedience of the order for combat, indicated how much the deterioration of discipline had eroded the power of the officers. The only punishment for most mutinies and a lack of discipline within the unit was to relieve the commanding officer of his duties. Consequently, many commanders would not report that they had lost control of their men. They swept news of mutiny, which would jeopardize their careers, under the rug. As they became quiet in their complicity, the officer corps lost any remaining moral authority to impose discipline.

For every defiance in combat, there were hundreds of minor acts of insubordination in rear base camps. As one infantry officer reported, "You can't give orders and expect them to be obeyed."[36] This upsurge from below was so extensive that discipline was replaced by a new command technique called "working it out." Working it out was a form of collective bargaining in which negotiations went on between officers and men to determine orders. Working it out destroyed the authority of the officer corps and stripped the ability of the army to carry out search-and-destroy missions. But the army had no alternative strategy for a guerrilla war against a national liberation movement.[37]

The political impact of the mutiny was felt far beyond Vietnam. As H. R. Haldeman, Nixon's chief of staff, reflected, "If troops are going to mutiny, you can't pursue an aggressive policy."[38] Some men who did not resort to mutiny resorted to fragging.

There is one first sergeant the men of the 513th will never forget and that is Sergeant Click.

The moral condition of the unit was at its lowest. You might describe it by saying the unit, as a unit no longer existed. Constant berating from higher-ranking officers had utterly undermined the troops.[39]

On October 9, 1968, an article appeared in *The Boston Globe* stating that the commanding general of the fourth infantry division had stopped punishing non-saluters. The murder of American officers by our men was an openly proclaimed goal in Vietnam. As one GI newspaper demanded, "Don't desert. Go to Vietnam, and kill your commanding officer."[40] And they did. A new slang term arose to celebrate the execution of officers by dropping a grenade in their vicinity: fragging. The word came from the fragmentation grenade, which was the weapon of choice because the evidence was destroyed in the act.[41]

In all wars, troops kill officers whose incompetence or recklessness threatens the lives of their men. But only in Vietnam did this become pervasive in combat situations and widespread in rear base camps. It was the most well known aspect of the class struggle inside the army, directed not just at intolerable officers, but at "lifers" as a group. In the soldiers' revolt, it became accepted practice to paint political slogans on helmets. A popular helmet slogan summed up this mood: "Kill a noncom for Christ." Fragging was the ransom the ground troops extracted for being used as live bait.[42]

No one knows how many officers were fragged, but after Tet it became epidemic. At least 800 to 1,000 fragging attempts using explosive devices were made. The army reported 126 fraggings in 1969, 271 in 1970 and 333 in 1971, when they stopped keeping count. But in that year, just in the American Division (of My Lai fame), one fragging per week took place. Some military estimates are that fraggings occurred at five times the official rate, while officers of the Judge Advocate General (JAG) Corps believed that only 10 percent of fraggings were reported. These figures do not include officers who were shot in the back by their men and listed as wounded or killed in action.[43]

Most fraggings resulted in injuries, although "word of the deaths of officers will bring cheers at troop movies or in bivouacs of certain units."[44] The army admitted that it could not account for how 1,400 officers and noncommissioned officers died. This number, plus the official list of fragging deaths, has been accepted as the unacknowledged army estimate for officers killed by their men. It suggests that 20 to 25 percent—if not more—of all officers killed during the war were killed by enlisted men, not the "enemy." This figure has no precedent in the history of war.[45]

Soldiers put bounties on officers targeted for fragging. The money, usually between $100 and $1,000, was collected by subscription from among the enlisted men. It was a reward for the soldier who executed the collective decision. The highest bounty for an officer was $10,000, publicly offered by *GI Says*, a mimeographed bulletin put out in the 101st Airborne Division, for Col. W. Honeycutt, who had ordered the May 1969 attack on Hill 937. The hill had no strategic significance and was immediately abandoned when the battle ended. It became enshrined in GI folklore as Hamburger Hill, because of the 56 men killed and 420 wounded taking it. Despite several fragging attempts, Honeycutt escaped uninjured.[46]

As a Vietnam GI argued after Hamburger Hill, "Brass are calling this a tremendous victory. We call it a goddamn butcher.... If you want to die so some lifer can get a promotion, go right ahead. But if you think your life is worth something, you better get yourselves together. If you don't take care of the lifers, they might damn well take care of you."[47]

Fraggings were occasionally called off. One lieutenant refused to obey an order to storm a hill during an operation in the Mekong Delta. "His first sergeant later told him that when his men heard him refuse that order, they removed a $350 bounty earlier placed on his head because they thought he was a 'hard-liner.'"[48]

The motive for most fraggings was to change conduct. For this reason, officers were usually warned prior to fraggings. First, a smoke grenade would be left near their beds. Those who did not respond would find a teargas *[sic]* grenade or a grenade pin on their bed as a gentle reminder. Finally, the lethal grenade was tossed into the bed of sleeping, inflexible officers. Officers understood the warnings and usually complied, becoming captive to the demands of their men. It was the most practical means of cracking army discipline. The units whose officers responded opted out of search-and-destroy missions.[49]

An Army judge who presided over fragging trials called fragging, "the troops' way of controlling officers," and added that it was "deadly effective." He explained, "Captain Steinberg argues that once an officer is intimidated by even the threat of fragging he is useless to the military because he can no longer carry out orders essential to the functioning of the Army. Through intimidation by threats—verbal and written—virtually all officers and NCOs have to take into account the possibility of fragging before giving an order to the men under them." The fear of fragging affected officers and NCOs far beyond those who were actually involved in fragging incidents.[50]

Officers who survived fragging attempts could not tell which of their men had tried to murder them, or when the men might strike again. They lived in constant fear of future attempts at fragging by unknown soldiers. In Vietnam it was a truism that "everyone was the enemy"; for the lifers, every enlisted man was the enemy. "In parts of Vietnam fragging stirs more fear among officers and NCOs than does the war with 'Charlie.'"

Counter-fragging by retaliating officers contributed to a war within the war. While 80 percent of fraggings were of officers and NCOs, 20 percent were of enlisted men, as officers sought to kill potential troublemakers or those whom they suspected of planning to frag them. In this civil war within the army, the military police were used to reinstate order. In October 1971, military police air assaulted the Praline mountain signal site to protect an officer who had been the target of repeated fragging attempts. The base was occupied for a week before command was restored.[51]

Fragging undermined the ability of the Green Machine to function as a fighting force. By 1970, "many commanders no longer trusted blacks or radical whites with weapons except on guard duty or in combat." In the American Division, fragmentation grenades were not given to troops.

In the 440 Signal Battalion, the colonel refused to distribute all arms.[52] As a soldier at Cu Chi told the New York Times, "The American garrisons on the larger bases are virtually disarmed. The lifers have taken the weapons from us and put them under lock and key."[53] The U.S. Army was slowly disarming its own men to prevent the weapons from being aimed at the main enemy—the lifers. It is hard to think of another army so afraid of its own soldiers.[54]

During the first few months in-country, when the unit was being infused with other units, Jack L. Click was appointed first sergeant. He was the 15th or 16th first sergeant. Click was career military, a lifer. He was born and bred in Georgia and made no bones about disliking anything and everything north of the Mason-Dixon line. Previously, I had heard stories about such prejudice, but now it was real. Click was fair-haired, light skinned, lean and mean. His distinguishable Southern drawl followed him wherever he went. The first morning he took command of the unit, I took notice. There was something different about Click. His actions and characteristics were different from what we were accustomed to. Rumor had it that he had been a drill sergeant most of his career. He made no bones about telling us he was a taskmaster on special assignment to straighten out the 513th. We were growing weary of this phrase. Each morning in formation he continued to further degrade us with his southern sarcasm directed toward the reservists from Boston. Here we were in a combat zone with many concerns and each day it was nothing but chicken shit harassment. Did anyone have the common sense to realize we were an older mature unit? The average age was about twenty-five, maybe twenty-six, and if they let us be we would get the job done and done with pride. Our individual assignments would have been accomplished with the prevention of much heartache and agony. I guess this was too much to expect. We had hoped the harassment would stop when we got to Vietnam but it only got worse. Alcohol became a problem. Everyone was drinking heavily and many started doing drugs, especially those who had been infused into the

513[55] from other units. Drugs were everywhere. Most of them were purchased on the black market. Many times we paid top dollar to local Vietnamese for items clearly marked U.S. Government Issue, items like toiletries donated by major corporations and marked "not for sale" were hard to get through regular channels. Many of the men were volatile and yet others withdrew into depression. It took very little to arouse emotions.[55]

Next to our bunks we each had an empty orange crate. The crate was divided into two sections used as a night table with two shelves upon which we would place personal belongings such as family pictures, etc. I still have a 12-inch Christmas tree my fiancee Mary sent me which I kept on my orange crate for the longest time and continue to display it every Christmas as a reminder.

One day a Marine took his weapon apart to clean on his bunk. This was standard procedure. On his orange crate he had a picture of his wife who had recently sent him a Dear John letter. One of the men in his unit walked in the front door of the hooch and as he left through the rear door he said loud enough so everyone could hear, "Hey, Joe, is that your wife? What a dog!" A seemingly inappropriate comment that the average eighteen-year-old would blurt out without giving it much thought, nonetheless, characterizing a complete disregard for the sensitivity of another's feelings. Joe assembled his weapon with determination. After it was assembled he placed a magazine in his weapon. He exited the rear of the hooch and in the alleyway between hooches he blew away his nemesis.

Another GI had taken his M-16 and plenty of ammunition and climbed to the top of the water tower at the main entrance to Phu Bai. Nestled at the top of the tower he picked off two GIs at random as they were coming through the main gate. It was awhile before the chaplain Fr. Anderson finally talked him down. Many times the anticipation of something happening was worse than the occurrence. When we were under attack the adrenaline was high and one reverted to instincts. Nothing else mattered but getting through the moment.

Every first sergeant sang the same song about straightening out the unit and somehow, in the process, they would figure out it wasn't working and would back off and to their amazement it made life bearable for everyone. However, there was something different about Click. He was squared away and took pride in having his shit together when others were totally disillusioned about our involvement in Vietnam and simply went through the motions. Because we had no alternatives, Click's military mentality prevailed which is necessary to win most wars, but in an environment where flexibility was the key to survival and rules had to be broken, it was a hindrance. He gave several men article fifteens (misdemeanor offenses usually resulting in forfeiture of pay and restriction to one's hooch rather than imprisonment) for fatigues not properly bloused, hats on backwards and working without a shirt often resulted in this minor infraction and caused added tension.

Many of us had occasion to be out in the field at firebases in remote areas where there was no required mode of dress. As a result, the men staffing these firebases were left alone and the mode of military dress was not an issue. At Camp Edwards and Landing Zone Sally (LZ Sally) I sensed many of the men enjoyed a new found freedom devoid of petty regulations. However, some abused this privilege.

It was at a firebase north of Phu Bai where a young company commander, pissed off at two Vietnamese for supposedly informing the Viet Cong of the location of several strategic coordinates in the compound, took things into his own hands. One of the Vietnamese was found with a map in his possession with all key areas highlighted. The compound had been hit several nights in a row and even changing the location of the ammo storage facility and rearranging some of the key positions was to no avail. Of course the villagers were in a no-win situation. If the VC thought they supported our efforts, they were dog meat; and if we thought they supported the Viet Cong, they were still dog meat. They couldn't win.

For the past several evenings the VC zeroed in and were successful at hitting the ammo dump. The company commander was frustrated beyond control. While interrogating two Vietnamese in the center of the compound, he ordered a helicopter to hover over the suspected informers. He ordered one of his subordinates to secure two ropes at least fifty feet long, each capable of supporting the weight of a person, and to tie a hangman's noose at each end. He ordered the helicopter to land and instructed the men to tie a rope to each pontoon. He then ordered the helicopter to hover above the suspected informers and with a noose around the neck of each Vietnamese he questioned them about conspiring with the VC. The more he interrogated them the more frustrated he became at their purported indifference. The Vietnamese always appeared to have an inherent sarcastic grin, characteristic of their facial expression. Thus their grinning at him was misconstrued as subordinate arrogance. He asked them one last time, "Did you give our coordinates to the Viet Cong?" He spoke in English and with the noise of the helicopter rotors he was barely audible. The Vietnamese just grinned and ignored him. He then ordered the helicopter to take off and circle around the compound with one Vietnamese hanging from each pontoon of the helicopter. The CO then turned to the remaining Vietnamese and warned them of encountering the same fate if they betrayed us. Such actions, if not condoned, were acceptable. I sensed that many actually enjoyed the experience for it gave them a license to behave in ways that were otherwise unacceptable. Sadly, many men enjoyed the power bestowed upon them to play God. We all saw what happened to many of these men when they returned home! On the other hand, it's easy to Monday-morning quarterback the actions of any individual. We say we would react differently, and I like to think we would. Most of us will never find out how we would react. The name of the game was survival at any cost. That's the way it was.

We were concerned about surviving. Whether your hat was on backwards or your trousers properly bloused or your shirt sleeves rolled up or not rolled up, these matters were not a major concern to us, but to Click they were. He was persistent and relentless. Every day while in formation he harassed us. The situation was explosive. Then, one morning in formation after our usual ridicule session from Click, a GI standing behind me and to my left repeated under his breath, "I'm going to get that mother fucker, I'm going to get that mother fucker I'm ...." My eyes shifted to my left and I realized that I did not recognize many of the men. The remarks came from someone I didn't know. I was just as happy for I wanted to remain anonymous. As we broke ranks and proceeded to go to our duty stations, you could hear his continued rambling.

At first I didn't give it much thought because Click had a long line of enemies. However, the more I thought about his comments, the more I realized that if one verbalizes his feelings, many are harboring the same animosity. The stress level was high.

This time Click had gone too far. His character assassinations of many of the men were something we were not used to. Other sergeants ridiculed us but as a group and usually not individually and not to the extent Click pursued his assault. Click meant what he said about us not buying into the war and because of this he considered us to be less than patriotic. He was right on about our lack of enthusiasm for the war effort and especially about our lack of preparedness. We knew it was true, but we didn't want to hear it day after day. We were doing our best and, under the circumstances, we were performing as we should. The difference between Click and other first sergeants was that Click took everything down to a personal level. He was mean and character assassination was the last thing we wanted to contend with.

It was two in the morning when I was reporting for guard duty at one of the perimeter locations. As I walked to my guard post I passed a number of hooches reserved for NCOs. Suddenly, there was an explosion. I ran off the path behind one of the hooches and remained there. There was much confusion. I was puzzled because I hadn't heard the siren indicating in-coming, which was usually the case before an attack. The explosion was followed by yelling and screaming and calling for a medic. It was coming from Click's hooch, two rows over from my location. A grenade had been thrown under his bunk. He had been fragged! I ran over to see what was happening. What was left of his bunk was in the left hand corner of the hooch. His tent flaps were up so I walked around the corner of the hooch to get a better view. Scattered about were the remains of his belongings. As though it was permanently fastened to remain in the appropriate location, his footlocker riddled with grenade fragments was still at the front of his bunk. On the floor beside his footlocker was a family picture completely shredded. As I approached the front of the hooch, Click was being carried out of his bunk. He was gasping for air. They transported him to the medic station where they patched him as best they could and then medevaced him out. That was the last time I saw Click. I hurried to my guard post for I was already five minutes late, a seemingly inconsequential transgression which placed me at the scene of the crime and I was considered a suspect.

Emotions ran amuck! They ran from those who couldn't believe or didn't want to believe someone would purposely do this to those who were outwardly jubilant that Click got what he deserved. I didn't sleep that night thinking about Click. I knew he had a wife and children and thought about their reaction, and wondered if the army would tell them the true story that someone threw a grenade in his hooch; or would they cover it up like they covered up many other situations and say it occurred in the line of duty. Like many others, Click was a victim. He was consumed by Vietnam and didn't have the presence of mind to see it as it was, and as a result it ultimately destroyed him.

The next morning during reveille, I didn't want to fall in. I was depressed. I had enough. This place called Vietnam had taken its toll on me as it had on the many men who came before me. My place in formation was in the middle of the third row. I dragged myself into position. As I looked up, in the center of the company area I saw a large rock with a note on the rock secured by a rubber band. The company commander walked in front of the unit, picked up the rock, carefully removed the rubber band, opened the note and started reading to himself. As he continued, his face tensed up. He then yelled for one of the sergeants to check the crawl space under company headquarters. Upon checking the crawl space two claymore mines were observed in key locations ready for detonating. One was directly beneath the company commander's office area. The note also revealed that the company commander was next if he didn't stop fucking with us.

Typical of the military and perhaps deservedly so, the Click incident brought the wrath of the Criminal Investigation Division (CID) on the 513th. Also typical of the military and the times, CID wasn't as concerned about finding out who fragged Click but was more concerned in finding a scapegoat. Since I had been late in reporting for guard duty the evening Click was fragged and I was two hooches away on my way to my guard post, I had reason to be in the area. They said I had motive and opportunity. I was questioned extensively. The first time CID interrogated me it was in a small hooch with one rectangular table and four chairs: three chairs on one side of the table where three investigators sat, and one on the other side where I sat. The lead investigator looked up. He was a short, burly, no-nonsense individual. Considering the way he handled himself, I assumed he had been in the military for some time. He was direct and intimidating and I sensed they were looking for someone to pin it on.

"Sit up specialist," he barked, reminiscent of a teacher admonishing a student for slouching in his chair. I thought back to my senior year at Christopher Columbus High School when I had everything going for me and each day got better and better. Everything was a big joke. My mind was drifting to a time when I was sitting in Fr. Thomas' office for what now appeared to be a silly minor infraction of school rules. I had entered the forbidden zone. Anyone who went to Christopher Columbus (CC) High School or Jullie Billiart (JB) High School is well aware of the forbidden zone. The high school was divided into two schools: CC for boys and JB for girls. Swinging doors with frosted window panes separated the schools making it impossible to see what was happening in the forbidden zone—the girls' side. It was as though some mystery of unimaginable proportions would beset anyone who passed through the swinging doors; only akin to entering a black hole in the universe, destined for destruction. Never, never did the boys gravitate to the girls' side and never, never did the girls dare gravitate to the boys' side. Fraternization was restricted to an occasional glimpse of the debs as they left the cafeteria and the boys, anticipating lunch, eagerly entered a minute or two early.

One day I was late leaving the cafeteria for my first afternoon class. The students were lined up on the left and on the right. At the end of a long hallway were swinging doors. I had a special place in line up front, and as I proceeded between the columns of students, I accidentally "on purpose" jostled myself to the left and right as I zigzagged to my assigned place. Then none other than the class clown, Battaglia pushed me from the rear and then the unspeakable happened. I was thrust through the swinging doors, losing my balance and falling to the floor in the forbidden zone. With the absence of locker room facilities, the girls changed into gym clothes in the hallway. As I catapulted through the doors I was greeted by the yells and screams of the entire JB senior class of about 100 girls. The Boston Strangler himself could not have elicited a more horrified reaction. Lying on the floor I looked up to see Sr. Roberta, all six feet of her, with her hands on her hips. She grabbed me by my ear lobe and escorted me to Fr. Thomas' office. Fortunately, Sr. Roberta was very friendly with my now deceased cousin Rosemarie who graduated three years before me. Their friendship weighed in my favor.

Now, I was *not* sitting in front of Fr. Thomas and the penalty would be more than the two weeks detention dusting Fr. Thomas' office every morning before school and every day after school. I was scared shit!

The interrogator asked, "Specialist Masciulli, where were you the night Sergeant Click was fragged?"

"I was on my way to guard duty, Sergeant."

"Did you like Sergeant Click?"

"No, not especially."

"Why?"

"I had nothing in common with him. He was my superior. He did what he had to do and I did what I had to do."

"Are you glad he's no longer first sergeant?"

"It doesn't matter to me. We've had many first sergeants. I hardly remember them. They come and they go."

"Our records indicate that on the night in question you were seven minutes late in arriving at your post. Is that so?"

"Yes, Sergeant."

"Why was that?"

"I was taking a short cut through the NCO hooches when I thought I heard in- coming. I hid behind one of the hooches."

"Which hooch was that?"

"I'm pretty sure it was hooch number 12."

"Why were you at that location. Wouldn't it be easier to take the road by the mess hall? It's a shorter route."

"It's shorter, but I prefer this route because I find when going by the mess hall at 2 a.m., which I frequently do, I encounter rats trying to get in the barrels and some of them don't scare easily."

"You know that taking that route to get to your post gave you an opportunity to be in the vicinity of Sergeant Click's hooch when he was fragged. You had motive and opportunity. This makes you a suspect." I hesitated to react. Putting myself in a defensive position would only make matters worse. I needed time to think.

The lead investigator continued, "While we're conducting the investigation you're not to discuss the situation with anyone. Failure to do so is a punishable offense in and of itself. Do you understand?"

"Yes, Sergeant."

Before I left the lead investigator said, "We're interrogating everyone in the unit and then we will speak with you again. You can go."

They detained me for about two hours and finally let me go after they realized I had guard duty in a few minutes.

When I left the interrogation team I reported for duty and received permission from the sergeant on duty to take a half hour to put myself together. I knew they were putting pressure on every one to force them to confess, but I was still scared. There were two other reservists in the area. Were they also prime suspects? The investigators were desperately looking for a scapegoat. I went back to my hooch and climbed onto my bunk. Suddenly I felt something beneath me, a letter. Not recognizing the handwriting, I thought it was from one of the school age children who often wrote to keep our spirits up, so I put it in my pocket and didn't think much about it. I lay on my bunk and listened to the cadence of the rotors as the helicopters came in from the field. I was getting pretty good at determining how many helicopters there were by the intensity of their sound. This time there were six of them flying in formation. Finally, at dusk I reported for guard duty and longed for a quiet evening.

It was a quiet evening. At about 11 p.m. I took the crumpled letter out of my pocket and started to read it. It was from a 5th grader in Arkansas and read:

> Deer Soldier
> Tank you for makin Amerika a safe place. I pray for you and every body in Vietam. Come home soon.
> Chuck

How could I lose. I had a 5th grader in Arkansas praying for me. What I appreciated most was the picture he drew of a soldier, his right arm extended and his left arm firing his rifle in the air. I hoped that Chuck would never have to experience any Vietnams.

The interrogation continued until everyone in the unit was questioned. Most of the men were on duty or asleep at the time and did not have occasion to be in the area. Those who were on duty that night were questioned extensively.

A week later I was interrogated for the second time. I sensed the team was more adamant about incriminating me. Being one of the few people in the area at the time of the fragging put me in a vulnerable position. This time again I sat down and unknowingly slouched in my chair. The short, burly sergeant looked me in the eye and said,

"Specialist, sit up." I wanted to portray an air of confidence but I felt I was at the mercy of the team. He continued, "We know you were the one who threw the grenade in Sergeant Click's hooch. If you confess, we'll make it easier on you. We'll say the pressure just got to you. We can help you if you confess now, but if you confess later, things will be more difficult." He then stood up and leaned forward and with both hands on the table he looked me in the eye and yelled, "Do you know what the sentence is for attempted murder in the military? If they spare you, you will never see the light of day." They interrogated me for a couple of hours and again I left the team thinking I was being set up. Again I was told not to discuss the investigation with anyone. Paranoia was setting in.

I went back to my hooch and lay on my bunk thinking about what to do. Finally, I decided to talk to some of the members of the original 513th. A couple of hooches down were the men who worked in the motor pool, some of whom I knew from attending reserve meetings in Boston and would spend R&R in Australia. A level of trust and confidence had been previously developed and was later reinforced during our week together in Australia. I knew some of them had occasion to be on duty on the evening in question.

As I approached the hooch I kept thinking about the lead investigator telling me not to speak to anyone under any circumstances but I had to do something. What the hell, I said to myself. I'm dammed if I do and dammed if I don't. As I entered the hooch two of the men, Chucky and Danny were sitting on one of the bunks playing cards and drinking beer. I knew Chucky and Danny from our reserve meetings and knew they could be trusted. Since the rest of the men were in the company area playing volleyball, this was a prime opportunity to bring up the discussion. At first I was reluctant but soon eased into the conversation by mentioning it would be nice if the investigation would end so we could resort back to normal chaos. Finally, I came out and asked, "What do you think about the investigation?" At first there was a lull, soon broken by Chucky who spoke up and commented, "Once again they're trying to give us the green banana. If they thought they could get away with it, they'd pin it on their mother."

I then asked, "Have you guys been interrogated yet?"

Danny laughed as he commented, "Have we been interrogated?"

Then they both laughed and simultaneous commented, "We're prime suspects."

"What do you mean you're prime suspects?"

Chucky who was always straightforward replied, "I mean they told me I was a prime suspect. They told me not to speak with anyone and they would enjoy hanging me if they found out I did otherwise."

Danny added, "The first time they questioned me they insinuated I was responsible and the second time they accused me and wanted me to confess. No way am I going to confess to something I didn't do. Believe me if they detect a weakness, innocent or not, you're dead."

Chucky answered, "Those bastards are messing with our brains again. Go through the motions and watch what you say. They're waiting for one of us to screw up so they can get us."

After speaking with Chucky and Danny, I felt some relief and realized more than ever that CID was looking for a scapegoat. Now I clearly understood how an individual under such intense pressure could admit to something one didn't do. The investigating team had a tendency to wear you down. I always thought it bizarre that someone could admit to something one didn't do. Consider a young eighteen-year-old GI who has never been away from home and subject to intense investigation and believing in motherhood and apple pie, and above all, believing in the infallibility of the military of the 60s, this concept is not far fetched.

Two weeks had passed. I knew CID was continuing with its investigation so I wasn't surprised when I was again called to meet with the team. This time I walked into the hooch with a predetermined idea of what was coming. I had thought about what I was going to say. The only thing I could do was to tell the truth as convincingly as I could and pray they believed me. Whether they had enough evidence or not to begin proceedings was immaterial.

It was the monsoon season and had been raining for several weeks. Everything was wet and muddy and my rain soaked poncho added to a feeling of melancholy. I walked into the hooch removed my helmet and left my poncho on. I approached the team, "Specialist Masciulli reports as requested, Sir."

This time the investigation team was accompanied by a captain from the judicial branch of the military, Judge Advocate General (JAG). Now I knew they were trying to press charges. No doubt he was present to determine if they should begin court martial proceedings. The question was, "On whom?" The three investigators were also present this time but the captain controlled the meeting.

"At ease, Specialist. Take a seat."

This time I sat up straight because to show the slightest weakness would be my death knell. I sat erect in the chair and glanced down at the writing on the table which read:

> **From night to night my journey**
> **The long pilgrimage before me**
> **From day to day my journey**
> **The stories that will be forever.**

My mind wandered. I felt clammy, cold, depressed and miserable. I hadn't received any mail in a week. Mary wrote daily but why no mail? What about my parents and friends? I felt abandoned wondering if all the sacrifices we made for this small country meant anything. I prayed to God for guidance and hoped my children and grandchildren would never experience anything as horrible as Vietnam. War truly sucks but I thought the only way we can understand the devastation it causes is to see it, day after day, and see how it tears at the soul of an individual and destroys them. I naively thought Vietnam would be the war that would prevent other wars. I was wrong because as time goes on generations forget and become more willing to pick up arms. Time and the passing of those who fought these wars lessen the pain and suffering. Each generation forgets, and we repeat the same thing again. History has proven this to be true. If we could only pass from generation to generation the psychological trauma caused by war, the perpetuation of the human race would be assured. In Vietnam there were no winners no matter what your situation, just various degrees of losing. By all standards we in the 513th were not losers because we came home. We had been hit 26 times—two direct hits. One individual was wounded and we had two attempted suicides. Statistically we survived. Yet many Vietnam veterans continued to be plagued by the demons of alcoholism, drug addiction, negative relationships and post traumatic stress. But we made it. Others were at the wrong place at the wrong time and didn't make it.

The lead investigator continued, "Specialist Masciulli, we're questioning you because you were in the area of Sergeant Click's hooch when he was fragged and you had motive and opportunity to throw the grenade in his hooch. Is that not so?

"Yes, I was in the area of Sergeant Click's hooch. We discussed the circumstances of my being in the area several times. I was going to my guard post when I heard the explosion. I thought it was in-coming and hid behind hooch number twelve. Yes, I was in the area but I did not throw a grenade in Sergeant Click's hooch!" We went over the events of the evening again and again and again.

Finally, being totally frustrated with the process I turned to the officer in charge and asked, "Sir, I request legal representation?"

No one spoke. Then the short stocky sergeant looked up and said, "Okay, let's go over everything again from the beginning." We went over everything again and again. I once again asked for legal representation and again I was ignored. Then at the conclusion of our meeting I was warned not to discuss the situation with anyone, no exceptions. Before I left, the Captain asked, "Specialist, is there anything else you would like to add to your statement?"

"Yes Sir."

"What's that Specialist?"

"Sir, if I'm considered one of the prime suspects I would like the record to indicate I request legal representation."

"Okay Specialist. We'll get back to you. You're dismissed."

As I left, I saw one of the other members of the unit enter. Again I went back to my hooch and lay on my bunk. I thought about legal representation but how would I begin? Where would I go? Were there any good military lawyers in Phu Bai? I decided to wait and see what developed. I couldn't believe what was happening. The following week other members of the unit were further interrogated. Slowly, the men started talking about our experiences with the team and we started to realize they pulled the same tactics on many of the men. The investigators stayed in the company area for a while and then one day they left as quickly as they came.

This was the turning point in our tour of duty. From this time on the enemy within the ranks was no longer a threat. Our internal battles were minimal. Now all we had to worry about was "Charlie" and getting home safely.

Chapter 18

Boll Weevils

When we look back on a bad experience, we look for the good or the humor in that experience as a defense mechanism no matter how minuscule. We tuck the bad away for there's no sense in dwelling on the unpleasant. In retrospect I remember several incidents that now appear humorous such as the story of the gunnery sergeant and the boll weevils. I was preparing breakfast one morning and the order of the day were pancakes. I went to the storage area and pulled out fifty pounds of pre-mixed pancake batter. When I opened it, I didn't notice anything unusual at first. However, when I added water to the mix, I noticed several boll weevils floating on top of the water. Further investigation revealed a large infestation of boll weevils in the pancake batter. Inclined not to think for myself, since the gunnery sergeant had often warned us not to, I went to the rear of the mess hall where he hung out, usually drinking coffee and puffing on a butt, and I commented, "Sarge, there are boll weevils in the pancake mix. What do you want to do?" He paused a moment and looked around as though the answer were somewhere in the mess hall. Then his eyes got wider. The wider they got the more they contrasted against his black skin. I then knew he had a solution to the problem. He asked, "Is that the only pancake batter left?"

"That's it Sarge," I responded.

"Well, we have some guys coming in from the field and I already told them they were having pancakes. They'll be disappointed if we don't give them pancakes. So we have to serve them pancakes." He then took me aside and put his arm on my shoulder. Then in a manner in which a Dutch uncle would give one advice, he said, "Put blueberry mix in the pancakes." Not knowing if I understood him correctly my immediate response was, "What?"

"Shh! Be quiet!"

He then leaned over. His breath smelled of cheap booze and his hair smelled of pot. His clothes smelled of buffalo dung. Then I remembered Clarence telling me she used dried buffalo shit to fuel the fire over which she dried his fatigues. He leaned closer and whispered in my ear, "Put blueberry mix in the pancake batter. This way the boll weevils will blend in with the blueberry mix and they'll never know the difference." I thought a moment and remembered that in the military, especially in the Marines, when given an order you disagree with, like a good boy scout, you always, always obey the order and complain later. Well, I thought, to whom would I complain and what good would it do, and then I'd probably wind up on every shit detail from Phu' Bai to DaNang, so I decided to put blueberry mix in the batter. As I walked away, he winked as he whispered, "Masciulli, that's our secret. Oh, by the way, you can work the grill in the officers' mess." This was my reward for being such a super trooper.

It was always better to work the grill in the officers' mess hall. There were fewer people to serve and the officers in general weren't as rude as the enlisted men as long as everything was done by the book. Also, their social graces were usually, but not always, a cut above enlisted men.

I set up the grill, and like a good boy scout, I followed the gunnery sergeant's orders and added blueberry mix to the pancake batter and, to my amazement, to a less discerning eye it wasn't noticeable. However, in a place where we were accustomed to paying attention to detail, I figured it would only be a matter of time before someone recognized the deception.

The first few officers had been served and everything seemed okay. I did notice that one of them had left his pancakes without trying them. I then realized he recognized the infestation in the pancakes but decided not to make it an issue. Considering there were many more serious concerns we all had, this was truly not very important but nonetheless should not have occurred.

About ten minutes before the end of the mess period, just when I thought the gunnery sergeant had succeeded in his evil deed, to my astonishment in walked a one star general. At first I thought someone had reported the boll weevils in the pancake batter, but the expression on his face was too pleasant. As he approached the grill, immediately we all snapped to attention. It may not have been necessary since we were in the mess hall, but a one star general, especially in Vietnam was akin to God the Father.

"At ease," he commented. "What's for breakfast, Specialist?"

I swallowed hard and answered, "We have blueberry pancakes, sir."

"Are they good?" he asked.

I hesitated before answering. Before I could say anything again he asked, "Well, are they, or are they not? Speak up son!"

"Yes sir they're very good."

"Good, I'll have three of them with lots of blueberries."

I mixed up the batter and placed three relatively large amounts of pancake mix on the grill. Whenever one of our unwelcomed friends floated to the top, I politely camouflaged it by pushing it underneath the blueberry mix. At the same time I was conjuring up a game plan in case he discovered our ruse. I was an E-4 and would probably make E-5 before I left Vietnam. Rank wasn't terribly important to me, but if he found the boll weevils in the mix, he would probably reduce me to an E-2. The only E-2s I knew in Vietnam screwed up big time. This would be terribly humiliating. I would be lower than whale shit in an organization where rank was everything. An E-4 or E-5 was respectable, but an E-2 meant I would get every detail and would be stigmatized. In grammar school and high school the Franciscans preached humility and brotherly love, but here in Vietnam as an E-2 it would have new meaning. I decided if anything were to happen, I would tell the truth.

I looked over at the general's table. At first he seemed to be enjoying his pancakes. After he wolfed down his second pancake he paused and looked down at his plate. As he moved his head closer to the plate, I could see his eyes getting bigger and bigger. He then took his fork and moved it around in his plate like a child playing with his peas. He put his fork down, approached the grill and said, "Specialist, do you know there's something in the pancake batter that doesn't belong there?"

I nervously stared straight ahead. This was it, my military career flashed in front of me as I prepared to bear the ultimate humiliation and accept a reduction in rank to E-2 or possibly E-1. Who knows, I thought, he may even ship me to parts unknown.

"Yes, sir!" I nervously responded.

"Why did you serve them?"

"I was ordered to do so, Sir!"

"Ordered? Who ordered you to serve them?"

"The gunnery sergeant did, Sir!"

"What's in there anyway?"

"Boll weevils, Sir!"

"How did they get there?"

"They were in the pancake mix, Sir!"

"And you served them like that?"

"No, Sir! I added blueberry mix!"

"For what?"

"To camouflage the boll weevils, Sir!"

"And who told you to do that?"

"The gunnery sergeant did, Sir!"

"Where is the gunnery sergeant, specialist?"

"He's at the rear of the enlisted men's mess hall, Sir!"

"You come with me," he bellowed.

He immediately left the officers' mess and proceeded through the swinging doors through the kitchen and into the enlisted men's mess hall. All the way I could hear individuals calling, "Attention! Attention! He went on his way and I followed. As he entered the enlisted men's mess hall the men snapped to attention. He walked down the rear of the mess hall and bellowed, "Where's the gunnery sergeant? Where's the gunnery sergeant?" In Marine Corps regalia the gunnery sergeant walked forward and presented himself. "Gunnery Sergeant Jones, at your request, Sir!"

The general asked, "Sergeant, did you order this specialist to put blueberry mix in the pancake batter to hide the boll weevils?"

The gunnery sergeant looked around the mess hall as he often did looking for answers. I then realized this was serious. My question was whether I would escape the general's wrath or not. The general paused a moment. He was visibly upset. He walked closer to the gunnery sergeant and in a barely audible tone I heard him say, "Boll weevils in the pancake mix." He then ripped the stripes off the gunnery sergeant and confined him to quarters pending a court martial. Later we learned he was reduced from E-8 to E-5.

While he was confined to quarters, I wanted to speak with him but never did. If he were a member of the original 513th and I felt confident in him backing me in case of trouble I would have figured a way out. Nevertheless, I did feel badly for him. He had been in the Marine Corps for fifteen years, married with three children and now he was reduced to an E-5 only one rank higher than me. Unfortunately that was Vietnam, every man for himself.

Chapter 19

Fighting Boredom

In Vietnam my life consisted of two extremes. Many times, I was completely bored and time weighed heavily as I wondered what might be coming next. Other times, the adrenaline flowed and I was caught up in chaos. Had I been given the choice, I would welcome boredom. Usually I would find ways to amuse myself.

Another reservist named Danny had the bunk next to mine. Danny was just out of high school and nineteen years old. I was twenty-seven. A significant age difference especially when you're young. Danny was somewhat naive and prone to exaggeration. One night at about two in the morning he came banging on the back door of the mess hall yelling, "Let me in. Let me in." Earlier in the evening rumor had it that he had been in a fight with one of the marines and he was hurting. We opened the door to the mess hall and there stood Danny. He was bleeding profusely from his nose. It appeared to be broken. I ran to the rear of the mess hall and seeing him bleeding I remarked, "Danny, what happened?"

"You'll never guess what happened? You'll never guess what happened?"

"Well, what happened, Danny?"

"I got in a fight with a kangaroo and it kicked the shit out of me."

"What?"

"You heard me. I got in a fight with a kangaroo and it kicked the shit out of me!"

Next to the mess hall was a Quonset hut staffed with a Navy medic. We summoned the corpsman who came and patched him up. We let Danny's story ride. At least in his presence we did. In the future, whenever something bad happened there was some consolation in blaming it on the infamous kangaroo.

One day I was lying on my bunk enjoying a Garcia Vega cigar, and Danny was relating one of his exaggerated tales. I would take a long drag and watch the smoke rings slowly rise and fade away to nothingness. I would then hold my cigar in a vertical position to keep the ashes from falling. Danny seemed amused by this and asked, "What are you doing?"

I answered, "Sometimes when I smoke a cigar I like to see how long I can smoke it without letting the ashes fall. Once, using two common pins inserted at each end of the cigar, I smoked it within an inch of the end and guess what? The ashes didn't fall. Not bad."

Danny commented," That's nothing, I do that all the time."

I said, "I'll tell you what. We'll make a little wager. I'll bet you twenty-five dollars your ashes fall before mine."

"You're on, old man," Danny answered.

Jokingly I quipped, "Don't you know I'm the master of this game. I'll even wait until you smoke your cigar so that it's the same length as mine."

Danny smoked his cigar down. We took turns slowly dragging on our cigars then carefully moving them away to watch the smoke rings rise in the air. Our ashes were about three inches long and were still intact. We were now attracting the attention of the other guys in the hooch. My turn was next. I took a long slow drag and as I pulled the cigar away, the ashes began to crumble but not enough to fall. Danny was next. He had done well up to this point and it looked as though he might pull it off. He slowly brought his cigar to his lips. He carefully took a drag and, afraid to move the cigar, he barely moved it. It was about an inch away from his lips. In the meantime, I glanced to the right of the hooch and noticed someone was coming. I also remembered that when the screen door was opened it created a draft. Just as I saw the door open, I cupped my free hand around the cigar ashes to protect them from blowing away. Danny's ashes fell and blew all over his face. Thus, the difference in wisdom between being nineteen years old and twenty-seven years old rose to the level of expectations. Danny asked for a rematch. I assured him that at some future time I would give him an opportunity to redeem his honor. Working with Danny was akin to working with a juvenile, always eager to roll up his sleeves and dig in, but never paying much attention to details, which always got him in trouble.

Like the time we were making pizza for the evening meal. The exact proportions of yeast to dough were always clearly defined. Difficulty arose when preparing pizza for hundreds of men. The amounts become difficult to comprehend. The recipe called for one pound of yeast to one hundred pounds of flour and let it set in order to rise. We placed the flour in large vats resembling bathtubs and asked Danny to mix in the yeast to make the dough. He mixed the yeast in and we placed the dough on several long tables to rise. The dough began to rise and continued to rise and kept rising and rising. At first we would walk over and pierce it, causing it to deflate, but as quickly as it was deflated it started to rise again. We realized there was too much yeast in the dough. Danny had mixed ten pounds of yeast to a hundred pounds of flour instead of the required one pound of yeast to one hundred pounds of flour. We knew if the gunnery sergeant saw it he would get upset so we decided to throw it out and start again. If we used it for pizza it would have large air pockets in the pizza. We put the dough in two large Dempsy Dumpsters and several fifty-gallon cans used for rubbish and tightly capped them. We went back into the mess hall to start again. As we worked the dough it continued to rise and periodically we would hear *Pop! Pop! Pop!* as the tops of the garbage cans came off as a result of the rising dough. Dough crept into the crevices of the dumpster. It was everywhere. To remedy the problem, we stationed Danny out back with his bayonet and every so often he would pierce the dough to deflate it. Fortunately, the gunnery sergeant never caught on.

Then there was the time Danny claimed he could outdo cool hand Luke. One night we were watching the movie "Cool Hand Luke" for the hundredth time. There was a scene in the movie where Luke eats twenty-five hard-boiled eggs in one hour. Danny boasted he had achieved this feat several times and would like an opportunity to prove himself which we graciously gave him. "I'll tell you what," said Danny, "I'll bet you twenty-five dollars I can do it. The only difference is I have to drink a glass of water between each egg to wash it down." Sounded reasonable to me, so the race was on. Little did he realize drinking large amounts of water would not help. I went to the mess hall and handpicked twenty-five of the largest eggs I could find without the gunnery sergeant seeing me. I hard-boiled them and also filled five canteens of water to wash the eggs down. I brought along an extra bucket just in case he became ill. Danny carefully peeled and ate the first egg and you could tell he enjoyed it. The second egg also went down with ease. He then took a glass of water. The third, fourth, and fifth eggs were no problem.

Danny did okay up until the thirteenth egg, and then he began to labor. He insisted on drinking more water. Of course, we accommodated him. The fourteenth egg presented a problem. The egg was slightly discolored. I thought it looked bad but he cracked it open and when a dead embryo fell out we were all amazed and began laughing. Evidently one of the uncooked eggs was mixed with the cooked ones and it just happened that this uncooked egg contained a dead embryo. We decided not to let the embryo count as an egg and we would be just as happy if he consumed twenty-four eggs. Then between the fourteenth and fifteenth egg he began straining. As he peeled the fifteenth egg the sight of the dead embryo in the bucket with all the egg shells was too much for him to bear. Fortunately I had brought the extra bucket in case of emergency. Danny unleashed a barrage of partially consumed hard-boiled eggs and a few egg shells. I didn't take many pictures in Vietnam, but the one of Danny laboring over the bucket vomiting up his eggs was one I couldn't resist.

Chapter 20

Cody

Today was my lucky day. Mail call was good to me. After duty I returned to my hooch and found no less than five letters waiting for me on my bunk. It was natural not to receive any mail for a while and then to receive several letters at once. Letters from  home were priceless. Mail call was always the highlight of my day. Today I received three letters from Mary. God bless Mary, she was always so faithful in writing every day. I have her letters saved in chronological order and read them every now and then. Today I also received a letter from Mom and an unexpected letter from a childhood friend, Cody, who was also in Vietnam. Cody wasn't his real name but like everyone else who grew up in the North End of Boston, he had a nickname. The psychology of North End nicknames is a study in social behavior.

We were in grammar school at the time and one day during spring vacation we were at a local movie theater in the West End of Boston called the Lanky, short for the Lancaster Theater. Rainy Saturday afternoons undoubtedly drew all neighborhood kids to the Lanky. We each had a quarter and spent fifteen cents for admission and saved a dime for a Joe and Nemo hot dog, purchased at the famous Scollay Square Joe and Nemo's. On this particular Saturday we were watching a third rate science fiction movie. It was about an alien named Cody who came to earth from afar to set up his new empire on earth. We all agreed that the alien resembled Cody, thus the nickname Cody was affectionately bestowed. He was about 12 years old at the time and the name stayed with him through high school and college. We were so accustomed to calling him Cody that the nickname didn't appear to be going anywhere. To refer to him by another name, even his real name, seemed awkward. I was ecstatic to hear from Cody. He was in Chu Lai, south of DaNang, and I was in Phu Bai, north of DaNang. Occasionally we wrote to each other and surprisingly neither of us mentioned Vietnam in our letters. The tone of his letters had deep-seated feelings about the war but why dwell on it. In our letters we usually wrote about our plans for the future in the real world after our tour of duty was over. In grammar school and high school, Cody was always the prankster. He was full of mischief but most of his mischief was benign. Like the time we bet him twenty-five cents to go up to the meanest nun at St. Anthony's School and look her in the eye and tell her he loved her. In the 7th grade twenty-five cents was big bucks and required an arm-twisting collection from several 7th graders. We never thought he would keep his part of the bargain but he did. When the big day came, Cody walked up to Sr. Mary Stella Maris as she faithfully guarded the front hall of St. Anthony's School against any hooligans as they returned from recess. He looked her straight in the eye and said, "Sr. Mary Stella Maris." She turned and asked, "What is it?" He then let it out, "I love you Sr. Mary Stella Maris." That did it. There was absolute silence in both the girls line and the boys line. Sr. Mary Stella Maris remained stoic. It was as though she had a special vision from the Blessed Mother herself. Sr. Mary Stella Maris was so stunned she ignored him. The least Cody could expect was a year of detentions and coming to school at 7:30 every morning to dust off the queen's desk and wash the blackboards. For weeks we waited for the gauntlet to drop but it never did. Later we heard that on that memorable day one of the students actually saw a twinkle in her eye and an ever so faint smile. This was a first for Sr. Mary Stella Maris.

Then there was the time when Cody was spending a few days with us at a summer cottage in Dracut, Massachusetts. Across the lake from our cottage was an island accessible only by boat. The previous summer, a young twenty-one-year- old woman was murdered on the island. Her body was dismembered and parts of her arms and legs were found floating in the lake by one of the local fishermen. Later they captured the villain, a patient who was recently released from a mental institution. Everyone was abuzz about the incident and although it was a random act of violence, we were all understandably apprehensive.

Once after a late dinner and shortly before dusk on a hot summer evening, Cody and I decided to take a swim before hitting the feathers. Cody ran ahead of me as he was inclined to do to dive off the dock into the lake. What I forgot to tell him was that a man with one leg swam the lake every evening at dusk. He would remove his prosthesis, place it at the corner of the dock, and dive in the lake. As Cody ran down to the dock to dive in the lake he tripped over the man's prosthesis and went tumbling into the lake with the wooden leg. Cody came running out of the lake with the wooden leg in his hand yelling, "It's a leg! It's a leg!" After feeling the leg he realized it was artificial. We then placed the leg on the dock and waited for the owner to return from his swim. When we handed him his wet leg, with shoe and stocking attached, all we could do was to keep apologizing while the owner just laughed and laughed all the while. At least he had a sense of humor.

Then there was the time when Cody and I went to a wake at one of the local funeral homes in the North End. Italian wakes are always emotional. However, this wake was exceptionally emotional because a young 8th grade boy, a victim of a fatal hunting accident was laid to rest. As Cody and I entered the narrow doorway leading to the bier, a large Italian woman dressed in black slowly walked in front of us. The back of her dress was slightly elevated causing the insides of her thighs and kneecaps to be exposed. She had on heavy black nylons rolled down to about two inches above the knee. One had a hole causing her thigh to protrude through the hole. She had difficulty walking and wavered to the left and right as she walked. While firmly holding her shopping bags with her right hand, she held on to the side of the wall with her left hand. When the door to the parlor swung open a glimpse of the corpse triggered her reaction.

She yelled, "Figlio di mamma. Che peccato. Il marito di Gelsomina è morto! My son what a sin. The husband of Gelsomina is dead!" She then passed out blocking the doorway to the parlor. The funeral director, whom we recognized as the father of a fellow North Ender, asked us to help pick her up and move her onto the sofa in his office. He then broke a vial of smelling salts and placed it under her nose. She awoke and while making the sign of the cross kept repeating, "Il marito di Gelsomina è morto. Che peccato."

The funeral director responded, "Signora, questo non è il marito di Gelsomina. Questo è il figlio di mamma Rosa. Il marito di Gelsomina è alla casa di Dello Russo a Medford. This is not Gelsomina's husband. This is mamma Rosa's son. Gelsomina's husband is at Dello Russo's in Medford." The old Italian lady paused, took a sip of water, looked around and when she realized she was at the wrong wake, again she started crying

Just looking at Cody made one laugh. He was always upbeat and looked on the bright side of life. I was pleased when he asked me to meet him in DaNang. It was Wednesday when I received his letter and learned that he would be at the South China Beach USO on the following weekend. As long as I could get someone to pull duty for me, I could probably get a ride early Saturday and return on Sunday. I was fortunate to get someone to cover for me.

The following Saturday I managed to get a ride down with a convoy.

I had been through the Hai Van Pass before, and always marveled at the terrain and how vulnerable we were from both sides of the pass. It was only 60 miles from Phu Bai to DaNang, but it took at least 2.5 hours especially during the monsoon season. I arrived at the DaNang USO club at China Beach and left my name. Every few hours I checked back, but Cody was nowhere to be found. At midday on Sunday, I was doubtful if I would see him and had an opportunity to catch a flight back to Phu Bai, thus avoiding the Hai Van Pass. Things being so uncertain, I thought it would be a long shot to link up together, but it was worth the attempt. Later that week I received another letter from Cody telling me he was detained leaving Chu Lai. A few months later we made the same arrangements, but this time my flight out of Phu Bai was cancelled and the only alternative was to hop a ride with a convoy leaving at 6 a.m. That morning the monsoons were in full force and bad weather was forecasted for the next few days. Even the convoy was delayed a few hours because of bad weather. I decided the ride would take too long and I didn't relish the ride through the pass, so I stayed in Phu Bai.

While Cody was in Vietnam he received two Bronze Stars. He returned home six months before my return home and I am proud to say he was a member of my wedding party. For a while, after that, we maintained a fairly close relationship. When we got together we never spoke about Vietnam, but he knew as I knew that things had changed. Shortly after he returned home from Vietnam, and a few months after my wedding, he was killed instantly after he lost control of his car and hit a bridge abutment while returning home from a date with a local acquaintance. With Cody's passing, things changed even more. For the longest time when the old gang got together, his absence made relating to one another awkward. With time this passed and we learned to include him in our conversations as a way of remembering him.

Chapter 21

Moving to the Education Center

I had been in-country five months and still had seven months before my tour was over. It was still an uphill battle but I thought of the halfway point coming closer and the one week R&R I had to look forward to after six months in-country.

One morning while working in the mess hall, a colonel and a civilian named Orville walked in just as we were closing. You could always pick out civilians and reporters because of the way they dressed. Although they wore military uniforms, they never had their pants bloused and their uniforms were usually baggy and awkward looking. This was a dead give away. One time, a first sergeant, not realizing Orville was a civilian, tried to give him an Article Fifteen because his pants were not bloused. Orville politely told him to stuff it. Orville and the colonel had come in from the field. There was mud caked on their boots and on the bottom of their trousers. It was late and the mess hall was closed, so we were not obliged to serve them. Three of us were assigned to the officers mess. We were standing at the corner table when they walked up to the grill. We each looked at one another reluctant to get up and serve them, but we knew we should. Finally, I got up and walked toward the grill just as the Colonel asked, "What's for breakfast, Specialist?" This time we had pancakes without boll weevils. I immediately responded, "We have some pancake batter left. I could make you some pancakes."

"Fine, I'll take two."

Orville also asked for two pancakes. Orville was in his forties but looked much older. He was retired from the military. Many lifers, like Orville, had spent so much time in the military that when they retired they couldn't deal with the lack of structure and gravitated toward occupations that were structured; in a sense, as close to the military as one can get and still be a civilian. You could tell he smoked because he had that puckered look around his mouth from inhaling so often. His face had that weathered look like he was out in the cold too long. If one looked closely you could see the blood vessels in his face were ruptured, which I attributed to drinking. It came as no surprise when I later realized he was a chain smoker and each evening he had five or six drinks before he went to bed. He often smelled of booze. Word had it that Orville was assigned to a Chemical Unit on his last duty assignment and he had something to do with pesticides and defoliants.

I overheard them talking about his mission. He was in Phu Bai to set up an Army Education Center. Orville was employed by the United States Armed Forces Institute (USAFI), a division of the University of Maryland, Far East Division, and was in Vietnam to establish General Education Development (GED) programs for GIs interested in working toward their GED certificate. I heard the Colonel tell him he could take one of the empty hooches and set up the Ed Center in the front and he could bunk down in the rear of the hooch.

On a regular basis I would see Orville in the compound and occasionally would drop by the Ed Center to see how he was progressing. We spoke often and he knew I taught electronics in the real world. He was also aware that I would go back to teaching when I returned home and that education was my ambition. One day he mentioned he had two GIs at Camp Eagle who were interested in getting their GEDs. They needed tutoring in math and science and he asked me if I wanted to accompany him to Camp Eagle twice a week to provide tutoring. I immediately complied. At first I tutored when I was off duty, but when he asked me to teach a three-semester-hour course in electronics offered by the University of Maryland (Far East Division) through USAFI, I was ecstatic. This was my opportunity to find some sanity in a niche in which I felt comfortable. Orville made the arrangements and after six months in-country I was transferred to the Army Ed Center. No longer would I be at the daily whim of a gunnery sergeant assigning me where he pleased. At least now I belonged somewhere. At least I knew where I was going everyday.

Although we didn't have much in common, Orville learned to rely on me to assist him in setting up the Ed Center. Phu Bai was our home base and we would go to the different firebases with materials and supplies to help GIs prepare for their GEDs.

Chapter 22

R&R

After six months in-country I was entitled to ten days of rest and relaxation (R&R). At first I put in for Bangkok but opted not to go since I didn't know very many people going there. When I realized some of the original 513th were going to Australia, I put in for Australia and so off I went with Kevin, John and Gerry (the Irish Mafia). We spent ten wonderful days in Australia. The first two days, I stayed in my hotel room enjoying a private room with a nice clean bed and fresh sheets. It was heavenly being shut off from the insanity of Vietnam, enjoying the simple peace of mind and having room service bring up my meals. The luxury I enjoyed the most was going to the bathroom in private. One of the things that disturbed me most about Vietnam and one of the utmost indignities was to have to relieve myself in the presence of GIs to my left and to my right and sometimes facing me.

While in Australia we went to rugby games in the day and went clubbing at night. The infamous King's Cross area, similar to

Boston's former Scollay Square, provided all sorts of adult entertainment, especially for GIs. On Sunday mornings it was exciting to see the deep green hillside dotted with men all dressed in white. They were bowling on the

green. From their Aussie kangaroo hats to their white polished shoes, this presented a spectacular contrast against the blue skies and green hillside. From a distance sheep lazily grazed on the hillside adding to the serenity. I was fortunate to help shear the sheep. West of Sydney was the bush (forest) inhabited by aborigines which was less tranquil than the peaceful hills of Sydney.

The Irish Mafia and I managed to get tied in with the South Civic Junior League in Sydney. I was impressed at how openly they included us in their inner circle, especially when in the states the compassion for the military was at such a low point. We were not accustomed to such good treatment and relished every moment. The League sponsored a rugby team and owned a building in downtown Sydney where it held many activities, the proceeds of which financed the rugby team. Each floor in the building had a specific purpose. The fifth floor held sports facilities such as bowling alleys, gymnasiums, swimming pools, handball courts, etc. On the fourth floor was a juice bar with dance halls and recreation lounges where juveniles and young adults would gather and socialize while their parents engaged in adult activities. On the third floor were several adult lounges and many excellent dining facilities. Here we spent most of our evening hours. On the second floor were several cinemas which featured entertainers such as Tom Jones. The first floor was all gambling, similar to our gambling facilities in Connecticut. In many ways, I likened Sydney and its harbor to Boston, especially the Beacon Hill area because in Boston we could walk along Beacon Hill and, every now and then, get a glimpse of the Charles River. In Sydney you could do the same.

One afternoon we were walking along a street in downtown Sydney that ran parallel to the harbor. Occasionally we would get a glimpse of the water from one end of a street that ran perpendicular to the edge of the water. It was lunchtime and many were walking around the harbor enjoying the fresh air. From the hilltop we noticed a commotion developing and a crowd gathering at the shore. A closer look at the harbor revealed an individual with a large bull horn yelling, "Now turn around and swim very slowly." Further observation revealed that several GIs had decided to go swimming in shark-infested Sydney Harbor in spite of all the warning signs. Many office workers would feed the sharks during lunch hour encouraging their presence. As we moved closer three GIs were swimming to shore as six to seven sharks fishtailed back and forth about ten feet behind them. When they finally made it back to shore the lunch hour crowd of several hundred Aussies let out a tumultuous roar of jubilation in honor of the GIs successfully making it back to shore unharmed. It appeared the police and the Aussies were more concerned about the GIs than the GIs were of themselves. They were intoxicated beyond control and could care less.

Going back to Vietnam after R&R was a complete downer. The only consolation was that I had now been in-country eight months and had four more to go. R&R had to be taken after seven months in-country for if it were any sooner I'm sure the desertion rate would have been higher than it was.

I recently saw a documentary about a GI who received several commendations for valor during his first tour in Vietnam. While on R&R on his second tour, he went AWOL from Australia. He assumed a new identity and settled in New Zealand. After thirty-two years his daughters, who were infants at the time he went AWOL, tracked him down and convinced him to report back to his unit and face the music. I was intrigued by his story. In watching him as he was questioned, I could empathize with him and share his pain. He was eighteen at the time, almost ten years younger than when I was in Vietnam. He had already served one tour of duty and received several commendations but did not finish his second tour. The interviewer asked, "Why did you go AWOL?" He responded, "After one tour, I no longer believed in what I was doing. I tried to go back to Vietnam and I wanted to go back, but I just couldn't get back on the plane. If I went back, I know

I would have come home in a body bag so I did what I had to do." He didn't say much during the interview, but exuded a sense of simplicity and sincerity that was uniquely distinguishable. Everyone picked up on it. He appeared to be a genuinely nice guy who got caught up in a bad mess. I thought of how easy that was to do and how our society eventually came to its senses about Vietnam, and how we emerged as a forgiving society about many issues concerning Vietnam. His sentence was minimal with no time served. Had it been Korea, WW II, or the war in Iraq, society probably would not be as forgiving. In retrospect would it have been immoral to go AWOL during Desert Storm, Korea, WW II, or the latest war with Iraq? Yet it was okay to do so in Vietnam. Although as individual soldiers we ultimately made the final determination, does societal approval make it moral, and its disapproval make it immoral? What about all those guys who went to Canada and have since received amnesty? I have compassion for an individual who couldn't face going back, but then I lived with many men who went back to Vietnam after R&R, who were just as depressed, including me, and with many others who seriously considered going to Canada, but decided not to. Well, why then did we go back? The answer is simple. We felt some type of vague, undefined responsibility. The members of the 513th were and still are conscientious people who always wanted to do what was right. The problem was no one knew what was right and what was wrong and to what extent this responsibility should have manifested itself.

When I arrived back in Phu Bai, Orville was not feeling well, but he continued his chain smoking and heavy drinking. I came to realize this was his death wish. When he was in the Army, he had served one tour of duty in Vietnam. When he retired he asked for more by coming back as a civilian. He seemed to thrive on confusion. The more confused things were the more he seemed to perk up. As a matter of fact he became excited when we were under attack in our bunkers awaiting in-coming. He would then talk about the incident for days on end as though the only excitement he got out of life was by living on the edge.

Much to my surprise when I reported back to the Ed Center after returning from Australia, I had orders to go to Bangkok. Surely this had to be a mistake because we were only entitled to one R&R per tour so I was told. I later found out this wasn't so. I asked Orville what these orders meant and, typical of a lifer, he commented one night after downing almost a half bottle of Jim Beam, "Orders are orders and you do what you're ordered to do."

I replied, "I don't think I should take a second R&R. Do you?"

"Why not? If you have orders to go, you go. I know several GIs who did. It's perfectly okay."

Not feeling comfortable, I spoke with the first sergeant at 26th General Support Group and realized some men received more than one R&R during their tour. When I showed him my orders he commented, "In the military we do nothing without orders. Furthermore, if you miss your plane to Bangkok, which is early tomorrow morning, then you miss your R&R. To cut you another set of orders is virtually impossible." I would have given an eyetooth to be anywhere but in Vietnam. After speaking with two of my supervisors, I decided to go to Bangkok.

I barely had time to unpack before I was off again. Staying in Bangkok for seven days would be great. Everyone in Vietnam counted the days and the wake-ups they had left for their tour of duty to be finished. This would be seven less days I would have to count. When I get back to Phu Bai, I would be in the short-timer category. Just thinking about it made me feel good. It made the light at the end of the tunnel a bit closer.

It was 6 a.m. when I reported to the airfield. On the same flight was

Gus, one of the marines in my hooch. I wasn't especially thrilled to link up with him, but I decided to stay with him for the time being and then gracefully find a way to be on my own. I was always more comfortable alone. I considered myself responsible for my actions, but to be responsible for someone else's made me feel uncomfortable. Gus was from Chicago and had joined the Marines just out of high school. He was an eighteen-year-old and of Polish ancestry. Like many kids out of high school in the 60s he wanted to make an impact. This was his second R&R in Bangkok and he was familiar with the routine. He sat beside me on the plane and drank heavily.

" Where are you staying?" he asked.

"The Parliament Hotel. It's in downtown Bangkok."

"That's great! As a matter of fact, that's where I'm staying. Why don't we get adjoining suites? We can raise hell together. You know you can do anything you want in Bangkok. Prostitution is legal and the girls are checked out regularly for syphilis or clap. As a matter of fact we can rent a couple of broads for the whole week for next to nothing or we can have a different broad every night. Whadda ya say?"

I was reluctant to commit myself. As a stall tactic I responded, "Well, let's get settled first and then I'll think about it."

When we arrived at the hotel Gus ran ahead and before I could check in he asked for adjacent suites with an adjoining door. I didn't like this idea. Gus had some problems at Phu Bai and was inclined to become volatile at the slightest provocation. I thought it best not to upset him. Little did I realize that at the core of his volatility was a serious drug problem.

When I finally checked in, I purposely left the adjoining door to our rooms closed. However, it wasn't long before he knocked on my door shouting, "Hey man, I called down and requested a few broads. They should be here any minute. Come on in. Let's get started."

When I walked into his room he had an array of drugs sprawled across his bed, including several exotic bongs the likes of which I have never seen. Just then three Thai prostitutes appeared at the door ready for business. I felt uncomfortable and instinctively realized I was putting myself in a precarious position. For seven months I had made it through Vietnam. Knowing the severe penalty for drug possession, I would be damned to have made it this far only to rot away in a Thai prison the rest of my life.

"Hey Gus," I yelled, "I have to get something. I'll be right back."

Fortunately, my duffle bag was still intact. I quickly gathered my belongings and quietly left my room and reported to the concierge. She was a beautiful Thai woman with long silky, jet black hair. I ran up to the front desk yelling, "My room is terrible, I want a room on the other side of the hotel. It's too noisy and I saw several lizards crawling up the walls." Little did I know that most of the rooms have lizards entering through the open veranda.

"Sir, I sorry, but this all we have available."

"Well, I'll go somewhere else, that's all."

"One minute, sir."

She walked into a back room to consult with someone and after a minute she returned. "Sir, we have cancellation. It in east wing on other side hotel. It quiet. You like?"

"Yes! Yes!"

I grabbed my duffle bag and belongings and quickly moved to my new location. I hesitated to tell Gus of my change in plans and felt uncomfortable about leaving him so abruptly, but I had no alternative and had to protect myself. My new room was near the rear exit allowing me to come and go, thus avoiding Gus. I also had ten days before I would see him on the plane back to Phu Bai. This was ample time to think up a story about my leaving him so abruptly. Once settled, I rested awhile before going out for the evening.

An hour later, I awoke refreshed and decided to walk down to the center of Bangkok and ask someone to clue me in about the evening activities. Cab drivers were always available for a fee. As I walked down by the river, I noticed many sampans along the edge of the river with kids playing on the deck. After seeing the living conditions on these sampans, the small three-room apartment we had in the North End was heavenly. The children had no idea they were impoverished. I'm sure they would be fine as long as they stayed that way and didn't experience anything different. They appeared happy. I flagged a cab and asked the driver to take me to one of the clubs. He drove down several narrow streets and stopped in front of a nightclub called the Manhattan. Many of the clubs catered to GIs and were named after cities and towns in the states to make the GIs feel at home.

As I entered the Manhattan the contrast between the bright sun and the darkness caused me to wait for my eyes to adjust. I walked into a large dance hall. The music was deafening. On the left of the dance floor was a bar with several cocktail tables. GIs were swarming all over the place. On the dance floor were no less than a couple of hundred Thai women, dancing together to the loud music. It had been a long time since I had seen two women dancing together. In Italian families, women dancing together is very common, especially at family and social functions. I suppose it's because the men don't dance and probably consider it to be less than macho and the women like to dance so they dance with each other. Each woman wore a similar type dress, about six inches above the knee, tastefully fitted, and not tight. On the shoulder of each dress was an identifying number. GIs would observe the women dancing and when one had an interest in a particular woman, he would signal to Papa-son who also was the equivalent of a bouncer. Papa-son would then shine his flashlight on the number and the number would glow. Once the escort came to the table, she was then asked to show her health card. If the GI was still interested Papa-son would recite the litany of her services and the cost, based on a daily or weekly rate. The daily rate decreased as the number of rental days increased. Papa-son would collect the money in advance and the GI would have to leave his name, military ID number and the address of the hotel where he could be reached.

At the end of the session the GI would have to return the escort to Papa-son. Failure to do so would bring the wrath of the Bangkok police to your room. With the assistance of the Thai police, Papa-son kept things well under control. At the end of each session the local doctor examined the escort. Only then was her card signed indicating she was okay. It was strictly a money making proposition and ran very efficient.

It was 3 a.m. when I returned to the hotel. The cab driver dropped me off at the rear of the hotel. Entering the rear door I heard a commotion coming from the front lobby. I looked down into the lobby from the second floor balcony and saw Gus and two other GIs, whom I did not recognize, being dragged through the lobby shackled in chains followed by three prostitutes. I asked around but no one seemed to want to know what had happened. I decided it best if I went to my room pour myself a stiff drink and sleep it off. That was the last time I saw Gus.

I finally awoke at 10 a.m. feeling somewhat strung out from the activities of the previous night. I decided to relax by the pool with a cup of coffee. Gazing at the pool closely, it appeared to have green slime floating in certain spots so I hesitated to go swimming. I looked around for something to read and the only thing I could find was the *Army Times*. Of course this was exactly what I wanted to read on R&R. According to the Times everything was going great in Vietnam. We were winning the war and for every GI we lost, the enemy lost at least a million. I often wondered if the people who wrote these articles were on the same planet for it amazed me how, week after week, they would come out with the same bullshit and everyone knew it was propaganda, yet it continued. I didn't know anyone who actually believed it but I'm sure someone must have.

As I read the *Army Times*, I glanced up and recognized the person in front of me as the woman who was at the front desk when Gus was escorted out of the hotel shackled in chains. She was also the same woman who managed to get my room changed. I decided to approach her and as I was about to speak to her a young gentleman approached and asked, "Excuse me sir, may I be of some help?"

"As a matter of fact you can. Last evening I was out on the town and found most bars very accommodating with many beautiful women. However, I found that most of them catered to the GIs and their needs. I was hoping I could experience more of the Thai culture and try its authentic Thai food instead of what was offered at most hotels."

We conversed for a while and I came to realize he was the husband of the young woman who had my room changed. Both were school teachers at a local elementary school and worked at the hotel part time. His name was Tran Van Nguyen. When I tried to find out more information about last night and the whereabouts of Gus, he was evasive and didn't seem to know much, or perhaps he didn't want to know much. After a while I developed a rapport with Tran and his wife and it was then that he revealed it would be awhile before Gus would be back. Gus wasn't allowed to speak with anyone and legal representation from the states or the military looked dismal if not impossible. The legal system in Bangkok, if you can call it that, believes in swift justice. Although they put on a facade of providing legal representation, it's a Kangaroo court. Everything is done in a matter of hours and sentences and fines are swift and severe. Twenty-five years hard labor and a stiff fine are customary for possession of a minimal amount of marijuana. Gus' sentence was never revealed. However, I did find out he was literally sent up the river Kwai to work in the jungles with the elephants clearing trees to be used for carving teakwood ornaments. I later found out that the drug dealers would sell drugs to the GIs and inform the police of the transaction. The police would then apprehend the GIs, take whatever they had as a fine and sentence them to a stiff penalty. They were famous for apprehending GIs shortly after they began their R&R because this is when they would have the most cash. Considering the average GI had anywhere from five hundred to one thousand dollars when he arrived on R&R, this was a great sum of money. After the bust, the GIs would be fined and sentenced. The police would receive the money and retrieve the remaining drugs, pay off the drug dealers and the court officials, keep their share of the pie, give the drugs back to the dealers and the cycle would begin again.

I decided to maintain a low profile and stay close to the Nguyens for they appeared to be people I could trust. The next day Mr. and Mrs. Nguyen invited me to the elementary school where they taught. I was impressed that the children had next to nothing for supplies and materials and yet they wanted to learn. They were attentive and well disciplined. A remarkable contrast to many of our public schools in the states. However, they pay a stiff price for this structure and discipline, one that I would not be willing to pay. Bangkok was not a democracy but a dictatorship. We all know what happened to their neighbors in Cambodia, also a dictatorship, as a result of the Khumer Rouge.

The next day was Sunday and the Nguyens asked me to accompany them on a boat ride to the village of their ancestors where they would have their relatives prepare dinner. I was excited. We proceeded north in a glorified sampan. Certainly, we traveled no more than 15—20 miles an hour. The river appeared unusually calm and the canopy was so dense in many areas it bridged the river and blocked the sun creating a macabre atmosphere. Although we could not see many of the birds and animals you could hear them through dense foliage. The only time they stopped singing was when we caused a disturbance in the water. We traveled north along the bank of the river until we came to a fork and headed right. Two and one half hours later, we arrived at our destination. We arrived at a clearing dotted with several huts along the bank. The native women were washing their clothes and smoke was billowing from most of the huts. We pulled the boat ashore and proceeded to one of the huts.

The Nguyens brought me to a hut close to the edge of the river. They introduced me to an old man and woman whom they called Mama-son and Papa-son. I knew these were the parents of either Tran or his wife. Later I learned these were his wife's parents and his parents came from another village farther north. He also revealed that his father had died in the war but his mother was still alive and well. War seemed to be a national pastime in many of these third world countries, and I wanted to ask in what war his father died but at the risk of becoming to personal, I hesitated. The Nguyens spoke English far better than I spoke the few words I knew in Vietnamese. My knowledge of Thai was nil, so I depended on the Nguyens to translate as we exchanged cordialities.

After a few minutes Mama-son started to prepare dinner. In one corner of a large room there was fire pit over which she prepared the meals. She used previously stacked fire wood for fuel and from the river she filled a large caldron of water and started to heat it. A second time she went down by the edge of the river and lifted several rocks as though she knew what she was looking for and where to find it. She lifted a large rock and quickly pulled out of the river four large crustaceans the likes of which I have never seen. Making a pouch with her apron she placed them in the center to take back to the hut. What she pulled out of the river were not crayfish and they were certainly not lobsters. All I can recollect as I looked at our dinner was that they resembled extremely large cockroaches at least fourteen inches long. She then put them in the cold water. She added herbs and spices, many I had never smelled and have never experienced. She let this cook for several hours. In the meantime I received the grand tour of the village. The one word that can best describe it is surreal. The people were self-sufficient. They hunted, fished and grew crops. They made their clothing from animal skins. From each hut spewed smoke resulting in a haze canvassing the village. This contributed to the surreal atmosphere. The children amused themselves by playing games with sticks and others willingly helped their parents. They appeared happy and had no knowledge of our culture and did not realize that according to our standard of poverty they were miserable. Hence, should we have also helped them out of the darkness?

Returning from our walk through the village, we went back to the hut and sat on the floor around a slightly elevated platform that served as a table. Mama-son served me dinner in a dish made out of hard clay. As was customary she wanted me to sample the food and give my approval. I looked down on my plate and for a moment I thought of the small three-room apartment in which I grew up in the North End and how Mom would cringe at the site of a cockroach. We lived over Giro's restaurant and periodically the restaurant would have to be exterminated, which was a common occurrence in many North End restaurants. As a result the cockroaches would migrate upstairs to safer quarters. They had to come up three flights of stairs to get to our apartment but they would converge with a vengeance. The only way to rid us of these pests was to exterminate our apartment. This was no small task for after we exterminated, Mom would religiously wash all the dishes and pans and everything that was exposed to insecticide. Then the cockroaches would migrate to the fourth floor to my Aunt Rosie's apartment. When she exterminated they would schlep back downstairs and Mom would get upset and the saga would repeat itself. I wondered what Mom would do under the present circumstances?

I looked down at my food, politely smiled and broke off the leg of what looked like a cockroach, dipped it in a dark sauce and tasted it. It was extremely hot and spicy. It wouldn't be my first choice on the menu but after making such a fuss about wanting authentic Thai food I had no alternative but to turn to Mama-son and gesturing with the thumb of my right hand I commented, "Number 1." Tran relayed this back to Papa-son and we all started eating. It seemed the more I ate the hotter it became. I maintained a smile, but with every morsel I had apprehensions. Although I was accustomed to hot food this was very different and I knew I was going to pay for it. Shortly after dinner I was happy when Tran suggested we move along. Already, I was starting to feel ill and we had at least a two-hour ride before us. I thanked Mama-son and Papa-son for their generous hospitality and immediately found a comfortable position in the back of the boat. I wanted to sleep but didn't feel comfortable doing so. As we started down the river, it started drizzling and it felt refreshing on my face. I started fading in and out of consciousness and asked for water. We were warned never to drink the water in Thailand but I felt I was burning up. It was all I could do to maintain my composure. Tran, finally thinking something was amiss, turned to me and said, "Hey GI, you okay?"

"Oh I'm fine, just a little tired. We only have another hour. We'll be back to the hotel soon and then I can rest."

The rain intensified. It seemed as though the rain was always more intense in the Orient than in the states. I pulled my poncho over my head and tried to maintain my composure. I did not want to get sick in front of my acquaintances and reveal that I was running a fever. We pulled into Bangkok Harbor, thanked the Nguyens for a wonderful day and headed to my room. I finally thought the worst was over but was gravely mistaken.

I lay on the bed and watched the ceiling spin round and round. I looked at the walls and it appeared that lizards were crawling up the walls. When I tried to zero in on one of them, it blended in with the flowered wallpaper; and just when I stopped looking to question myself, it would move up the wall, similar to seeing something out of the corner of your eye fleeting across the room and you ask yourself, "Was that a mouse?" It was hot and muggy and I was burning up. I took my cloths off and lay on the bed looking at the ceiling fan that was now turning at full speed. I was sweating profusely. I was always a healthy person and took care of myself, especially in Vietnam. I took my malaria pills on a regular basis and made sure I always had my insect repellant with me. I also made sure I used water purification tablets when it was necessary and slept with my mosquito net securely fastened at the bottom to prevent rodents from making themselves too comfortable. Now I was too sick to call the doctor. I did not have enough energy to get out of bed. I looked up and noticed the ceiling fan was rotating off balance. I thought it might break loose at any minute. Suddenly the room started rotating, following the regular cadence of the fan. I lay in bed all night hoping I would feel better. Morning came and I felt worse. I thought if this is how it is when one is deathly ill, then death would be a blessing. No wonder many would rather die than be miserably sick. I lay in bed sweating profusely. I focused my eyes on a spot on the wall only to realize it was a lizard when it suddenly jumped. I felt like I wanted to barf but I couldn't. I finally made it to the bathroom only to sit there and ponder my dilemma. It felt good to have privacy, especially since I was ill. I would take a cold bath to reduce my body temperature, but it took all my energy to get to the bathroom and back to bed. I thought I should put on some shorts in case I died in bed. In Vietnam, I often thought of dying and always prayed I died with dignity. At least if I died in bed and not on the throne, and having on shorts rather than being found in the nude like in one of those serial murder mysteries, this would give me a measure of dignity. It was still hot and humid with no relief in sight. In the heat of the day it must have been at least one hundred degrees with the only air coming from the fan. In spite of it all, I valued the fan for it was better than nothing.

I continued looking up at the fan and as the blades turned round and round, I focused my attention on one of the blades. As it rotated, the catchy cadence of its sound led me to believe some of the ball bearings were worn out. I was in a semi-catatonic state and in spite of feeling ill, I enjoyed the sense of numbness. It provided me with an escape mechanism. I truly didn't care what happened! It was easy to tune out the world. I resigned myself to the fact I was ill and just wanted to lie there and do nothing. When I returned home, I often used this technique of withdrawal. It provided me with a way of dealing with the assholes of the world in a semi-positive manner rather than lashing out at them.

About 4 p.m. there was a knock on the door. I thought it was my imagination. When I heard a second knock, I wasn't up to it but I decided to answer it. I slowly walked to the door and asked, "Who is it?" The voice from behind the door answered, "It's me, Tran. You okay?"

"Yes, I'll be okay but I feel a little sick. Please, you bring me three liters of bottled water. Leave behind door."

Tran replied, "Maybe I get doctor?"

"No! No! I'll be okay. Just bottled water please."

Shortly thereafter Tran left several liters of bottled water behind the door. It wasn't until after midnight that I managed to drag myself to the door to retrieve the water. I drank some water and tried to get some sleep but it was impossible. The Americans had just landed on the moon and the noise from the open courtyard made me well aware of what was happening.

I tried to determine if it was the water I drank on the boat that made me sick. This didn't seem possible since I was feeling ill before I drank the water. Perhaps it was the dinner that was cooked with water from the river? Although Ma-ma-son supposedly boiled the water, perhaps it wasn't boiled long enough to kill the bacteria present in the look-a-like lobster, to which my system was not accustomed. Whatever the reason, whatever I had was nasty.

The second day of my illness, my body ached and all I could do was lie there and pray it would soon pass. The third and fourth days passed as miserably as the first two. Then early in the morning of the fourth day, there was another knock on the door. A voice whispered, "Hello GI, this is Tran. I bring doctor. Please open door. I mustered enough strength to get to the door. As soon as I opened the door Tran looked at me and commented, "GI you velly sick you need doctor." The doctor came in the room and examined me only to speculate that I had a bug and that it could be bacterial if it came from the water. He recommended that I go to the hospital. I chose not to do so and asked him for medication. I declared nuclear war on my illness. I tanked up on medication, took a sleeping pill he prescribed, went to bed and finally slept.

Forty-eight hours later I awoke. I had been ill for six days and was at least 15 — 20 pounds lighter. At least I could move around and would be able to make the flight back to Phu Bai. The last thing I wanted to do was to miss my flight and be declared AWOL.

Chapter 23

Back to Phu Bai

We circled around DaNang several times before we received clearance to land. It was early afternoon and rather than spend the night there, I wanted to get a flight back to Phu Bai before dark. I managed to hop a flight on a C130A transport plane that flew to Phu Bai twice daily. The cargo area where we sat was filled mostly with Vietnamese. They had their entire belongings in large sacks they carried on their heads. Some were fortunate to have suitcases. Others had chickens in crates and a few also had calves. This was the last flight back to Phu Bai, and there didn't appear to be enough room for all of us. The pilot expressed concern about the heavy load. We all sat on the floor as we were about to take off. One of the crewmen spoke on the intercom and informed us that three short bursts on the horn meant we should get ready to ditch and should sit in a tight ball and prepare for impact. We taxied down the runway, picked up as much speed as we could, and sluggishly lifted off. Anyone who has flown in a C130A knows how it never seems to get off the ground, but somehow it eventually does. We gained altitude very slowly, just enough to clear the mountain range along the eastern seacoast of Vietnam. Suddenly I heard a jolt and we started to lean to one side. One of the engines had failed causing the plane to lose altitude. The Vietnamese were yelling and screaming as there belongings shifted to one side of the craft. The chickens were now flying about the aircraft adding more chaos to a bad situation. The calves were whining because they sensed fear of what seemed inevitable. There was barely room to move as we all piled on one another. I remembered what the crewmen said and placed myself in a tight ball, said an Our Father and asked God for help.

Just then three short blasts were sounded on the horn. We continued to lose altitude. The inevitable appeared at hand. I was lying on the right side of the plane and could hear the whining of the engine as the pilot was trying to restart it.

Suddenly I heard the roar of an engine and realized how happy that sound made me feel. Just as suddenly as the engine failed and we were thrown into chaos, we were now back on track. The plane stabilized. I gathered my belongings and after settling down I nestled into a lethargic complacency. Everyone sat there looking at each other. That thousand-mile stare, I now so often learned to recognize, became more prevalent as I continued my tour.

I still had a fever and was feeling nauseous but was glad to get back to Phu Bai. Although I had orders to go to Bangkok, which I confirmed with my superiors, I was paranoid and felt guilty about going.

After I arrived in Phu Bai, I reported to the Education Center to see what was going on. In front of the Ed Center hooch was a note written on a piece of plywood that read, "Education Center closed until further notice." I decided to check in at Headquarters 26th General Support Group. When I arrived there was a great deal of activity. The preceding evening we had been hit and now they were assessing the damage. The company clerk, whom I did not know, was a Specialist 5th class, one rank higher than me. I had been put in for Specialist 5th class before I left for Bangkok and felt his equal and didn't feel intimidated saying, "Excuse me specialist, I'm Specialist Masciulli. I'm assigned to the Education Center. I've just returned from R&R only to realize the Ed Center is closed." Before I could continue he interrupted, "Oh yes, the CO has been looking for you. Now I sensed a problem. Until this time I had remained anonymous. I found a spot in the Ed Center and had hoped I could ride out my tour in anonymity. I was afraid this was about to change. The Company clerk then instructed me to report to the CO on the double. I entered the CO's office and reported as requested. "Specialist Masciulli reports as requested sir." I stood at attention and the phone rang. I knew he was pissed off by the way he answered the phone. He was curt and appeared irritated. Also, when speaking to the CO, he would usually put you "at ease," which meant you could spread your legs and stand with both hands behind your back in a relaxed position. Since he required me to stand at attention during his phone call, I sensed I was in serous trouble. After his conversation, he slammed the phone down and looked up at me and asked, "Specialist Masciulli, where the hell have you been?

I began to answer, "I've been on R&R in…."

He interrupted, "You had no authorization to go to Bangkok. Your request had been cancelled. As far as the Army is concerned, you've been AWOL. I've already commenced court martial proceedings. You reservists, you're all alike. You're dismissed."

I answered, "But sir…."

He interrupted, "I did not give you permission to speak. Furthermore, Mr. Orville has been medivaced to DaNang. He has liver cancer and is not expected to make it. In his absence I expect you to take over his duties until his replacement arrives. God only knows when that will be. In the meantime move your gear into the Ed Center. You can stay there. Now get out of my office." When I left his office I felt like a piece of shit. Will it ever end, I thought. Every day it was something different in this Godforsaken place. I decided the best I could do was to go to the Ed Center and try to get some courses underway.

Nights continued to be boring unless we had in-coming. The men continued to sit around drinking 3.2% beer and smoking pot to relieve the boredom. Maybe if I got some courses underway it would weigh in my favor. If I were to be court-martialed and reduced in rank I would be lower than an E-4. This would be humiliating, not only for a guy with a degree in engineering, but for anyone. Going home with a rank lower than E-4 was unacceptable.

On my fifth day back from Bangkok at 2 a.m. when most of us were asleep, the all alert was sounded. "Wake up! Wake up! Hurry up. Get in the bunker." We all grabbed what we could and made a beeline for the bunker. Some had helmets and a few were fortunate enough to grab their flak vests as they exited the hooch. We crouched down with our hands covering our ears. This time it seemed worse than ever. As often as I heard the sound of in-coming, it seemed to get worse and worse. I can only compare it to the sound of several bolts of lightning striking within one hundred feet. The sound is deafening. A new GI, one whom I had never seen before sat in the corner with his hands cupped over his face. He was crying. When the all clear was sounded, I waited a moment before I exited the bunker. I turned and commented, "Come on. Let's go. That was the all clear. We can go now."

He continued to cry and mumbled, "I can't."

"What do you mean you can't go? Let's get the hell out of here. This place is cold, damp and miserable. Let's try to get some sleep. We'll need it."

Again he repeated, "I can't."

"Why?" I asked.

"I messed myself, that's why."

"Okay," I replied. "Stay here. I'll go back to the hooch and get a pair of clean shorts and a towel. The only available water is in the mess hall which is too far to go. I think I can find some soap and water behind the Ed Center. That should help." After gathering some hygienic materials, I went back to the bunker with several canteens filled with water and a wash basin. I waited outside while he cleaned himself. As we walked back to our hooch not a word was spoken.

When we arrived everyone was all wound up. Like many other nights, I was afraid tonight was going to be another wasted, sleepless evening. Some of the guys were drinking and smoking pot. There was much noise and cussing at Charlie for the harassment. I left and retreated to the loneliness of the Ed Center where I could be alone with my thoughts. Being alone never bothered me except when we received in-coming and I couldn't exit quickly enough. Then I would crawl under my bunk. The vibration would disturb some of the resident vermin and they would scurry by a little too close for comfort.

It reminded me of my throwing out the garbage when I lived in the North End. In the alleyway behind my building at 460 Hanover Street across from the Coast Guard Base were twelve garbage cans enclosed in wooden frames with wooden covers where we would throw the household garbage. On my way out for the evening it was my job to bring the garbage down to the yard and drop it off in our assigned barrel. I would then exit through the open gate on Commercial Street. Often, I would run into two very attractive girls as they ran down the stairs singing in harmony to ward off any unwanted vermin. We referred to them as the German girls because their mother was Italian and their father was German. In the 50s, this was rare in the North End of Boston where most residents were of Italian descent. One evening I was wearing my Sunday best anticipating a very special occasion. As I opened the cover to the barrel, I heard a noise in one of the empty barrels. Instinctively I looked in the barrel before I inserted the rubbish and a rat jumped out. Quickly I reared back to avoid it. Not quick enough because his tail brushed my cheek. As I lay beneath my bunk during in-coming seeing a vermin run by, I was reminded of the unusual texture of a rat's tail and how unsettling it would be if I died alone in the rear of the Ed Center in Phu Bai.

The next month brought progress to the Ed Center. I managed to get a few GED courses under way in preparation for High School Equivalency exams. Nights continued to be boring. However, knowing what the alternative would bring, I welcomed the boredom and two nights a week I taught a course in Basic Electronics. This kept several GIs and me busy during the evening hours rather than sitting around drinking and getting into trouble. I also helped set up a few courses at some of the firebases. This gave me a great deal of satisfaction and things progressed so well that one day a newcomer named Dennis Weaver was assigned to the Ed Center to help out. Dennis was considerably younger than me. He was eighteen and hailed from Wisconsin. He was young and impressionable like so many others. Everything was flag waving, motherhood, apple pie and "kicking ass," especially the gooks, as he so often referred to the Vietnamese. I never got close with Dennis and perhaps for good reason. When I think of Dennis, I think of Wisconsin and Gouda cheese. I had purchased a small refrigerator from a GI who finished his tour. He sold it to me for short money. Coming from a large extended Italian family, I received at least one package of goodies a week from relatives. I would put all my goodies such as pepperoni, pickled artichoke hearts, pizzeles, Italian cookies and many more in the refrigerator. Often, I would notice Dennis and some of the students would help themselves. This was fine with me for all my life I was taught to share what I had. One week Dennis had received a package of Gouda cheese containing six individually wrapped pieces and placed them in the refrigerator. One day I came in from the field at 7 p.m. I had not eaten since morning so I ran to the Ed Center and all that was left in the refrigerator were three pieces of Gouda cheese. I can still envision the three pieces of cheese neatly wrapped in individual containers. I was so hungry I ate all three pieces. I did something I so often reprimanded my sons for doing, I left the empty packages in the refrigerator.

I went to bed that evening not having the slightest inclination of my dastardly deed. The next morning Dennis was late for duty. He arrived at the Ed Center a half hour late. His hair was disheveled for he just rolled out of the sack and had missed breakfast. Immediately he went for the refrigerator, opened it and saw the three empty packages. He yelled, " Where is my Gouda cheese?" One of the students in the Ed Center who was often accused of raiding the refrigerator looked the other way. Again Dennis bellowed, this time with more determination, "Where the fuck is my cheese?" Suddenly there was a lull in the Ed Center. He then removed his bayonet from its case and placed it against the throat of the suspect and threatened, "If you don't tell me who took my cheese, I'm going to slice your fucking throat from ear to ear." You could hear a pin drop in the Ed Center. I knew something more than a few pieces of missing cheese was wrong but I couldn't put my finger on it. I had no alternative but to turn to him and admit, "I arrived late from the field and had not eaten since morning so I helped myself to your cheese. I apologize if I have offended you and I assure you I will replenish your cheese twofold as soon as possible." The silence in the Ed Center was striking. No one said much to Dennis. He sat there for the longest period of time, staring at the wall, perhaps embarrassed to say anything. That evening I wrote home to Mary, my wife to be, and insisted she send me at least three large packages of Gouda cheese. As soon as it arrived, I placed it in the refrigerator with Dennis' name on it and a note that read, "Please do not touch." Later I came to realize Dennis was heavily into drinking and doing his share of drugs. This accounted for his unusual change in personality. From this day on I maintained a cordial but distant relationship with Dennis for I was always cautious of him turning against me or someone else in the Ed Center.

Chapter 24

118 Days and a Wake Up

I was in-country a little more than eight months. This made me feel good. Only four months left in this hell hole. Now, I was considered a short timer which was the rite of passage for which we were all striving. The rite of passage was approaching and hopefully, Vietnam would soon be behind me with only four more months to go. Assiduously, I counted the number of days and the number of wake-ups I had remaining before my departure. It was common practice to greet newcomers by reminding them, "I have one-hundred days and a wake-up" or "fifty days and a wake-up." Time was everything.

Since Orville was very ill, Dennis and I decided to visit him in DaNang. We managed to sneak away under the ruse of picking up supplies for the Ed Center. The CO gave us little resistance because it was policy that when taking such a long trip, we traveled with someone. I drove and Dennis rode shotgun. The ride south along Highway 1 was beautiful. It was mid May and hot. Many of the beaches were pristine. Looking across the South China Sea my imagination lulled me into believing I was elsewhere; perhaps on Cape Cod or the coast of Maine with all its splendor and tranquility. Today even the Hai Van Pass seemed palatable. We approached an old discarded Army truck weathering in time. Its stillness was broken by the sound of the canvas cover flapping in the breeze against the side of the truck. The sound brought me back to reality. Instinctively I knew how quickly everything could change for the worse. Finally arriving in DaNang, we approached the infamous China Beach area.

Everyone who has been to Vietnam has experienced first hand the China Beach syndrome. For a price anything could be purchased at China Beach. We stopped at one of the traffic lights when two Vietnamese prostitutes approached the jeep and offered their services. One reached into the jeep and grabbed Dennis' crotch saying, "Hey GI, you horny, vely vely horny? Me horny too. Me take good care of you and you take good care of me." "How much?" said Dennis. She then blurted out the litany of her services and added, "For you, me give special price, only ten dalla."

Dennis immediately responded, "Ten dollars! No dice. Too much."

"Hey GI this DaNang special only good for today, tomorrow twenty dalla. Ten dalla cheap for rich Amelican."

Dennis quipped, "Ten dollars too much."

She answered, "Ten dalla not too much. GI you bu cu dinky dow." She then placed her right index finger and thumb to her right temple and rotated them back and forth indicating he was crazy.

"Okay, I bu cu dinky dow but ten dalla still too much. Good-by."

"GI you wait. I give you special, special price only seven dalla." With what appeared to be her final offer, Dennis decided he would go with her and catch up with me at the hospital. I wasn't thrilled about his leaving and going off alone, but I had no alternative. I asked him not to be too long. I had little, if anything, in common with Orville, and Dennis' presence would make the time pass quicker. Orville was a man of few words. Even at the Ed Center and at night just hanging around, I had difficulty conversing with him. I felt sorry for Orville. How sad his life must have been for him to want to return to Vietnam a second time. How unfortunate it was that the only time he would get excited was when we were under fire or when total confusion ruled. Many men signed on for an additional tour, but they were much younger than Orville and had not yet figured out what was happening. Orville was older and should have figured it out by now but he didn't. When I walked into the hospital room, Orville had just woken up. I tried to be as upbeat as possible and greeted him, "Hi Orville, how are you?"

"Not so good," he answered, "I'm afraid, I have liver cancer."

I didn't expect him to be so quick to tell me of his illness. It made me feel very uncomfortable. I began searching for something else to say and must have sounded trite when I commented, "That's too bad, I'm sure there's something they can do for you."

"They recommended that I go back to the states for treatment but I've decided to stay here." He spoke as though he had already resigned to dying without a fight and Vietnam was as good a place as any to pack it in. His comments raised a red flag. Why in the name of God's world would anyone want to die in such a horrible place and without the presence of family?

I decided to make small talk and gather more information about him. The small talk would do him good to occupy his mind, if only for a brief moment. I knew he was from Georgia so I decided to focus on his home state.

"Where in Georgia are you from?" I asked.

"A small town south of Atlanta called Macon. You probably never heard of it," he replied. "Where are you from?"

"I'm from a small Italian neighborhood in Boston called the North End. Not many people from Georgia come to the North End, that's for sure," I laughed.

He answered, "Not too many Italians are in Macon either. Macon is a small farming county where they grow Elberta peaches. You like peaches?"

"Yes, especially in wine."

"In wine? What a beautiful way to ruin a perfectly good peach."

I continued, "Are you married?"

"Not now, although I was married to the same woman for twenty years."

"Any children?"

At this point I was asking too many questions, but at the risk of just sitting and looking at each other with nothing in common, I continued, "Any children?"

"Yeah. Three, all girls and all pains in the ass."

"Do they also live in Macon?"

"They used to, but God only knows where they are. I haven't heard from them in years. Just as well." Just then his nurse walked in and asked me to step outside.

"How well do you know Orville?" she asked.

"I worked with him at the Ed Center for a short period of time."

"Do you know any of his kin?"

"No, but that information must be in the personnel file."

"I looked in his file for next of kin and tried contacting people whose names were listed but with no success."

I continued, "Well, from what I understand, he is friendly with Dennis who also works at the Ed Center. I think they were together on their last duty assignment. Dennis will be coming along shortly. Maybe he can help you."

Just then Dennis walked into the room. I felt a sense of relief for I didn't want to be in a position where I would be responsible for being the only one Orville knew and relied on in his last days. There was a chaplain assigned to the hospital, but one chaplain assigned to so many made it difficult to provide him with the consideration every individual deserves in his or her last days. I decided to leave. I politely wished Orville my best and left. I knew it would be the last time I would see him so as I left I told him I'd remember him in my prayers. He just looked at me with that infamous thousand-mile stare and nodded.

Dennis stayed with Orville. As I walked to the jeep I walked through some of the wards. All I could see were beds and beds of injured GIs. I sensed that somewhere life was normal, but not here. As far as I was concerned my whole world was at war. The thought that most people in our society didn't care about Vietnam as long as it didn't affect them personally ripped away at my insides. As I approached the jeep Dennis called, "Hey Ralph, wait up." When he reached the jeep he shook his head and sarcastically commented, "Poor bastard only has a few weeks to live, at that. His nurse spoke to me as though I was his long lost buddy and next of kin. I couldn't wait to get the hell out of there." I thought Dennis' comments were a bit cruel.

I asked, "Well, what did you tell him?"

"I told him I'd be back to see him again."

"Did he say anything?"

"Yeah, he asked for a bottle of Jim Beam."

"I told him I would bring him a bottle the next time I came. That is if there is a next time."

"Do you think that's realistic?"

"Maybe not. At least it will give him something to look forward to."

Dennis' comments didn't help the situation. I had hoped he would have spent more time with Orville.

It was still early and the market section in DaNang was bustling. Slowly, we drove through the center. It was a daily occurrence in the market that fruits and vegetables and all items for sale be displayed making it difficult to maneuver with the jeep. At the end of the market district, we again approached the China Beach area when Dennis asked me to turn right down one of the side streets. No wonder Dennis was in a hurry to leave the hospital. He was to rendezvous with his China Beach damsel to resume where he had left off. I dropped him off and drove to a secluded end of the beach, pulled the jeep off the road and waited on the beach in the one-hundred degree heat. There was concertina and barbed wire strung along the shore with barricades to prevent anyone from coming ashore. I thought of how foolish I must have looked sitting in the blazing sun in full gear all alone and thought the MPs might pick me up. I thought of Orville and Dennis and how different our backgrounds were. Again, I thought of how he decided to stay in Vietnam away from his family and how he would die there and how, when Dennis asked him if he could get him anything, all he asked for was a bottle of Jim Beam. He didn't ask for family or friends or letters to be written to loved ones or to take care of his affairs. All he asked for was a lousy bottle of Jim Beam. I realized it wasn't only Orville who was messed up but he was the rule rather than the exception. He was a microcosm of Vietnam.

I realized in retrospect that he was the typical Vietnam veteran looking me in the face and telling me he didn't care, and all he wanted to do was to drink his pain away. He was the personification of a fair percentage of GIs who served in Vietnam and had to learn not to give a shit, forsaking their ideals in order to survive. They were a segment of our society who had no support back home, screwed up on drugs and booze, and complicated by a war that no one wanted or much less cared about.

Chapter 25

God Bless America

A week after we returned to Phu Bai we heard that Orville had taken a turn for the worse and finally succumbed. Dennis and I were now in charge of the Ed Center awaiting a replacement for him. Since I outranked Dennis, I bunked in the rear of the Ed Center and escaped guard duty. This was a definite plus. Each day I became more anxious and less tolerant and wanted to go home in the worst way but still had four months to go. We continued to travel to various locations in an attempt to encourage GED programs and we were able to start a few more courses. Basic supplies were always difficult to get and yet at times the almost impossible became a reality.

One morning, about 2 a.m., I was asleep in the Ed Center. It was in the middle of the monsoon season and it had been raining for some time. Everything was damp and the dirt roads turned to mud. The hooches became muddy and nothing was clean. Through the cracks in the hooch, I saw the headlights of a 2.5-ton truck. A faint voice from the front of the truck could be heard, "Hey Ralph! Hey Ralph! Are you in there?"

"Who is it?" I responded.

"Who the hell do you think it is. It's me Ed."

"Ed who?"

"You know Ed, the corpsman in the Quonset hut next door. Your neighbor."

"What is it?" I answered. "Is something wrong?"

"No, nothing's wrong. As a matter of fact everything is just fine."

"Well, what is it?"

"Would you like a baked stuffed lobster and baked potato?"

Not knowing if I heard him correctly I answered, "What the hell are you talking about? You've had too much to drink."

"I'm talking about a baked stuffed lobster and a baked potato. I even have drawn butter. Do you want one? As a matter of fact you can have two."

"Give me a break, will you! It's two in the morning and pouring like a bastard. You wake me in the middle of the night and ask me if I want a baked stuffed lobster with drawn butter and baked potato. Half the time we can't get basic supplies and now you have baked stuffed lobster. What have you been smoking?"

Getting more upset by the moment and wanting to sleep, I blew him off.

"You're just like Charlie. You're fucking with my mind. Just let me go back to bed."

"Ralph, I'm serious." As he came closer he reeked of booze. He continued, "We hijacked a truck that had picked up 25 baked stuffed lobsters from a ship in DaNang. They were bringing them to the officers club to celebrate the anniversary of the founding of the Marine Corps. It's tough shit for those jarheads. We confiscated them at the entrance to the compound just outside Highway 1. We gave the truck driver some bullshit story about us being from the Criminal Investigation Division (CID) and we had authority to confiscate any unauthorized deliveries. Since I had no manifest for any lobster deliveries, I did what any patriotic young blooded American would do. I had to follow orders. To add insult to injury, I was just covering the gate for one of the guards when these two jarheads (marines) came driving up to the gate bombed out of their minds. I took the truck. Hurry up so I can ditch the truck behind the mess hall. That should blow a few minds. Anyway, we can appreciate a lobster dinner a hell of a lot more than they can. I'm sure they'll be pissed but that's the way it goes. Myself and the other corpsman have three each in the Quonset hut. The others we gave away, with the exception of a few. If you want them, you should take them right away, else they'll go bad." The Italian in me rose to the occasion. Ed left me two lobster dinners and parked the truck behind the mess hall. I sat on my bunk, retrieved some wine we had hidden in the supply room behind the Ed Center, and in my solitude thought of home and how fortunate I was to have baked stuffed lobster. I had an uneasy feeling about eating alone. I wished I had someone to enjoy it with. However, I didn't feel uneasy enough to pass up a rare find, even though it was 2 a.m. Somehow it just didn't seem real.

Shortly after Ed dropped off the truck he returned with a bottle of Jim Beam. He reeked of booze. He poured two stiff drinks and insisted we have a drink together. He began to talk.

"You know, some GIs say Phu Bai is all right, but I think Phu Bai sucks. What do you think?"

"No matter how bad it seems to be, it can get much worse. Just think of that reserve unit that was activated with us. You remember when we were in DaNang and the powers to be were undecided whether they would go to Phu Bai or we would go south in their place. Well the other night they were all smoking pot and drinking as reservists are inclined to do. They were bombed out of their minds when they got hit. They were overrun. They suffered a lot of casualties. Just thank

God you made it this far. In a couple of months you will be home with your family and this will be nothing but a bad dream."

"That's the point, what family? Today I received a letter from my wife. She's leaving me. I have a little girl too. I've never seen my little girl. Is this screwed up or what? The least the bitch could have done was wait until I got home and I got my head screwed on right. I had no idea." He downed his first drink and poured a second stiff drink and lit up a joint. "What can I do?"

I knew it was going to be a long evening. I listened as he told me about how he and his wife were childhood sweethearts who went to high school in Berlin, New Hampshire and how they participated in ski jumping together. He rambled on and all I could do was listen. I knew he wasn't interested in what I had to say, but just wanted to vent. This was fine with me. After downing almost a full bottle of Jim Beam he wrapped himself in an American flag and started to sing the National Anthem. Eventually he crashed on an extra cot we had in the rear of the Ed Center. He laid on his back intoxicated beyond control and finally dozed off, half singing, half crying.

The rain had intensified and between the smell of the lobster and Jim Beam, I decided to air out the hooch. The rain was coming from the left side so I rolled up the canvas flaps on the right side of the hooch hoping to get some cross ventilation. It was now 3:00 a.m. and we still had three hours before reveille. I was grateful that it was a quiet evening. The rain was coming down so hard, even Charlie probably thought it was a bad evening for harassment but then he always screws with our minds when we least expect it. I decided to try and get a couple of hours sleep before morning formation.

About an hour after I had dozed off, I looked over at Ed and heard him choking. He was gasping for air. I ran over to his cot only to realize he had regurgitated his lobster and was choking on his vomit. He was turning blue. I turned him over, extended his head over his bunk and slapped him on the back. Fortunately, he started vomiting again. I was relieved. When he stopped vomiting he went back to sleep.

Tomorrow would come soon and we were leaving at dawn for Camp Eagle. I decided to try and get some rest and finally dozed off but not for long because shortly thereafter a drop of water dripped on my forehead and startled me. At first I didn't think much of it, but about ten minutes later I felt another drop. I looked up and saw water coming from a crease in the canvas. It continued, drip…drip…drip…. Half asleep, I talked myself into thinking it would stop. Looking up a third time, still half asleep I noticed the dripping increased. I looked up the fourth and final time only to notice the canvas was starting to rip. Suddenly as if the war lords looked down on me and cast a hex of unimaginable proportion for enjoying the two lobsters, the canvas tore in half and I was deluged. It had been raining for days and the accumulation of water in the tent flap soaked all my belongings. I looked over at Ed, he was an absolute mess still wrapped in his American flag covered with vomit and water. I looked closer to see how he was doing. As long as he was sleeping and okay I let him sleep. Everything was drenched. It took a little effort but the next morning I managed to confiscate a field stove from the mess hall. Clarence and I cleaned the hooch and washed my clothes including the flag. I put my clothing and boots in a large pan which I retrieved from the mess hall, covered the top and set the stove on low to dry out my clothes. To my surprise it worked. We kept the field stove behind the Ed Center. Periodically, Clarence and I would confiscate kerosene for fuel. She even started drying my fatigues over the field stove on a regular basis. There was a faint smell of kerosene in my clothing, but anything was better than the smell of buffalo shit from using dried dung as fuel. I chalked it up to another crazy evening in Vietnam. I was eternally grateful for not being out in the field in such miserable weather, and always in the back of my mind I thought of how, in a nanosecond, things could change.

With mixed emotions I was waiting for Orville's replacement. Dennis and I had the run of the Ed Center and did pretty much what we pleased. As long as we ran a few GED courses and occasionally showed up in some of the outlying firebases we were okay. With a new NCO in charge, things could change. The worst-case scenario was being transferred out of the Ed Center to a location where they needed a warm body. The thought was frightening.

Chapter 26

The Fresno Connection

I had about three months left in-country when I discovered the Fresno connection. One of the original members of the 513th was interested in going back to college and wrote a letter to the admissions director at Fresno State College in California, expressing an interest in returning to school. If he were accepted as a full time student, he would be eligible for early release which could amount to a maximum of three months early-out. In order for this to come to fruition, he needed a letter on school stationary signed by the admissions director, indicating that he was accepted at the school. The letter had to be submitted to the Education Center and after the appropriate "forms" were filled out, the request was submitted to headquarters. Since there was no one officially in charge of the Ed Center, I assumed the responsibility of making sure the forms were meticulously filled out and only one way—the Army way, right or wrong. I learned early in the Army, as with all government organizations, that the process was always more important than the product. Many men got screwed royally for mistakenly putting misinformation or incomplete information on the many forms we had to fill out. If information was left blank, a clerk who didn't have a clue and could care less about getting it right usually filled it in. As a result, you could conceivably wind up in Goose Bay, Labrador or worse, in the middle of the jungle performing some ludicrous high risk task deemed necessary to the war effort. Assured that all the forms were completed properly, I signed them and sent them forward with some reservation. Since everything was legal and in accordance with Army regulations, the worst thing that could happen would be that the request would be rejected requiring someone of higher rank to sign. When gambling against the possibility of getting out of Vietnam three months early, indeed a small price to pay. I signed the request and sent it along. To my amazement the request was approved. This opened Pandora's Box. Immediately thereafter I had four requests that were approved, then six more which were also approved. It appeared that the Dean of Admissions at Fresno State College was a dove and wrote acceptance letters with the slightest provocation. Either that or Fresno State College had a very low enrollment and needed students badly. Having been affiliated with a technical college in Boston, I am personally aware of the intense pressure that can be brought to bear on admissions directors when enrollment is low.

When I arrived home, I found out that none of these men ever went to Fresno State after all but switched to one of the local colleges in Boston when they got home. Others just didn't go and to the best of my knowledge nothing ever came of it.

One day, the new director of the Education Center, Sergeant Fred Foster, finally arrived. He hailed from Butte, Montana and was an E-7. He was young for an E-7, but he had previously spent time in Korea where he advanced rapidly. After his tour in Korea he re-upped having been in the military for nine years when he arrived in Phu Bai. His claim to fame was that he graduated from high school and was friendly with, then little known, Evel Knievel. We would laugh in amazement when he told us stories of how Evel Knievel would ride his motorcycle up the front stairs of the high school, and how he even tried to jump the Grand Canyon on his motorcycle. We always laughed with skepticism and privately joked about the phantom, Evel Knievel. Little did we know that there was a daredevil, Evel Knievel, and he did try to jump the Grand Canyon. In another daredevil attempt Evel Knievel broke every bone in his body trying to break a world record for jumping over a record number of cars while riding his motorcycle. Even that wasn't enough for the famous Evel Knievel.

He later bounced back stitched together with all kinds of plates, nuts and bolts in his body and attempted to jump the Snake River Canyon by propelling himself on his motorcycle tethered to a parachute. To the best of my knowledge this also failed.

Sergeant Foster had a little bit of Evel Knievel in him. He was upbeat and positive, a rare combination for anyone in Vietnam. One idiosyncrasy I thought somewhat unusual was the sadistic pleasure he received in taping the sound of in-coming as it struck the compound. During the day he would often play it and replay it in the Ed Center while Dennis and I would cringe at the sound. One day I finally asked him if he would stop this nonsense. He was very apologetic and complied with my wishes. With his arrival, Dennis and I were concerned about having to resume guard duty or being transferred. Guard duty was something we would have to contend with anyway, but being reassigned at this late date and not knowing where was unsettling. When Sergeant Foster went to headquarters, he produced some creative scheduling assigning Dennis and me in the field regularly so we couldn't possibly be available for guard duty. We were ecstatic. Anything to stay out of harm's way. From this moment he gained our confidence and our trust. Two years after I returned home I called him in Butte, Montana and asked him to recommend me for a teaching position. He gave me a glowing recommendation which undoubtedly helped. In a way Sergeant Foster was one of the few high-ranking NCOs I found to be sincere and truly concerned about our welfare. This partially restored my faith in the military, especially since I considered him a lifer.

I was getting more excited as each day went by and looked forward to Mary's letters informing me about the details of our upcoming November wedding. There were times when it was the last thing on my mind and I seriously doubted whether it would ever come to fruition. Nothing excited me except the thought of someday, with the grace of God, I was going home. This is what I lived for. Often, I thought Vietnam would never end and I would be stuck here all my life, or just when I would be leaving for home, something bizarre would happen and I couldn't go home. I always wondered why Mary was always upbeat, bubbly and enthusiastic, especially in her letters, and continues to be so. Why did she always consider the glass half full while I considered it half empty?

Chapter 27

Early Outs

Periodically, we continued to get hit and many of the "old timers" were getting careless. When the sirens would go off, they weren't as quick at getting to the bunker as they were when first in-country. As a matter of fact the sirens would go off and some would even ignore them and consider it an infringement on their beer drinking and stay in their hooch. Others were determined not to let it bother them. They even wore ear plugs so they could sleep through the roaring sounds of sirens. It was a "Que Sera, Sera!" attitude that if their names were on a projectile it was going to happen anyway. I had a different outlook. I wanted to have the satisfaction of knowing I did everything in my power to stay out of harm's way. I like to think I lived as though it depended on me, but I prayed as though it depended on God.

I began to notice changes in the Phu Bai area. First, the chaplain's tour was over. He had gone home. We were waiting for his replacement, but it had been three weeks since Father Anderson had left us and God only knew when his replacement would arrive. I missed Fr. Anderson and missed receiving general absolution, absolution without confession, and Holy Communion, especially before going into the field. One day, I realized that many of the members of the 513th would be leaving with early-outs. When several started to leave, it became even more depressing. Even a few more weeks in Vietnam seemed unbearable, especially with about thirty percent of the original 513th now on their way home and others on different assignments.

Shortly before my tour was over my replacement finally arrived. I was thrilled and so was he. I was excited because this brought me one step closer to going home and my replacement was ecstatic because his MOS was 11 Bravo, Infantry. He was out in the field when he was transferred from one of the firebases along the DMZ to the Ed Center. He still had six months to his DEROS date. I was determined, as he was, to make sure he fit in. Within a week or two he fully understood the routine and I started to coast. Even though my slot had been filled, I was now available for guard duty. One day, I had just returned from Landing Zone Sally when my replacement told me the first sergeant for the 26th Group wanted me to report to him as soon as I got back. I reported to his hooch. From the outside, it looked like any other hooch, but as I entered I was flabbergasted. It was hard to believe we were in a combat zone or even at war. He certainly didn't lack accommodations including air conditioning, and he had two generators going at all times—one for two AC's and the other for lights, refrigerator, television, etc. Looking around, and seeing all these niceties, I became upset. It brought to mind the old story of the disparity between the haves and the have-nots, an old story I had seen throughout the year between officers and high ranking NCOs and enlisted men. As often as I saw it, it was especially difficult experiencing this distinction which was flagrantly prevalent among fellow Americans of a higher rank. I calmed down by telling myself I should be above this by now and would be going home soon and this would be nothing but a bad dream that I should forget. When I approached his hooch, the first sergeant was sitting on his footlocker. He looked up at me, handed me two pieces of paper and said, "Good Luck." My orders were finally cut! I was dumbfounded. I looked at the orders and zeroed in on my DEROS date, August 17, 1968. I was leaving Phu Bai for the states on 17 August 1968. I now had twenty-five days and a wake-up left in-country.

Returning to my hooch, I found it empty. This gave me an opportunity to study my orders. I lay on my bunk examining every word, making sure I didn't miss any important detail. I decided to write Mary and tell her the good news.

Dear Mary,

My scheduled date to leave Vietnam is 17 August.
I should be in Ft. Lewis for out-processing on 18 August.
Out-processing takes about 15 hours and operates 24
hours a day. Therefore, I should be home between the 19th
and 24th of August.

All my love,
Ralph.

I sent the letter off immediately telling myself all I had to do for the next twenty–five days was to keep cool, and hope and pray I didn't find myself at the wrong place at the wrong time.

I continued to pull guard duty regularly. Two days before I left Vietnam, I was pulling guard duty alone for the last time and was guarding a location on the perimeter of the north side of the compound. The area was remote and in the distance I could see the lights from the 24th Corps, a couple of hundred feet to my left, across Route 1. I was positioned in a guard tower, approximately 30 feet high, looking out into a field strewn with devices to prevent Charlie from sneaking up. The field was well lit with the glare of the lights facing away from the guard tower. The lights were blinding, preventing Charlie from looking directly at the tower and this enabled me to see out in the field. The guard tower also had emergency battery-operated lights that were focused on the field. When all other lights in the area went out, the emergency lights would switch on and, in my opinion, be a most distinguishable target.

I was looking out into the surrounding area thinking of how peacefully quiet everything was and hoping it would stay that way. My thoughts were filled with going home and our November wedding. For the first time I believed I was going home and would get married and live a "normal" life. Suddenly, I looked up and from a distance I saw the trajectory of in-coming and heard that recognizable high-pitched sound as it continued on its way. No, not now I shouted. Suddenly the all alert was sounded. The generator station at 24th corps received two direct hits. All power was lost to the Phu Bai area. The emergency lights went on which meant the guard tower was now visible. In the tower we had a telephone that was powered by a hand-cranked generator. As the telephone began ringing, I looked up to see additional in-coming in the distance. Contrary to everything I had learned about abandoning my post, I was a sitting duck in the guard tower. I knew it was absurd to stay at my assigned location, but I also knew the officer in charge was trying to locate me. He was more concerned about protocol than common sense. I decided to leave the tower. The phone continued to ring. Below the tower was a bunker. I jumped down on the roof of the bunker and crawled inside. There I remained in deep solitude, afraid to lift my head up, while the shelling continued. I crawled into the corner of the bunker and forced myself to think of happier times. I thought of anything that would bring relief. I thought of my wife to be, Mary, and how she faithfully wrote to me every day. I thought of letters I had received from friends and relatives. I thought of high school and growing up in the North End and how much fun we had as kids. I thought of Christmas and the New Year, of birthday parties and holidays, and sitting around the kitchen table for hours laughing and talking, and most of all, I thought of how I always took life for granted. I prayed. During this time the phone kept ringing and ringing. It was absurd to climb the tower to answer the phone. I knew I was going to be called on the carpet about my whereabouts so I formulated a game plan. An hour passed. Once the all clear was sounded, I quickly climbed the tower and picked up the phone, "Post #2, Specialist Masciulli speaking, can I help you sir?" The voice at the other end responded, "Specialist

Masciulli, this is Captain Toomey. I've been trying to locate you. Where have you been? Did you desert your post?"

"No, sir, there was activity in the brush about 150 feet to my right. I went down to check it out. It appears some of the Vietnamese women who work in the compound were leaving and when they heard the all-alert they hid in the brush off the access road until the all clear was sounded. We have no electricity, but everything is secure at Post #2."

"You know you can get court-martialed for leaving your post?"

"Sir, I thought…." He snapped, "Specialist, you're not here to think. It's my job to do the thinking. You do exactly what I tell you to do or your ass will be in a sling. Get it." I then heard the phone slam. Here I was in the middle of nowhere with less than a week to go. Not only did I still have to contend with Charlie and getting my ass shot at, but I also had to contend with major assholes like Captain Toomey who were all over the place and often presented as many problems as Charlie.

Soon guard duty would be a thing of the past. More importantly, I wouldn't have to put up with any more Toomeys. This alone was better than pulling guard duty. Toomey was typical of company commanders I experienced. He had a high regard of himself and portrayed an air of arrogance. He wouldn't think twice about putting you in harm's way to save his own ass. Everything he said and did gave me the impression he thought his life was more important than mine. I definitely wouldn't trust him in combat and would do everything within my power to avoid his leading me not only in battle but anywhere. No thanks, but I'd take my chances alone. No doubt he would only make matters worse.

The next day the captain called me into company headquarters and, once again, read me the riot act about leaving the guard tower during in-coming. I listened without commenting. I figured that was the best thing I could do. I let him play God. He seemed to get a tremendous amount of pleasure knowing he had me in the palm of his hand and my life depended on him.

"By the way Mas-cuuu-lee-lee, didn't your name recently come across my desk?" he asked.

"Yes sir."

"For what?"

"Sir, my DEROS date is 17 August. I just received my final orders. I'll be going home next week."

He looked at me for a few seconds with that thousand-mile stare I learned to recognize and understand before he said, "You're dismissed."

I had five days and a wake-up left. Each day I became more excited. I decided to pack four days in advance. This way I would have time to think about items I may have forgotten. I laid everything on my bunk including all of Mary's letters, one for each day. I looked at my belongings and laughed. When I first arrived in-country I brought two over-stuffed duffle bags. Now my belongings occupied half a duffle bag at best. The important items in addition to my letters were the rosaries Clarence had made and the few pictures I had taken in Vietnam, thinking they would only remind me of something I wanted to forget. Although I only took a few pictures, I managed to get pictures taken by others in the unit when my boys wanted to see more pictures of Vietnam. I kept one pair of fatigues which I would wear to DaNang and packed a pair of class A's. I kept an Army field jacket, now a little torn and snug, but still able to occasionally wear.

I also brought along a pair of combat boots. My orders indicated I should dress in class A's for the flight home. Rumor had it they would not let you on the plane unless you were in class A's. Moving thirteen times in one year, I learned to manage with bare necessities. Since most of my supplies were GI issue and would have to be turned in when I checked out of Phu Bai, I traveled light.

I counted the days and I couldn't believe I now had one day and a wake-up. During the day I signed out at the different stations and turned in all my gear. I was in my hooch all checked out by 5:00 p.m. I had a 4:30 a.m. wake-up call for my ride to DaNang, so I thought I'd get some rest. I knew the next few days were going to be filled with excitement and emotion and although I was too keyed up to sleep I lay on my bunk. On the orange crate I used as a night stand was a note from Clarence that read, "GI me see you tomorrow at 4:30 a.m." Since Clarence was still working in the mess hall, it was no problem for her to be in the company area early the next morning.

It was now about 8:00 p.m. and you could hear the USO show down by the airfield. Most of the men were at the show. I was alone in the hooch, lying on my bunk, anticipating the next three days and wondering how I would react when I got home. Would everything be as I left it and could I simply pick up where I left off and block out the year? I knew the show was over because I could hear the men singing, *"I want to go home."* They always sang along to this song at the end of all USO shows. It was around nine o'clock when the men started trickling back from the airfield. As usual they were grumbling about the quality of the show. DaNang was where they brought the McNamaras and other high-ranking officials to impress them with the war effort. This is where all the quality USO shows performed. Phu Bai was farther north than DaNang, had less visibility, and a lot less brass than DaNang. The quality of entertainment was so poor it could only be considered pathetic. Most of the entertainers were aspiring Asian rock stars. At times it was so bad, I was embarrassed for they had no inclination they were making fools of themselves. Fools though they may be, I was eternally grateful for their effort to entertain us for it provided me with a sense that someone in this God forsaken place was trying to make life just a little brighter.

When the men returned they continued drinking and smoking pot. They felt no pain. Most of them were relative newcomers with only one who had been in- country more than six months. The infusion program must have been successful for now there wasn't one member from the original 513th in my hooch. Attention now turned to me when the new hooch commander, a big burly GI from South Dakota, yelled across the hooch, "Hey Mas-cuuu-lee-lee, tomorrow's your big day. You have one more wake-up in this hellhole. Good luck to you! Right now I'd give my right arm to be in your shoes." I didn't bother to answer for I knew going home was an extremely sensitive issue and not wanting to flaunt my fortune in the face of another's misfortune I low keyed his comment by responding, "You know, when I first arrived in-country there was one individual who came over with the 513th and had two weeks left in the reserves."

"Whadda ya mean, he had two weeks left in the military when he came over? Why would the Army do that?"

"You're not supposed to ask why. But this is what they did. As a matter of fact he was in my first hooch. It was heart wrenching to see him come here, spend a week in-processing and then the other week out-processing. Sometimes it seems like you will never get there but with the grace of God eventually you will." To avoid further conversation I walked out the rear, took my beach chair on the way, and climbed up on the bunker. Opening a can of warm beer, 3.2% alcohol, I sat out looking off in the distance and after taking a couple of swigs, I decided to leave it. It's amazing how much warm beer was consumed daily. Occasionally in the distance you could see the sky light up from activity in the field. Big Bertha, a 155mm Howitzer, positioned at the perimeter made her presence known. At night the sound would cause the hooch to vibrate but tonight I didn't mind because tomorrow I was going home. When things quieted down, I took a walk around the compound, strolling by the mess hall, down by the Ed Center, through the NCO hooches and past Sergeant Click's former hooch and along the perimeter. I stayed far away from the guard posts fearing the guards may challenge me. Most of the hooches were now filled with faces I didn't recognize. I thought of the many people the war had affected and of the original 513th, many of whom were now home, getting on with their lives. I thought of the many lives that have crossed my path: especially the arrogant Sergeant Click and his misfortune, the ignorant Gunnery Sergeant and his insensitivity, Orville for the price he and his family paid for his making the military a career, Dennis and his Gouda cheese, and Clarence for her simplicity and bad luck yet unwavering faith in God, and I thought of all the others who but for a brief moment made an impact on my life.

On my way back I noticed a light coming from the corner of Sergeant Foster's hooch. I had said good-by to him earlier in the day but felt the need to be with someone I liked and trusted during my last evening in Phu Bai. As I approached his hooch, Sergeant Foster was sitting on his bunk writing a letter. When he recognized me he whispered through the mosquito net, "Hey Ralph, wait on. I'll be right out." He walked out with two paper cups and a bottle of Chevas Regal scotch. He insisted we have one last drink together. We talked and drank for three hours.

Sharing my feelings with others was something I always felt uncomfortable with and had a tendency to mask. Tonight was different. It was my last night in Phu Bai and Sergeant Foster seemed to be in a talkative mood. He asked, "Now that you're going home tomorrow and Phu Bai will be in the past, you think it was all worth it?"

"Worth what?" I answered.

"Worth all the people, heartache, time, money, effort, etc."

I hesitated to answer knowing he was a lifer or as close to one as you could get. Lifers were usually all blood and guts. Until now we had worked together and avoided any discussion about the politics of the war. Discussing the pros and cons of the war was something I purposely avoided in order to maintain healthy relationships. This could acerbate a bad situation and serve no useful purpose.

I finally answered him, "I suppose history will have to make that determination."

"What determination?"

"Whether the war was justified or not. What do you think, Foster?"

"I have serious doubts."

"You're not supposed to have doubts. You've been in the military for ten years and it's your career. Top sergeants usually don't talk like that unless they're reservists. Besides, what do you have doubts about?"

"About everything we're doing. Obviously, I can only compare this entire situation as it relates to me. When my heart isn't in what I'm doing, it never turns out right. All I see around me are GIs going through the motions, counting the days until they go home and getting messed up in the meantime."

"That's a simplistic assessment. It goes far beyond that."

"In what way?"

"You may think it's easy for me to say everyone should do his time. I did two years in the military and you did ten years. It's not that easy.

201

We live in a great country. Yes, we have problems, but it's still the best of the worst. We both profited from its educational institutions. We have the opportunity to work hard and make something of ourselves. This is not so in many other countries. My parents worked hard, as I'm sure, your parents did, to provide us with good upbringings. My Dad and Uncle Joe both served in WW II. Uncle Joe was wounded in the South Pacific and received a Purple Heart. My future father-in-law was in WW I. He's a member of the *Forty and Eight* and never lets me forget it. He said the army used to transport them in cattle cars with forty men and eight cattle in each car. Furthermore, I don't think there's any future for any of us in war and wars usually further divide the people. On the flip side I've spent some time in several third world countries and realize we're dealing with a different mind set that doesn't value life as we do, and has nothing to lose.

As a result it forces us into confrontation. I don't see this as being the case in Vietnam. Men with huge egos orchestrate wars and sometimes they sacrifice lives rather than admit they're wrong. They don't know how to back off with dignity. No matter what the outcome of this mess, the brass will probably find a way to declare victory and say we won because we killed one million Vietnamese to every GI killed. Yet we had no alternative but to go. Not to go was against the very fiber of our being. You know as well as I, many did what they had to do to avoid what we are involved in. History will show whether they did the right thing or not. We can't judge them. History will also judge what we did here. Perhaps, personally, we didn't make a significant contribution to the war effort, but we answered the call in spite of our feelings about it and we did the best we could. What more could they ask?"

We spoke about our futures and how we were going to move on with our lives when we got home. We discussed family and friends, hopes and dreams and past disappointments. It was two in the morning when I arrived back to my hooch. With three and one half hours to go before reporting to headquarters, I decided to get dressed. Clarence had laundered a pair of fatigues which I donned. I stripped down my bunk, rolled up my mattress and laid on the springs using the mattress as a pillow. I was ready to leave Phu Bai.

Chapter 28

Leaving Phu Bai

I lay on my bunk and every fifteen minutes I looked at my watch: 2:00 a.m ... 2:15 ... 2:30. Finally it was 4:45 a.m. It was time to go. I took one last glance at my bunk and the orange crate I used as my desk and wondered who would take over when I left. I hoped he would be as lucky as me. Leaving the hooch I saw Clarence and one of the other mess hall workers walking toward me. She yelled, "Hey GI, good luck." I dropped my duffle bag as she approached, I was confronted with a bittersweet feeling that left me lost for words. We were friends and our relationship was always platonic. She was slightly older than me, but when I looked at her I saw an old lady, not even of my mother's age, but more of my grandmother's generation. The war had taken its toll on Clarence. I was sad, yet happy at the same time to be leaving. However, knowing the war was impossible and the situation, especially at my lowly level, couldn't render a positive contribution, I was happy to be leaving. I hugged Clarence and bid her farewell, picked up my duffle bag and walked down the road to headquarters. Several times I was tempted to turn around and wave, but each time I convinced myself not to look back, but to look ahead. The last thing I heard Clarence say as I entered company headquarters was, "GI, you number one."

The flight schedule was posted and I managed to catch an 8:30 a.m. flight to DaNang on a military transport, C130A. Several times I had flown from Phu Bai to DaNang. It wasn't the most comfortable flight and it usually carried a substantial amount of cargo and a fair amount of GIs. On a space-available basis, it also carried Vietnamese refugees relocating to DaNang. I felt safer taking a quick flight rather than a truck ride through the Hai Van Pass which takes several hours. As usual the aircraft was congested, but I managed to work my way to a spot in the center of the plane. Next to me were Mama-son, Papa-son and their three children. The children were wearing Ho Chi Min sandals, sandals with straps made from tire tubes cut in strips and secured to the sides of the soles. The soles were made from the inside of the tire, the curved part where the side wall meets the bottom of the tire, cut to fit the arches of their feet. Just think of it, they'll last at least 50,000 miles. Anything we discarded such as tires, tubes, crates, boxes, pallets, to name a few items, was always put to beneficial use.

Around 11:00 a.m. I arrived in DaNang and still had twenty-three hours to wait for my flight to Ft. Lewis. As far as I knew Ft. Lewis was one of the out-processing stations, if not the only one, for GIs coming from Vietnam. Therefore, it was open twenty-four hours a day, seven days a week. I checked in to make sure I was on the roster and was happy to find out I would be flying to Ft. Lewis on TWA and not on a military transport.

It was August and the heat was unbearable. It was at least in the 90s even at night. Although I did not sleep for 36 hours, I was not tired but was anxious to get going. I changed into my class A uniform and even though Clarence had laundered them, they were wrinkled from the humidity. There was a holding barracks for GIs in transit where I managed to hang out until morning.

I was at the airfield at 6:30 a.m. the next morning. Woe if I missed my port o' call, I would have to wait several days or more to catch another flight. As usual the airfield was humming with activity. Helicopters were coming and going in all directions. On one runway cargo planes were landing and taking off at regular intervals. Yet on another, fighter jets, one right after another. Supposedly, DaNang was the busiest airport in the world at the time. We lined up at the edge of the runway and waited for our flight, while our orders and boarding passes were checked. It was 8:00 a.m. when our flight finally arrived. It taxied to about three hundred feet from where we were lined up. I didn't expect the plane to have any passengers aboard, but when they lifted the little shades on the windows, probably down for security reasons, I saw a great deal of movement. When the stairway was wheeled up to the door and the plane began unloading, I was surprised to see GIs descending the stairway. Everything became quiet as they passed within six feet of us. It was akin to walking through the receiving line at a funeral and not knowing what to say. They stared at us and we stared back at them and although nothing was said, they sensed our anxiety in that far away look and we sensed their innocence. They seemed to share the pain we experienced as we shared the pain they anticipated. The GI next to me broke my concentration when he whispered in my ear, "Those poor, poor bastards." Before I turned to see who it was, I responded, "Yah, poor bastards." All the while I was thinking they all have three hundred and sixty days and a wake-up. They would all be sent to different locations and some would never return. Who's going to be lucky and who's not? Perhaps the 5th GI in line will be okay, but the 6th and the 15th will not make it! Is it luck or Providence?

I turned to see who spoke to me. It was none other than Butch! Yes, the guy I shared my tent with at Camp Drum for two consecutive summers. The guy I went to Aberdeen Proving Grounds with. Yes, the guy I wanted to choke at Aberdeen because he was such a slob. The guy who was my soul mate because we had the same Military Occupational Speciality (MOS). Actually, I was happy to see Butch. We checked our boarding passes and laughed when we saw we were sitting next to each other. When the word was given to board, three hundred men broke ranks and made a mad dash for the plane. Butch and I found our seats and settled in. Everyone was bubbling over with enthusiasm. The stewardesses were very patient while trying to calm us down. It was evident they had been through this before. When we quieted down, the plane taxied down the runway. The captain announced over the intercom, "Welcome aboard. I'm glad you all made it. This is TWA Flight 762. Our next stop will be Ft. Lewis, Washington. In a minute or so we will be airborne." When we heard the landing gear come up and lock into position, three hundred men started stamping their feet and at the same time let out a tumultuous roar. Never have I experienced so much excitement at any one time. The stewardesses liberally passed out alcohol. I poured myself a large glass of scotch with little ice. The captain continued, "Sit back, relax and try to rest. We have a long flight ahead of us." For the first time in forty-eight hours I could sleep. I sipped my scotch as I looked down on DaNang. In the distance I saw the distinguishable plumes of smoke from the burning excrement. I laughed and shook my head in amazement. A couple of hours and a few scotches later, I finally dozed off, occasionally awaking to refresh my drink which lulled me back to sleep.

Twenty-two hours later at two in the morning we approached the runway at Ft. Lewis, Washington. I looked out the window and it was pitch black. We landed on a remote runway, distantly located from the airport facilities. Deplaning the aircraft, I was taken by the change in temperature. When we left DaNang it was humid, close to one hundred degrees. It was now frigid, approximately low twenties. We stood shivering, standing at attention beside the plane, and when the "at ease" command was given we moved closer together to keep warm. We huddled together for at least half an hour before I saw the headlights of two five-ton army trucks approaching. The trucks pulled up and two NCOs jumped out and ordered us to strip down to our shorts, but to keep our boots on and to throw our clothing in the back of the trucks. Our clothing was brought to another location and burned to prevent the possibility of the spread of infectious diseases. I purposely kept my field jacket, knowing if I stayed in the middle of the huddle the NCOs wouldn't see it. After disrobing, we huddled even closer and waited and waited. We were cold, tired, miserable and hungry. We waited a half hour in the cold before two more five-ton trucks approached. Then, to my utter amazement, I looked at the top of each truck to see a hose, mounted on tripods, pointing in our direction. "What's this?" I asked myself. I had no idea what was happening. Then the spraying started. We were being de-liced! They hosed us down with a heavy mist of disinfectant resembling a smoke bomb. Now, totally pissed off, miserably cold as a result of leaving a tropical climate and waiting in the middle of nowhere in frigid temperatures stripped to our shorts, we were being de-liced. Butch turned and asked, "When does this shit end?" I responded, "It ends when we get the hell out of here." I took my field jacket, which I was fortunate enough to hold onto, and wrapped it around Butch and myself. We continued to wait for an additional forty-five minutes.

In the distance, I saw the headlights of several busses approaching to pick us up. Still in our undershorts, we were transported to the out-processing center where we were each given a new class A uniform and a ticket that entitled us to a free steak dinner at the out-processing mess hall. After taking a quick shower I donned my new class A uniform and decided to have a final steak dinner in the military. Across the center of the mess hall was a large faded torn banner, once white, but now yellow from smoke, with the inscription, "Welcome Home." It had been awhile since we had something substantial to eat. Butch and I lingered over our food rather than wolfing it down as we were accustomed to.

The first station was finance where we received final payment for our services. We were paid in cash as was customary at the time and finally purchased our plane tickets to Boston. Butch and I, once again, managed to book the same flight home. When I opened my pay envelope to hand the cashier the money for my ticket, I realized I had been overpaid by $500. If I decided to clear up the money issue immediately, I feared we might not get the same flight home. I decided to purchase the ticket and worry about the overpayment later. I still had two more stations to visit; namely, debriefing and to pick up my separation papers. I honestly wanted to return the money fearing twenty–five years down the road I would receive a call, or worse, a visit from Uncle Sam telling me I owed a phenomenal amount of money because of the interest compounded over a twenty-five year period.

I decided to report to the finance office. The clerk, who appeared to be running the show, instructed me to take a seat and wait. I waited an hour before I had a chance to mention my plight to him and informed him of my dilemma, but he wasn't at all concerned. Rather than taking my cue from the clerk, to be on the safe side, I asked to speak to the payroll officer. Another hour passed, and I started to doubt if I would make my flight home. Only after I heard the payroll clerk speak to the finance officer did I realize they wanted me to go away. I now knew it would cause more problems to give the money back than it would to keep it. When I finally spoke to the payroll officer he gave me two alternatives. The first was to report the discrepancy to central finance which was closed and would not open until Monday at 9:00 a.m. It was now Friday evening and I would have to stay at the out-processing barracks for three nights and report back to finance on Monday morning. The second alternative was to continue on my way with the very remote possibility they would find the error. I decided to take the second alternative and continue out-processing.

It took less time than anticipated to pick up my separation papers. Alas, I was on my way to my final debriefing. I walked into a small, smoked filled room, and sat at a wooden table across from one of the debriefing sergeants. He read a prepared statement that I barely paid attention to. It had something to do with revealing information that may be detrimental to the war effort. It was what he did next that blew me away. He looked me straight in the eye. Without blinking he asked, "Specialist, in order to maintain the integrity of

209

defeating communism in Vietnam, are there any recommendations or suggestions you would like to share with the military to improve the war effort?" I was absolutely dumbfounded! Was he serious or was he screwing with my brain? Was this the final green banana before I left? Was this my swan song? Maybe he was on drugs? The room reeked of cigarette smoke as evidenced by the huge round ashtray on the table filled with butts. I could also smell stale beer on his breath. I considered the possibility that for the last possible time they were playing with my mind. Nonetheless, where would I begin to answer such a question? I thought about his query. Immediately a rush of adrenaline went to my head. After a brief moment he repeated the question, this time with more determination. He looked mad as he repeated his question, **"Specialist, in order to maintain the integrity of defeating communism in Vietnam, are there any recommendations or suggestions you would like to share with the military to improve the war effort?"**

Where would I begin? The tone of his voice told me he wanted an answer and he wanted it immediately. It also told me the answer he wanted to hear. Indeed, there was a great deal I wanted to say. However, was this the appropriate venue with hundreds of GIs lined up, frothing at the bit to sign out and get home after a year of madness. Yes I was dumbfounded by the question, but I also knew the less I said the better off I would be in order to get home as soon as possible. The only sensible thing for me to do was to answer, "No Sergeant." I could see he was pleased with my answer because before I could finish my lengthy dissertation, he immediately stamped "okay" on the debriefing section of my separation papers and bellowed, "Next." That was my input to the war effort.

Chapter 29

Today's Military

When the Americans left Saigon and the famous picture showing hundreds of Vietnamese hanging onto the helicopter above the American Embassy was repeatedly televised, General Norman Swartzkoff in his book, *"It Doesn't Take a Hero,"* tells us he was so guilt-ridden about us leaving in defeat that he purchased a half-gallon of scotch and retreated to a motel room for the weekend. A few days later his sister went to get him and she brought him home. She found him intoxicated and  crying. This is one reason why he was so compulsive in maintaining control of the Gulf War and especially of controlling the press which had much to do and say about our strategies in Vietnam. He had a second chance and he was determined to do it right, thus redeeming himself. He was fortunate to have a second chance to make it good. Many did not.

As a result of Vietnam, we have acknowledged that to engage in a ground war on foreign turf, especially with such limitations, is futile. One does not necessarily have to be an authority in military science to understand a similar parallel. As a youth engaging in a game of "Hide and Seek" in the North End of Boston, North Enders had a distinct advantage. I can personally attest to running from the cops through alleyways and cutting through buildings, along rooftops and down fire escapes only to come out on a different street escaping from the cops. As we had the advantage on our turf, so did the Vietnamese have the advantage in a ground war on their turf.

The military of the 60s compared to the military of today is not only different in the enormous technological advancements we achieved during the last forty years but also very different in the cultural, social and the human relations aspect of military life. In essence the military has changed in many ways. Hopefully, we have learned from our past mistakes. In the Gulf War we presented an entirely different approach to fighting aggression than we did in Vietnam. At the time of our invasion of Kuwait I was upset at the thought of screwing it up but once we decided to invade, I received a great deal of satisfaction in seeing that we finally did it the right way. I remember watching the invasion on television and although it saddened me that we were at it again, I realized we had no alternative. The bottom line was we were in and out in no time. Perhaps the one lesson we learned is to rely heavily on technology rather than engaging in a ground war at the risk of sacrificing human lives. Whether the war in Iraq is a mistake or not remains to be seen.

In retrospect, I have had occasion to visit several military installations on the East Coast. I was always interested in observing the social and group dynamics among the personnel and would compare it to that of the military during the Vietnam era. I would sit in a coffee shop on base and observe the inter-personnel relationships among the various ranks. My perception is that the GI of today has much more self respect and respect for his fellow GIs than we had during the Vietnam era. There are three major factors contributing to this difference.

First, the peace movement of the 60s and the Vietnam War resulted in extremely trying times be it the rules of engagement in Vietnam, the corruption, or the simple nature of being in a no-win situation. These factors caused different behaviors and attitudes which resulted in less self respect among GIs. We lacked support. If we are foolish enough to put the military in the same position today as we did in Vietnam, I am inclined to think they would react the same way we did in Vietnam. Of course the argument could be made that once we start shipping enough GIs home in body bags and, if we let any war drag out as long as Vietnam, be it Korea, Vietnam, the Gulf, Kuwait, Saudi Arabia or Iraq, it will never be supported by the American public. Perhaps, as a nation we have become soft, and any interruption in our nice cushy way of life, no matter what the cause, will it not be supported unless we have instant success?

On the contrary we may be evolving to a level where we see the senselessness in war, and even if we strike hard and fast to win a temporary victory we prolong the inevitability of Armageddon because our enemies can attain biological weapons of mass destruction, thus leveling the playing field and retaliating! Therefore, we should negotiate at any cost?

Secondly, the lack of support we received at home was a major contributing factor in our differences of behavior. Although there will always be some criticism today, society views the military as a positive force which makes the military feel good about itself, resulting in its projecting a positive image back to society, thus the cycle is self perpetuating.

Finally, the Army of today is a volunteer army, supposedly, a significant portion of which is a highly skilled reserve component. The individuals who join today have greater skills and are better educated than ever before. They are committed to a cause. Its skill level coupled with high level technology make it the most efficient military since the beginning of time. During the war with Iraq we all marveled at what our military is capable of doing.

However this alone is not enough. The problem results in the advancement we have made in the weapons of technology as compared to the advancements we have made in the social sciences. Our social development on the whole has not progressed enough to cope with technology. That is the reason these weapons cannot be allowed to fall into the hands of the wrong people.

Since the beginning of time man has been readily willing to pick up his weapon, mount his steed and engage in killing his fellow man. The only difference between then and now is the weapons have changed. The concept of going to war is the same whether it be the battle of Hastings in 1066 or the war with Iraq in 2003. What has changed are the weapons.

The solution to an everlasting peace lies in identifying the behavioral traits inherent in the genetic code that causes violent behavior that makes men want to go to war. Once we identify these genes we can find out what gene makes us violent, etc. and alter the code to result in behavior beneficial to all. We do this now to prevent physical deformities. If technology continues to advance at the present rate and we continue to fall behind in social development, we are no better than children playing with A-bombs.

A month or so after I returned home from Vietnam, I had occasion to visit a local VA hospital. Many staff members and their patients had that long lost look on their faces so common in Vietnam. It was a form of warehousing the very people who put themselves on the line so we, supposedly, could have a better future. It was depressing. Thirty-five years later, I went back to the VA. The veterans are still there with their thousand-mile stares and although my perspective about many issues have changed over the past thirty-five years, I must acknowledge the VA has also changed and for the better. Attitudes toward veterans have changed and society is more willing to acknowledge that veterans had no choice but to do what they had to do. The people at the VA were actually helpful and are willing to please. They exhibit a level of consideration I have never been exposed to in any military or civilian medical facility, be it a primary care doctor, nurse, social worker or patient and I can only admire them. At first I was very suspicious, but I came to acknowledge the good that was being done. Often on Sunday mornings my wife and I attend the 10:00 a.m. Mass at the VA Chapel in Bedford, Massachusetts. We arrive early to assist in transporting wheelchair patients from their rooms to the chapel. Many have been wounded and many carry psychological scars. I have on occasion visited their rooms of which they are very proud. No doubt an offshoot of their military training. The pride everyone takes at the Bedford VA in caring for those that truly deserve it can only be considered admirable.

Chapter 30

Finally Home

Our flight was booked from Ft. Lewis to O'Hare Airport in Chicago and then on to Logan Airport in Boston—the final leg of my journey. With the exception of a few civilians, there were mostly military personnel on the plane. When we stopped at O'Hare to refuel, Butch and I were reintroduced to the real world. We sat in a small airport coffee shop watching the interaction among its patrons. It was fun just sitting and watching everything that was going on. Butch remained silent and so did I. Perhaps it was jet lag or just a sense of complacency, but we sat in the corner and remained quiet. I thought of how fortunate many of these people were, and how some of them had no clue about Vietnam. We were now officially civilians and if it were not for our uniforms we were part of the real world. Something still didn't connect, however, something was very different. I didn't feel part of the real world, but I assured myself it would soon pass when I got to Boston.

It was 8 p.m. and I knew it was after midnight in Boston. I considered not having Mary meet me at the airport. After all, I did give her a seventy-two hour window during which I would arrive home, so I couldn't expect her to stand by. Nevertheless, the thought of arriving home with no one to greet me was unsettling. I decided to call her. I let the phone ring and ring. I knew it would take awhile for her to answer in the middle of the night because the phone was in the kitchen and the bedrooms were on the second floor. I continued to let it ring. After twenty rings someone picked up, "Yellow. Yellow. Who's this?" I was always amazed at the way Mary's mother, Violet, answered the phone. She always answered with an emphatic enunciation of the word hello that always sounded like, "Yellow! Yellow! Who's this?"

"Violet, this is Ralph."

"Oh, Ralph! Where are you?"

"I'm at O'Hare Airport. Everything's fine Violet, may I please speak to Mary."

"Okay, just a second, I'll get her." It took awhile for Violet to get Mary. Her room was also on the second floor and she had to come down to answer the phone. Finally in a scratchy voice Mary answered, "Hello, Ralph? Where are you? Is everything okay?"

"Everything's fine. I'm at O'Hare Airport."

"Ralph, it's good to hear your voice."

There was much I wanted to say, but just couldn't. So many thoughts ran through my mind but they all seemed too heavy for what should be a bright moment. I simply repeated, "Yes, it's good to hear your voice. My flight to Boston will be leaving in an hour and is scheduled to arrive at 10 a.m. at Gate 9. There are about 15 GIs in line to use the phone. We agreed to keep the time down to two minutes so everyone could call home. See you soon. Love you."

"See you then. Love you too." Hearing her voice increased my level of expectation. It had been a year since I heard her voice.

The last leg of my journey was most difficult. Butch barely spoke while I kept staring out the window. I was trying to relax, but I couldn't. My mind kept racing around and around like a gerbil in a cage going nowhere. Never was I overly patriotic and never was I gung-ho about anything in life, but I always had a soft spot for the less fortunate. I thought of all the people I left behind. However, I was fortunate. I was going home. I should be jubilant. I should be dancing down the aisles. I should be yelling and screaming, "I made it! I made it! I made it!" I was happy but I was also sad. Why did I feel like I let someone down? I felt a certain emptiness, a feeling of abandonment, like I left at the worst possible time, just when everyone was jumping ship. Such a feeling I hadn't experienced since my high school days. It was akin to running away and leaving a close friend alone in a street fight in his time of need. Even when I was losing and managed to win, I never flaunted my achievements and tried to have compassion for the less fortunate.

As the plane descended through the fog, I looked out the window and recognized the crescent shape of Revere Beach. It was late August and the beach was packed with bathers frolicking in the surf and having a good time. I felt uneasy seeing so many people enjoying themselves. My mind momentarily flashed back to Vietnam and the disparity between the bathers at Revere Beach and the refugees of Colco Island. "We're at war," I thought. Why are all these people having so much fun? Don't they know there's a war going on and people are dying? What's the matter with these people?

Our plane touched down at Logan Airport and taxied to about 300 feet from the gate. Butch and I were sitting in the rear of the plane. We had no alternative but to anxiously wait for the others to clear out before us. We walked down the stairs to the tarmac and with our duffle bags slung over our shoulders, it was difficult dodging the passengers running to catch their planes. Everyone was in a hurry. I could see that no one cared. Why should they, Vietnam didn't affect them. Butch and I momentarily stopped on the tarmac. I didn't know exactly what to expect but I did expect something to happen. We put down our bags and looked at each other for a moment. Butch turned to me and apologetically said, "My parents said they would meet me at the airport deli which is down this way. I'll walk along the tarmac."

Still with an apologetic look on his face, he extended his right hand to shake my hand and said, "Good-by, Ralph." I looked at Butch and felt numb. I searched for something to say. I wanted to say something profoundly meaningful that would sum up the many moments we shared. There was so much I wanted to say to bring closure to our situation. I felt like crying but big boys don't cry. All I could do was to shake his hand and say, "Good-by, Butch." As I continued toward the gate I turned once to see Butch fade into the August haze with his duffle bag over his shoulder. That was more than thirty years ago. It was the last time I saw Butch.

I was in a hurry and ran toward the gate, anxiously looking for Mary. Feeling dazed from all the excitement and emotion, I feverishly looked up and down the crowded terminal, thinking I might have given her the wrong gate number. In the distance I saw a slender young woman. Interestingly enough, the first noticeable quality were her long slender legs. I attribute them to her mother, Violet, who always massaged them and pulled them when she was a young girl to ensure they stayed long and straight. Looking up I saw it was Mary. She heard me and ran toward me with tears in her eyes. "Welcome home. You finally made it home. Thank God." We embraced and sat in the airport for the longest time catching up on the past.

A couple of hours later we walked to the parking lot to pick up the car. Exiting the airport, we drove up the ramp leading to the Sumner Tunnel. We talked all the way and as we approached the tunnel, I turned to Mary and asked, "Please, drive through the North End."

Still feeling depressed, I thought driving through the North End would surely make me feel happy. We exited the tunnel, took a sharp right onto Hanover Street and continued past Tosi's music store where I took accordion lessons. Then past Barone's Drug store where I worked as a soda clerk for a while and then past Burden's Drug store where as a boy I made Tamarindo, a sweet concocted syrup made from the cola nut and professed to be a cure-all for little old Italian ladies. We turned left onto North Bennet Street and by St. Anthony's Church where I had been an altar boy for so many years. Then, by St. Anthony's School, where I attended elementary school and then by Christopher Columbus (CC) High School where I went to high school. I looked at the bath house where routinely every Wednesday and Saturday, I went for my shower with a clean change of underwear my mother neatly folded and left in a brown paper bag on the kitchen table for me to take to the bath house. We drove past the North Bennet Street Industrial School where I spent many hours playing ping-pong and basketball in Shaw House, and I thought of the seven summers I attended Boxford Camp as a camper and later as a handyman. We turned the corner onto Salem Street and luckily found a parking space across from Coogie's coffee shop. Mary pulled into the space and we sat watching the people coming and going from the small coffee shop where the problems of the world were solved and where I spent so much time hanging around while I was in high school. I wanted to leave the car and walk around and go into Coogie's but I still had my uniform on, which I admit, I was ashamed to wear. During the sixties wearing one's uniform in many locations would be like attending the St. Patrick's Day parade in Southie and flaunting one's Italian heritage. It simply wasn't a very wise thing to do.

Now it's very different. I believe that today, soldiers are proud to wear their uniforms, especially after the attack of 9/11/01, resulting in the destruction of the Twin Towers in New York City. Of course in uniform, one is looked upon with esteem. We have a volunteer army and those that join are committed to the cause. Vietnam was different, very different. There was no cause to be committed to. It reduced itself to saving one's hide and those of our fellow GIs. The war machine ran amuck and even those at the highest levels were caught in the quagmire, let alone the GIs. The GIs realized it was hopeless and everyone's survival became the major objective. Yes, at the time I was ashamed to wear my uniform.

There were several categories of GIs I encountered in Vietnam. First there were those whose perceptions were different from the beginning. Many were drafted and were never committed to the cause. They used the system to their advantage and enjoyed the chaos and lack of leadership. They could hide in the confusion occasionally challenging the system. Their goals were always to save their hides and those of their buddies. They depended on each other to get back home. These people were generally brighter than the rest and used their ability and knowledge of the military and the code of justice to achieve their goals. They were adaptable and flexible playing the game and pushing the system to the limit.

Then there were those who were extremely structured. They did everything by the book. They believed everything they were taught in training. When they tried to implement what they learned in training, it didn't work in the context of Vietnam. This group was so structured they couldn't cope with what they learned as being untrue. They now saw this as the ultimate contradiction and deception. This group suffered the most in Vietnam and they continued to suffer when they came home. When they figured out what was going on, some retreated to the freedom that came with being stationed at remote landing zones and firebases because it gave them liberties they couldn't enjoy now that they were no longer committed to the cause. I believe that in this group we find the drop outs, those who fit the typical stereotype of Vietnam veterans as being drug users and alcoholics who struggle to hold down a job and have trouble with relationships. They are suspicious of everyone and everything. They are angry. However, with help many still lead productive lives.

Finally, we have those who were crazy to begin with. It was either the military or jail. In fact the military may have saved some of them. They were gregarious and excellent fighters with no emotion or conscience about what they were doing. If we have to go to war, this is the group we want to fight our wars, but don't know what to do with them when they get home. They need that constant adrenaline rush that comes with a fire-fight to survive. Many are now in military prisons because of something trite that got out of control. Maybe we all have a little bit of this in us. When this group of GIs came home they were lost and many got in trouble and wound up in jail. These are the pseudo crazies who talk much about their Vietnam experience and are prone to embellish their experiences.

I couldn't believe that thirty-six hours earlier I was in Vietnam and now I was sitting in a car in front of Coogie's. It was culture shock. It was time warp. Looking out the window I recognized some of the regulars; the familiar faces of those who spent their lives hanging around on street corners. They were still there. The tourists were gathering in front of the Old North Church as they had done for years. I looked into Coogie's and Tony was sitting on his pear box behind the counter, half asleep, half snoring, smoking his Parodi cigar as he had done for years. He was still the same. I looked out the passenger side window and recognized a fellow North Ender who I went to school with. After St. Anthony's Grammar School Joe and I drifted apart. He recognized me in typical North End fashion as though my separation had caused me not to be on the street corner for a mere day or two. He tapped on the window and commented, "Hey Ralph, where've you been? Haven't seen you around. I still hang around in Carlo's pool room. Drop by sometime. We'll play shit eight." Nothing had changed, but something was very different. It was I who had changed. No longer did I belong. I was different. I now looked at my life as a precious gift from God to be cherished. Life was too important. As a young boy, I was told by nuns and priests how quickly my life could change in a heartbeat, how quickly I could be gone. Like most young adults, I believed it, yet maybe I didn't. I took life for granted, knowing I could never go back to that sweet innocence. I had seen too much and my outlook on life had changed. I was angry and wanted that innocent ignorance back. That playful silliness only the young of heart enjoy along with that idealism I heard so much about from the Franciscans and tried to emulate. That idealism that always made me look at the glass as being half full instead of half empty. That idealism we have when we're young and bright and just out of school. That idealism that makes you tackle a difficult challenge when everyone around you thinks you're crazy and you make it work. Physically, I was a young man, but mentally I was old. I was an old man in a young man's body. To think that we have to pick up weapons and kill each other to prove a point is mindless. Unfortunately, at certain times throughout our history, war may have been necessary and probably will be necessary in the future. If we don't blow ourselves into extinction, the future will portray our past as being no more advanced than that of the Barbarians or the Huns. Look at past time activities, they are no better than the Romans pitting one gladiator against the other. Just think about twenty-two men on a football field bashing heads together over a football or putting two men in the ring to see who is the better fighter. Most of us enjoy these activities, but they are fundamentally barbaric, especially when we eliminate the emotion. We are a society that expects hockey games to result in fights and the more violence we see the better the game. We want to see action because it makes the game more exciting.

I sat in the car and gazed out the window at the little coffee shop I spent so much time in when I was younger and thought of all the many American lives lost, eventually totaling 58,148. Supposedly up to one hundred thousand committed suicide after they came home while many others had psychological problems.

A good diversion from war is for everyone to experience war and see firsthand what it does to people, families, nations etc. If this were so, there would never be anymore wars because no one would go and you couldn't have a war if no one went. "Was it all worth it?" I asked myself, "Where do I go from here?" I wanted to retreat into a hole and stay there, far away from everyone and everything for the rest of my life.

In retrospect several questions still remain: Did the role of the Army Reserves and that of the 513th in Vietnam make a difference or not? The individuals and the units mobilized did an "outstanding" job to use that overstated Army phrase. The Army Reservists, however, were only a minor fraction of the total Army force involved. They did their jobs well. But whether they made any real difference in the war is debatable.[56] Perhaps no more debatable than the individual impact we all make in life. Most individuals work to support their families and make a better life for themselves and their loved ones. In essence to live the American dream. In reality, most of us, regardless of our profession or occupation, do not make a major impact on society. However, we do make an individual impact through families, friends, social organizations, etc., on the individual lives we touch on the way. So it was with the 513th. *We impacted one another and did what we were supposed to do. We never received any recognition for serving nor did we expect it. Most of us disagreed with the war since its inception; however, we answered the call, served our country well, came home, and continued on with our lives. This is all anyone could expect from the 513th and all that anyone can expect from any other individual asked to serve.*

I sat in the car, cradled my head in my hands and cried. I was sad. I should have been happy. I had come full circle, back to where it all began. I remembered that morning in Coogie's, discussing the Vietnam War, and how I was so confused. Now it was over for me, but it wasn't really over as it's never over for the Veterans of WW II, Korea, the Gulf War and other wars. I didn't feel like it was over. I still had that gut-wrenching, sickening feeling in my stomach. That same feeling I had when I first flew into DaNang. That same feeling when I saw them bombing Baghdad during the Gulf War and the same feeling I get when we invade Iraq or Saudi Arabia. I sat in the car and cried. Instinctively I knew it would never be over and each day, if only for a fleeting moment, Vietnam would always remain on my mind and hold a place in my heart for the less fortunate who didn't make it. The experience of war will always remain vivid in the minds of those who fought in them. Its impact is so great that we do not want to repeat it in our lifetime. However, every twenty years, a new generation comes along. They have yet to realize the impact of war and the evil quest for power and control among people and nations will always emerge, forcing us into other conflicts. Such is the history of mankind. Whenever I wonder whether Vietnam was worth it or not, I read this note I found taped to a name on the Vietnam War Memorial.

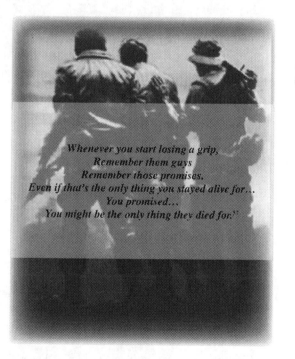

> Whenever you start losing a grip,
> Remember them guys
> Remember those promises,
> Even if that's the only thing you stayed alive for...
> You promised...
> You might be the only thing they died for."

Chronology of Events

The following *Chronology of Events and Notable Facts* have been taken from the Battalion Operational Reports, the Battalion Brochure and the Annual Historical Supplement of the Headquarters and Main Support Company 513th Maintenance Battalion.

5 Jan 66	LTC Eugene Martinez assumes command of the **315th** Maintenance Battalion.
31 Jan 66	The **315th** Maintenance Battalion Direct Support and Main Support Company was activated within the Army Reserves at the Boston Army Base and redesignated as the 513th Maintenance Battalion.
Apr 68	Ordered to active duty effective May 13, 1968 for a period of 24 months unless sooner relieved.
5 Jul 68	Assigned to Pacific Command upon embarkation with a ready date of 28 September 1968.
4 Oct 68	Advance party consisting of two officers and eight enlisted men arrive at Cam Rah Bay, RVN.
6 Oct 68	Advance party arrives Da Nang Support Command.
15 Oct 68	First half of main unit leaves US for Da Nang, RVN and on 16 October remainder of unit leaves US for Da Nang, RVN.
17 Oct 68	First half of unit arrives Da Nang, RVN and on 18 October remainder of unit arrives Da Nang, RVN.

19 Oct 68	Entire unit deploys to Phu Bai where it is assigned to perform its mission.
27 Oct 68	Convoy personnel leave Phu Bai for Da Nang to unload unit TO&E property.
29 Oct 68	Convoy proceeds from Da Nang to Phu Bai with equipment except for the M-88 and the "Dragog Wagon." They will follow by LST to Tan My Ramp. Convoy was without incident and all arrived safely at Phu Bai by 1700 hours.
1 Nov 68	Battalion Headquarters assumes command of the 67th Maint. Co., 178th Maint. Co., and the 578th Maint. Co. in addition to Hq. & Main Spt. Co.
3 Nov 68	Main Spt. Co. assumes its mission of providing Direct Support to non-divisional units in Phu Bai.
18 Nov 68	Main Spt. Co. is 100% operational and able to assume a mission consistent with its capability. Tech Supply operations are currently manual.
13 Dec 68	Battalion Headquarters assumes command of the 596th Maint. Co. The company has moved from Quang Tri to Gia Le.
26 Jan 69	Unit undergoes major inspection by the DaNang Support Command team. All areas were found to be satisfactory except electronics which was unsatisfactory.
31 Jan 69	A formation was held in recognition of Unit Organization Day. Hq. & Main Spt. Co., 513th Maint. Bn. was constituted as a part of the U.S. Army Reserves

on 31 Jan 1966.

Report Ending
Jan 1969

• All Battalion units are actively involved in security and defense measures associated with the perimeter sector in their Area of Operations. At Gia Le, Camp Eagle, and Camp Evans, our units are responsible for the manning and maintaining of an allotted number of bunkers. The Main Support Company provides approximately fifteen men to the 26th General Support Group which in turn is responsible for a perimeter sector at Phu Bai. In addition, the 26th General Support Group has initiated interior defense measures.

• All units are following the training outlined in the Battalion Master Training Schedule. A vigorous program is being installed. Weekly inspection of classes, lesson plans, and instructors is awakening units to the need and the value of a progressive training schedule and compliance with the mandatory subjects prescribed.

• Due to the great number of personnel arriving in-country in the last months, an orientation program for each unit is being emphasized. All in-country mandatory briefings and classes have a number one priority. Security and Vietnamese relations are being emphasized.

• In accordance with directions from 1st Logistical Command, extra classes are given on weapons safety focusing on the M16A1. At least one such class per month is mandatory.

- Crew-served weapons, M79, and shotgun classes and familiarization firing of the above are mandatory. All Battalion personnel will be familiar with each and every weapon used for interior and perimeter defense. This includes training with mines, flares, and booby traps.

- Morale in our units appears to be high.

16 Feb 69   Tech Supply reports that they are now completely converted to a mechanized stock control system.

13 Mar 69   ISG Jack L. Click medivaced.

31 Mar 69   Unit alerted that it will be visited by a group of U.S. Army Reserve General Officers during the week of 7 April 1969. The General Officers are inspecting activated reserve units and their progress is RVN.

8 Apr 69   Brigadier General Harkinson, Hq., 95th Division, visits unit.

9 Apr 69   Brigadier General Kauffman, Hq., 124th USARCOM, visits unit.

10 Apr 69   Brigadier General Booth, Hq., 81st USARCOM, visits unit.

21 Apr 69   LTC Douglas Knowlton, IG, Dng. Spt. Com. and his IG team conduct the unit's first AGI. Both the Main Support company and Battalion Headquarters received "Satisfactory" ratings. (Only ratings of "Satisfactory" or "Unsatisfactory" are given). However LTC Knowlton stated that in most areas the unit was superior.

29 Apr 69   LTC Charles E. Orr Jr. assumes command of the 513th

Maint. Bn. LTC Martinez is reassigned to 1st Log. Command.

Report Ending
Apr 1969

Crew served weapons and M79 classes—familiarization firing of same are mandatory. Battalion personnel will be familiar with each and every weapon used for interior and perimeter defense. This includes training with mines, flares, and booby traps. All mandatory subjects are being covered. In addition special courses in POW handling, storage, and firefighting have been given.

1 May 69   CPT Kenneth R. Grice assumes command of the Main Spt. Co., 513th Maint Bn. CPT Roughan is re-assigned to the Materiel Section, 26th GS Group.

21 May 69   596th Maint Co. re-assigned to a new area of operations farther south. The Battalion is now back to four companies.

30 June 69 Unit awarded "Best Maintenance Unit" in 26th G.S. group for the month of June, 1969.

21 Jul 69   Unit is again inspected by the DNG SUP COM CMMA team. This time all areas are passed. The Hq. & Main Spt. Co., 513th Maint Bn. (DS) is the first unit in 26th G.S. Group to successfully pass all portions of this inspection in calendar year 1969.

Report Ending
31 Jul 1969

• A vigorous training program is continuing within the Battalion. During the reporting period some of the more important classes given were a CBR refresher; survival, escape and evasion; SAEDA and Geneva convention.

• All units have been to the range at least once during the reporting period. Familiarization firing on all TO&E weapons was given to include M-16, M-79, M-60 and 45 caliber pistols.

• Weekly safety classes on weapons and driver safety procedures are conducted by all units.

• Physical safety training has been emphasized by all units with a practice alert being held in each unit at least once every two weeks.

• 9 May 1969 - A 122mm rocket hit the Tech Supply Building of the 513th Maintenance Battalion at Phu Bai. Heavy damage occurred to this building. No personnel causalities.

• 11 May 1969 - At Camp Evans a 122mm rocket landed in the 178th Maintenance Company area causing light damage to the orderly room and EM club. One individual was WIA.

• 10 June 1969 - Two rounds 122mm rockets landed in the shop area of the 513th Maintenance Battalion Phu Bai causing heavy damage to two 5-ton vehicles. No casualties.

• The infusion program, with the purpose of ensuring that any unit does not have more than 25% of the assigned DEROS in any one month has presented problems within the Battalion units, particularly the program 6 units, the 513th Headquarters and Main Support Company.

4 Sep 69   Unit received advance warning order that unit would depart RVN for CONUS on 3 Oct 69.

11 Sep 69   Major General Woolwine, commanding General, 1st logistical Command, visits unit.

23 Sep 69   Unit enters "Stand-down" phase in order to prepare for overseas movement.

26 Sep 69   A Departure Ceremony is held at the parade field in the 26th G.S. Group compound. The unit guide-on is presented a Vietnam Campaign Streamer by Brigadier General Gunn, Commanding General, DaNang Support Command. The unit was commended by General Gunn and Col. McCartney, Commanding Officer, 26th G.S. Group for the outstanding job it had done during its year in Vietnam.

2 Oct 69   Unit departs Phu Bai for DaNang.

3 Oct 69   Headquarters and Main Support Company, 513th Maintenance Battalion (DS), departs Danang, RVN, for CONUS.

Report Ending
Oct 1969   IV. OPERATIONS AND TRAINING

a. Training

Headquarters and Main Support Company, 513th

Maintenance Battalion (DS) conducted a vigorous training program in accordance with the Battalion Master Training Schedule (Annex C). In addition to the regularly scheduled weekly training, selected individuals attended the following courses which were conducted by Battalion, Group, or Support Command:

1. Field Sanitation
2. TAERS
3. NCR 500 Operation
4. Generator Operator and Maintenance
5. Fire Fighting
6. Convoy Operations
7. PLL
8. Preventive Medicine
9. Tire Inspection

In order to ensure that the hard-skill technicians are kept familiar with the latest equipment and repair techniques, 1st Signal Brigade and other major subordinate commands conduct in-country schools. Personnel from this unit have attended the following in-country maintenance courses:

1. ES-38 Photo Lab
2. Officer Machine Repair
3. Reefer and Air-conditioning Repair
4. Radar-Conograph Repair
5. AN/PPS-5 Radar
6. AN/GRC-163 Radio
7. AN/MPQ-4A Radar
8. AN/TRC-24 Carrier
9. AN/GRC-50 Radio
10. AN/GRC-106 Radio

11. Pulse Code Modulation (PCM) Radio

In addition this unit conducts cross-training and on-the-job training programs, using the guidelines set forth in the 1st Logistical Command Project Skills Charlie. These programs have provided the unit with vitally needed special skills when personnel shortages occur.

One final important part of the unit training has been safety training. It has been recognized that needless loss of manpower because of accidents could be greatly reduced if a vigorous safety training program was pursued. Therefore, weekly training sessions and seminars on accident prevention were held, emphasizing motor vehicle safety.

b. Weapons Training

Headquarters and Main Support Company, 513th Maintenance Battalion (DS) conducts range firing on a monthly basis. The purpose is to allow all replacement personnel to fire their assigned weapons as soon as possible after arrival. This also allows all personnel in the company to fire their assigned weapon (M16A1 Rifles), the M-79 Grenade Launcher, and the M-60 Machine Gun at least once every 3 months. Integrated with the Range Firing are classes on mines, flares, and booby-traps. Personnel who serve on the perimeter defense are given weekly classes on weapons training by the sector commander and his staff. Also included as part of weapons training are weekly classes on weapons safety, integrated into the weekly safety classes.

c. Combat Service Support Activities

Headquarters and Main Support Company, 513th Maintenance Battalion (DS) has provided, during the reporting period, for operating forces combat service support in the fields of Maintenance, Supply, Evacuation, and at times, Transportation. In addition to the wide range of maintenance support available in the unit shop areas, numerous contact teams have been sent out to assist operating forces, especially in the fields of Artillery, Tracked Vehicles, and Radar. Evacuation support is provided operating forces by the Service and Evacuation Platoon north from the Hai Van Pass to Hue, RVN. When requested and approved by higher headquarters, the transportation assets of this unit have been utilized in a support role for operating forces.

d. Combat Activities

The only combat activities members of this unit have participated in is in the active defense of one sector of Phu Bai Combat Base. The unit has provided from 13 to 28 permanent personnel as part of the perimeter defense force. These GIs are all volunteers and they live permanently on the perimeter. They engage in such activities as day and night patrols outside of the perimeter, the manning of listening posts at night outside the perimeter, and the manning of bunkers, observation posts, and flash towers inside of the perimeter. There have been no ground attacks on Phu Bai Combat Base since the unit has been stationed here.

V. PERSONNEL AND ADMINISTRATION ACTIVITIES

During the reporting period there was one AWOL in the Headquarters and Main Support Company, 513th Maintenance Battalion (DS). Thirty-four (34) Article 15s have been administered; 3 Summary Court Martials, and 5 Special Court Martials have occurred. There have been only 4 congressional or special interest inquiries. On the positive side ten (10) soldiers have re-enlisted, twenty (20) soldiers have been awarded or been recommended for the Bronze Star Award, and thirty (30) soldiers have been awarded or been recommended for the Army Commendation Medal.

SOURCES

513th Maintenance Battalion Brochure Support with Honor, 5 June 1966—April 1969.

513th Maintenance Battalion Operational Report, period ending 31 June 1969, prepared by C. D. Wilson 1 Lt., AGC.

513th Maintenance Battalion Operational Report, period ending April 1969, prepared by C. L. Short Cpt. AGC.

513th Maintenance Battalion Operational Report, period ending July 1969, prepared by C. D. Wilson 1 Lt., AGC.

513th Maintenance Battalion, Annual Historical Supplement of the Headquarters and Main Support Company, 17 Oct. 1968—30 Oct. 1969, prepared by Charles E. Orr Jr., Lt. Col., ordinance Corps. Commanding.

FAMILIES RUSH TO GREET THE RETURNING 513TH (Carl Pierce Photo)

513th Home From War

By STEPHEN KURKJIAN
Globe Staff

BEDFORD - Sixty seven men stood at attention in yesterday's early morning sun at Hanscom Air Force Base here and shivered.

But it was difficult to tell if it was the brisk wind or the excitement that was bothering them. The last time they'd been on the ground was in Da Nang, Vietnam, and they hadn't been home for a year.

An anxious crowd of 450 wives, parents, relatives and friends waited in a roped-off area while the members of the Boston-based 513th Army Maintenance Battalion started marching in their green fatigues to their loved-ones. They never made it.

With a cry of "there he is," the families broke through the rope and ran with open arms, and wet eyes, to their boys.

The unit had been activated in a nationwide call-up in May 1968 and had been stationed close to the Demilitarized Zone for 51 weeks.

Holding his eight-month-old son Daniel whom he was seeing for the first time, Sgt. George P. Hagan, 22, of Roslindale said: "All the guys are just glad to be back.

"We did our job well and we're glad it's over. My God, just look at this boy," he said holding his son. "I never knew how much I missed being away until right now."

513TH Page 25

See appendix for full text of articles

238

Our Heroes
Come Home

When Johnny comes marching home again, Hurrah, Hurrah.

See appendix for full text of articles

239

Marching to a happy reunion yesterday at Hanscom Field, Bedford were 67 Greater Boston Army Reservists, home after a year in Vietnam.

See appendix for full text of articles

240

BACK HOME—Lt Col Eugene Martinez of Winthrop arrives home with the 513th. (Carl Pierce Photo)

Boston Unit Kept Morale in Viet

★ 513th

Continued from Page 1

There were no traces of discontent over a delay for several months of the unit's shipment to Vietnam.

Commander of the unit, Lt Col Eugene Martinez of Washington terrace, Winthrop, said his men "functioned A-No. 1 in all areas. We fixed everything from shoes to radar. Once we left the state we had no problems and there were no battle casualties at all. They were real soldiers."

Most of the 231 members of the unit, which is stationed at the Boston Army Base, had arrived home during th the last 90 days in order to start college, teach school, for medical reasons or because their tour of duty had expired.

The 513th left Da Nang late Thursday aboard a four engine, C-141 jet transport which touched down at Hanscom at 7:35 a.m.

The crowd, many of whom had been waiting inside the hanger since before dawn, rushed to the roped-off area when the jet's engines came into hearing.

Capt Leo Cass, 29, of Town Hill st., Quincy, was greeted by his family and wife, Kaarina and their two children, Paul, 6 and Lisa, 2.

"We had no morale problems over there,"

manding officer of one of the battalion's four companies said, "We got over there and settled right down to work. You can be proud of these men. They performed like soldiers."

The soldiers and officers were given an immediate two-day leave. They will report to Fort Devens tomorrow and be processed for discharge from active service. Actual discharge ceremonies will take place Thursday at 2:30 p.m. at Fort Devens.

Sixteen members of the battalion filed suit in Federal court in Baltimore in October, 1968 to block their shipment to Vietnam. The suit charged that the unit had not been given adequate training in such areas as escape and survival.

Activated in May 1968 with 97 other reserve units throughout the nation, the 513th had been scheduled to be sent to Vietnam in August. However, because of the grumblings over inadequate training, the unit was given further instruction and training at Fort Meade, Md., and sent to Vietnam in October, after the judge refused to issue a restraining order to halt the shipment.

Capt Peter Beughan of Billerica said, "Most of the ones who made a fuss before leaving never made it over there anyway. Once we got to 'Nam there was no questioning. We did our

See appendix for full text of articles

REUNION—John Noble lifts his son Jeff high after returning from Vietnam. His wife looks on. (UPI)

FOR THOSE who sit and wait, the reward came yesterday at Hanscom Field, Bedford, when Mrs. Mary Ann Montague of Wayland hugged her husband, Robert, left, and Cathy Rush and William Wilder, right, both of Jamaica Plain, picked up where they left off a year ago.

See appendix for full text of articles

APPENDIX

Full Text of Articles

Army Denies
Training Charge

By WILLIAM A. DAVIS
Staff Reporter
Boston Globe 10/68

FT. MEADE, Md. Army officials on Sunday vehemently denied charges by 18 reservists that the 513th Maintenance Battalion, scheduled to leave for Vietnam Saturday, is inadequately trained and unfit for active duty.

The unit was stationed at the Boston Army Base until its activation in May. Most of its 215 members are from the Greater Boston area.

A petition was filed Thursday in Federal District Court in Baltimore for an injunction to prevent the 513th from being shipped overseas. The court will rule on it this week.

An Army spokesman said that the charges made in the petition have been investigated by the First Army Inspector General's office, the Fort Meade Training Section, and the 47th General Support Group, of which the battalion is part.

"The unit is properly trained and the charges are unfounded," the spokesman said.

The rebellious reservists claim that training performance records have been falsified and that the battalion has been given either inadequate or no training in areas such as use of the M-16 rifle, chemical warfare, physical fitness and survival.

One of the petitioners, Pfc. William J. Freedman of Beverly, has been quoted as saying: "We want to be properly trained so we won't be slaughtered when we go over there." Two of the petitioners have already been ordered to Vietnam as part of an advance party.

"I'm completely satisfied with this unit; I think we'll do an excellent job," said Lt. Col. Eugene Martinez of Winthrop, battalion commander.

Martinez, a combat veteran of World War II, described the petitioners as "some boys running scared and clutching at straws." The 18 don't reflect the unit, Martinez said, "and the other men are upset by what they've done."

The battalion handles all aspects of military maintenance "from the shoes on your feet to radar," he said, and is broken down into specialized platoons. Most of the men, according to Martinez, are working in the same areas they worked in as civilians.

"The unit has trained on the equipment it will use overseas and members have received advanced training in specialized areas at various Army schools since activation," he said. "The U.S. Army would never allow anyone to go anywhere untrained," Martinez added.

Martinez said the battalion is not a combat unit but has met Army requirements in basic military skills, including use of individual weapons. Many of the reservists had completed six months active duty before the call-up, he noted, and already had received their basic military training.

Charges that rifle range and physical proficiency test scores were falsified to meet training requirements were "malarkey," Martinez said.

"I'm a little disappointed in some of our young men," Martinez said.

The 18 members of the 513th are among hundreds of Army reservists mobilized in the last year who have brought court action to try to prevent shipment overseas, usually to Vietnam.

Some have based their actions on the "illegality" of the Vietnam War and the 1966 law under which they were called to active duty.

Supreme Court Justice William O. Douglas has found "substantial" questions about the law and has ordered the Army in several instances to delay sending reservists to Vietnam.

Army Admits Some Training
Of Hub Reservists Incomplete

By BERTRAM G. WATERS
Boston Globe, October 10, 1968

WASHINGTON The United States Army admitted Wednesday that a continuing investigation into the training received by the 513th Maintenance Battalion at Fort Meade, Maryland, had shown some of that training to be "incomplete."

A spokesman for Secretary of the Army Stanley Resor's office also said the Boston reserve unit would not be shipped to Vietnam this Saturday as scheduled, but that this was due to a shortage of aircraft and not to the investigation.

At least 92 of the unit's 250 men have signed affidavits supporting a law suit for them in Baltimore's Federal District Court and alleging that they have not received the training credited to them on Army records.

RESERVISTS PAGE 20

Judge to Hear Government
On Reservists' Case Friday

*RESERVISTS
Continued from Page 1

Meanwhile, a government attempt to dismiss the suit was not heard in Baltimore as expected Wednesday because no judge was available, according to Peter Sherman, the Washington attorney retained by the 513th.

Sherman termed the Army report a "significant" step in support of the injunction he hopes to secure.

U.S. District Court Judge Roszel Thomsen said he would be available Friday to hear the government's argument for dismissal, which is based on the contention that courts are not equipped to decide what constitutes "adequate" training.

The interim report issued by Resor's office at first claimed that only a few men were missing a limited amount of training, and that completion of training would not hold up the scheduled deployment. This settlement was later rescinded by a spokesman who stated that the large number of affidavits available resulted in a study requested by the Senator Edward M. Kennedy.

In those affidavits the enlisted men swear that they have not received training in everything from first aid to repairing tanks, and that the records showing that their training is complete are false.

Among the complainants is an acting Sergeant John P. McAbee, who swears he took part in falsifying records of class attendance, physical training, chemical warfare, and rifle training, all on orders from officers. McAbee was shipped to Vietnam last week before Sherman could get a court order preventing his deployment.

Interviewed Tuesday, several members of the 513th said their battalion commander, Lt. Col. Eugene Martinez of Revere, Mass, told them he knew they had not had all their training, "but they would get it in Vietnam."

Others said another officer had admitted it would be "nine months" in Vietnam before they could possibly perform their support mission which involves everything from typewriter repair to sewing up torn tents.

The delay in court action Wednesday had left little time for a hearing on the merits of the affidavits, which must follow the original motion for dismissal, until the Army said deployment of the 513th had been delayed. Pressed for a new departure date, the spokesman said such information is "classified".

Also not available was the number of men believed inadequately trained, or the amount of class or field time needed to train them. It was unclear whether the interim finding was based on training records believed to be accurate, or falsified, as the men allege.

Hub Reservists Lose Bid to Stay Viet Duty

Boston Globe, October 14, 1968

BALTIMORE, MD. U.S. District Court Chief Judge Rozell C. Thomsen today dismissed the complaint of 92 Greater Boston Army reservists that they should remain in training at Fort Meade until they are qualified to perform their support mission in Vietnam.

The reservists, through Atty. Peter R. Sherman, had brought suit in that court on Oct. 2, stating they were not properly trained for Vietnam duty and asserting that records which said so were false.

RESERVISTS Page 26

Sen. Ted Challenges Army Sec.

*RESERVISTS
(Continued from Page 1)

Atty. Sherman said he would be here tomorrow and go before the U.S. Court of Appeals seeking an immediate injunction against shipment of the men to Vietnam.

Meanwhile Secretary of the Army Stanley Resor issued an opinion to the effect that an investigation showed the reservists training was incomplete.

In a response to U.S. Senator Edward M. Kennedy who had written him about the reservists' allegation, Secretary Resor said that additional training sessions have been conducted and will be completed before the men are sent overseas.

"But," said Resor, "I see no reason why plans concerning deployment of the unit should be affected by the investigation of allegations that training records were falsified."

Sen. Kennedy, in reply to Resor, said, "I can only conclude that a substantial segment of this military unit would have been deployed to a combat area on schedule without having this required training had the matter not been raised."

"It does not suffice to say," Kennedy added; "that these men will receive all necessary training before they leave."

"The large question now is: could the same situation occur in another unit; is our military effort being affected by the military deficiency; in essence, are our servicemen endangered in combat situations as a result of insufficient training?"

"It appears that we were confronted in this case with a situation in which our young men were being sent into combat without receiving the minimum training required."

"I am disturbed by this casual, approach to a situation which is potentially very serious"

247

Reservist Issue Raises Question of Standards

By BERTRAM G. WATERS
Globe Washington Bureau
Boston Globe 10/68

FT. MEADE, Md. As Bill Delaney recalls it, the war games last summer were a disaster.

"We climbed on the trucks at the motor pool, and on the way out we were attacked by an "aggressor" force, suffering 100 percent "casualties" with 85 percent of our vehicles "destroyed."

After we set up our perimeter defense, Col. Brian made a speech: He told us we were the sloppiest unit he had ever seen, and made us go out and do it again."

Last week Delaney's unit Co A, 513th Maintenance Battalion, Army Reserve was sent to Vietnam as an infantry support group.

Bill Delaney, who has doubts about the unit's ability to survive under combat conditions, should be along for the ride, but got a reprieve when his brother was sent first. A pleasant, soft-spoken 25-year-old with two years of Boston College behind him, he remained at Fort Meade in another outfit when his company took off.

In the unit were at least 92 men who had signed affidavits saying their training was seriously deficient in some way, and that they were incapable of performing their mission, whatever that was presumed to be? They claimed they had never been given a mission since being activated at Boston Army Base last May.

During several weeks of court proceedings, they managed to interest Sen. Edward M. Kennedy in their plight, causing a "full" investigation by the Army into the alleged training deficiencies. A report issued last Monday said the Army was satisfied that all training was complete under the regulations.

"I had a discussion with a field-grade officer," said Delaney, who became a sort of unofficial spokesman for the group, and he told me it might be a question of standards. `Maybe the Army's standards are so low,' he said, "that you men don't feel you really are qualified, while the army does.'"

In a reply to the Army's investigation report, Sen. Kennedy wrote: "I can only conclude that a substantial segment of this military unit would have been deployed to a combat area on schedule, without having received this required training, had the matter not been raised (by the men.)"

"It does not suffice to say that these men will receive all necessary training before they leave, in this instance. The larger question now is: could the same situation occur in another unit, is our military effort being affected by this training deficiency? In essence, are our servicemen endangered in combat situations as a result of insufficient training?"

Sen. Kennedy was so disturbed at what he called the Army's "casual approach to a potentially serious situation" that he informed the Department of Defense he would seek a Congressional investigation of resent training standards in the new Congress.

The courts including the U.S. Supreme Court did not feel they had jurisdiction in the case and refused to hear it, despite the efforts of a Washington attorney hired by the soldiers. It now becomes the responsibility of Congress to hear the tale of a unit that has had 10 different first sergeants since being activated, a turnover of nearly one-third of its enlisted men one attempted suicide, one near-breakdown, and passed no inspections.

In a rush move that coincided with Sen. Kennedy "investigation," officials at Fort Meade interviewed each man in the 513th as to his state of training, and then provided any training that was said to be lacking. This included two straight days of rifle firing. Part of it on the weekend, for those who said they could not use an M16, but with no loss of leave time as was originally threatened. What Delaney and others claim cannot be made up in this fashion in training in the military occupational specialty (M.O.S.), which prepares a man to fix typewriters and tanks, or learn to fill out orders. Most of the jobs supposedly held by the men of the 513th are basic and unsophisticated, but the group was frank to say that it feared for the safety of the troops it is assigned to support.

Out of the hassle, only one fact emerged with any clarity: The Army, and the reserves in particular, suffered, a black eye. It is still a hazardous business, at best, to be a "week-end warrior" for Uncle Sam in wartime.

Combat Ready?

Army Reservists who claim they are inadequately trained for Vietnam duty have brought suit in Federal District Court in Baltimore to prevent being shipped overseas until their training is completed.

At least 92 members of the 513th Maintenance Battalion at Ft. Meade, Maryland, have signed affidavits alleging falsification of records showing their training has been finished.

A Federal judge in Baltimore is expected to hear today a government motion to dismiss the suit.

Army Secretary Stanley Resor's office admitted Wednesday that an investigation prompted by Sen. Edward M. Kennedy (D-Mass.) has revealed that some of the training was "incomplete."

The Fort Meade incident is not the first in which Army Reservists have maintained that they were being moved to a combat area without sufficient training.

Two months ago an Army Reservist recalled to duty at Fort Lewis, Wash., complained to his California congressman that he was being sent to Vietnam as the driver of an armored personnel carrier although "I had never been inside one of those vehicles much less driven one."

The Reservist, PFC Carl R. Greene, a 1966 graduate of Yale, wrote that his lack of training reflected "disregard for life and property." He added that many of his friends at Fort Lewis also had been given credit for training they had not received in weapons and riot tactics.

As a consequence of his letter and others, Greene's unit, the 1st Squadron, 18th Armored Cavalry, was taken off orders for Vietnam and detained for further training.

The Army claimed the faulty records were a matter of misjudgment rather than fraud.

Whatever the reason for the inaccuracies, the fact they could occur suggests there may be others.

The government should consider whether these incidents warrant a thorough review of our military Reserve training practices.

Herald Traveler Washington Bureau

10/68

WASHINGTON Sen. Edward M. Kennedy said yesterday he would seek a Congressional investigation to check if reserve units are endangered in Vietnam combat situations by lack of training.

Kennedy, in a four-page letter to Defense Secretary Clark M. Clifford, urged the Pentagon to initiate a full investigation of "readiness, training and job classification of individuals and units presently on active duty and units that may be activated in the future."

Kennedy's decision to seek a full-scale probe of the training of Reserves grew out of his concern over charges by 92 Greater Boston men that they had not received all their mandatory training. The men are scheduled to be shipped out today and tomorrow.

Army Secretary Stanley R. Resor, who re-opened the Investigation into the readiness

Ted Asks Training Probe

of the 513th Maintenance Battalion at Kennedy's request, notified the Massachusetts senator yesterday that the unit had been found "adequately trained and fully qualified for Vietnam duty."

But Kennedy, in his letter to Clifford, said he felt Resor's investigation had left several substantial questions remaining and added that he was disturbed by the Army's "casual approach" to charges that official training records were inadequate or had been falsified.

"I have been to Vietnam," Kennedy said. I have seen the American fighting men in that country, and I know the intelligence, dedication, and valor that they bring to their duties. I believe it is vital to our servicemen, as well as to the security of our nation, that the caliber of the training should match the caliber of men.

KENNEDY said that he was very concerned with the fact that the substantial part of the 513th "had not received training in required subjects, including M-16 training." Before the investigation, he was even more concerned with the larger situation.

"My overriding concern is that inadequate training may have taken place in other instances in the past, and take place in the future, unless this problem is now resolved," Kennedy said.

He said he could only conclude in the case of the 513th that "a substantial segment of this military unit would have been deployed to a combat area on schedule without having received its required training, had the matter not been raised."

"IT DOES NOT suffice to say that these men received all necessary training before they leave in this instance," he said. "The larger question now is: Could the same situation occur in another unit; is our military effort being affected by this training deficiency. In essence, are our servicemen in any way endangered in combat situations as a result of insufficient training?"

Kennedy said that when congress reconvenes in January, he will "request that an appropriate committee of the Senate conduct an immediate and thorough study of the administrative, investigative and procedural methods by which our armed services assure compliance with the Army and the Department of Defense regulation regarding the activation and training of reserve units."

Devens Unit Wins Delay in Viet Duty

Asst. U.S. Atty. John Wall informed a three-judge Federal court today than an order sending the 107th Signal Corps at Fort Devens to Vietnam has been rescinded.

He made this statement to the court after Atty. Moses Falk had urged the court to issue a temporary restraining order, barring the government from shipping the members of the Signal Corps unit on Monday.

"The attorney for the members of the unit is under a misapprehension" said Wall, as he informed the tribunal of the cancellation of the Vietnam order.

Wall said further that no order will be issued sending the 107th Signal Corps or any other reserve outfit abroad until after the U.S. Supreme Court has ruled in the Morse Case.

Judge Bailey Aldrich of the U.S. Court of Appeals presided, flanked by Judge Andrew A. Caffrey of the Federal Court in Boston and Judge Hugh Bownes of the Federal Court in New Hampshire.

Atty. Falk had asked the court to issue a temporary restraining order to halt the dispatching of the Signal Corps to Vietnam.

He argued that the government had no right to ship the Signal Corps overseas because there has been no declaration of war by President Johnson or by the Congress.

Named as respondents in the current petition are President Johnson, members of Congress and officials at the Pentagon.

Atty. Falk pointed out to the court that Justice William O. Douglas of the Supreme Court had issued stays in several cases of a similar nature.

But Wall told the tribunal that Chief Justice Warren and four or five other justices of the court had denied stays.

Falk argued that the government had no right to activate the 107th Signal Corps because no governor of any state had given his consent.

The 107th was activated last May Most of the members were attached to the National Guard in Rhode Island and other members were reservists from various sections of the country.

Falk said to the court that until President Johnson or the Congress declare a state of war or a national Emergency, the government has no right to commit any reserve outfit to duty in Vietnam.

"These men are being shipped to Vietnam to be shot at and to shoot " said Falk, "these men are being deprived of their life, their liberty and their freedom."

Falk asserted that men are being forced into combat in the name of peace. "The only recourse we have is with the judiciary" Falk said.

251

Viet Shipment Disputed
Ruling on Mass. Reservists Today

Boston Globe October 1968

WASHINGTON Government attorneys today will move to dismiss a suit in Federal court in Baltimore which seeks to delay the departure for Vietnam of an Army Reserve unit on the grounds that its men have not had adequate training.

The unit is the 513th Maintenance Battalion, stationed at Ft. Meade Maryland. Its 250 members include 150 men from greater Boston.

Senator Edward M. Kennedy, after being advised of the men's complaints, directed a letter Monday to Army Secretary Stanly Resor asking that the departure of the men, scheduled for Saturday, be delayed "until an appropriate inquiry is satisfactorily completed.

A spokesman for the Army said Tuesday that Resor had received Kennedy's letter and had referred it to the military authorities to investigate.

However, the same official said that Resor had not made any decision as to delaying the shipment of the troops to Vietnam. "Obviously a decision will have to be made quickly," the spokesman said. Kennedy has not received a reply from Resor.

Pentagon Says G.I.s Won't Leave Saturday.

A congressional liaison officer at the Pentagon told a Kennedy aide that the men are not scheduled to be shipped out Saturday and that no schedule for their departure has been set.

But Kennedy staffers were skeptical. They had been advised Oct. 2 that two members of an advance unit of the battalion who were involved in the complaints would not be moved overseas until an investigation was completed.

The following day the two men were moved to the west coast and shipped to Vietnam.

More than 100 members of the battalion have signed affidavits claiming they did not receive adequate training for combat.

Kennedy wrote the letter after a lawyer for the complainants consulted with a Kennedy staff member and explained that the men were not charging they were illegally called to active duty.

On Monday the Supreme Court refused to delay the departure for Vietnam of 867 other Army Reservists at Ft. Meade and Ft. Lee, Va., who contended their call up was illegal and that they had not been credited with time already spent on active duty

Members of the 513th have not contended that activation of their unit was illegal.

In his letter to Resor, Kennedy said, "I do not question, nor do these men question, their obligation as Reservists on active duty.

They only question their preparedness to fulfill their Reserve obligation."

Cong. Bradford Morse of Lowell, Mass, last Friday called on Defense Secretary Clark Clifford to investigate the charges of the Reservists. Morse's office said, he had not received a reply from Clifford yet.

Among the complaints listed by the men was that their military specialties had been changed several times in some cases since their call up, and that records had been falsified to indicate the men had

attended classes when they were in reality not present.

A decision in the case is expected to be handed down in the Baltimore court today. The court earlier had rejected a request for a temporary restraining order to prevent the shipment of the battalion's advance party overseas.

Today's arguments will be based on a similar request for a restraining order barring shipment of the remainder of the battalion.

BOSTON HERALD TRAVELER

THE WEATHER SUNNY, WARM
HA 6-3000

TUESDAY, OCTOBER 15 1968 52 PAGES
TEN CENTS

Army Ships 513th to Viet Today

Reservists Viet-Bound
After High Court Acts United Press International

WASHINGTON The Army is going ahead with plans to ship to Vietnam 236 reservists who lost a Supreme Court appeal to stay their transfer while its legality is being decided in the courts.

Justice William O. Douglas protested the court decision, which involves the language of the reservist's military contracts with the Government, as one touching on a "credibility gap" problem between citizen and their Government.

Meanwhile, Sen. Edward M. Kennedy has demanded a full investigation of the charge by 16 Boston area Army Reservists that they are inadequately trained and thus not prepared for assignment to Vietnam combat duty.

An aide in Sen. Kennedy's office at Washington said the Massachu-

setts's Senator has intervened on behalf of the men and written the Army to hold up their orders for Vietnam duty until a "full investigation is conducted."

Also backing up the claim of the 16 soldiers, members of the 513th Maintenance Battalion were 67 fellows. GIs, also from Greater Boston, who on Monday signed a statement that they, too, had not had adequate training, and also should not be sent to the war zone.

Justice Douglas had granted stays of the transfer orders pending Supreme Court action on the soldiers' appeals. But on the opening day of the fall term Monday, the court majority rescinded the stays. It will decide later whether to hear the cases.

The reservists involved in the action included 113 Cleveland, Ohio,

253

men of the 1002d Supplies and Service Co., stationed at Ft. George G. Meade, Md.; 13. New Yorkers in the 448th Army Postal Unit; 80 men of the 1018th Service and Supply co. of Schenectady, N.Y.; 43 men from New York and New Jersey assigned to the 74th Field Hospital Unit, and seven Mississippians, including ex-football star Joe Don Looney of the 173d Petroleum Co. All but the Cleveland group is stationed at Ft. Lee, Va.

The reservists are challenging the 1966 law which authorized the President to call up any reserve unit for two years without declaring a national emergency or eliciting a declaration of war from Congress.

Lawyers for the reservists argued in lower courts that the Army was going back on enlistment contracts with the petitioners. They said some contracts specified active duty service would be required only "in the event of a mobilization of emergency" and others "in time of war or of national emergency declared by Congress."

There has been no declaration of war or of national emergency in the Vietnam conflict.

Some of the petitioners already have served some active duty time which apparently will not count toward fulfilling the two years for which they have been activated, the lawyers said.

RESERVES Page 49

Hub Reservists Lose Viet Bid
October 1968

BALTIMORE   Two Army reservists from Boston lost a bid for a last minute reprieve in Federal court Thursday and began a long trek from Fort Meade, Md., to Vietnam.

Sgt. John MacAbee and Pvt. Robert Delaney of 53 Custer St., Jamaica Plain, were among 16 Massachusetts reservists suing to prevent their shipment to Vietnam.

The reservists, members of Headquarters Company, 513th Maintenance Battalion, U.S. Army Reserve, claim their combat training was inadequate and in conflict with Army regulations.

Their suit, filed by Atty. Peter Sherman of Washington, charges the Army falsified their training records.

Judge Roszel C. Thomsen refused to issue a temporary order delaying the departure of the two men in the unit's advance party. He set Oct. 10 as the date of a hearing on the government's motion to dismiss the case. The other 14, and more who wish to join their suit, are due to leave for Vietnam two days later.

Arguments on the request of Atty. Peter Sherman for postponement of departure of other members of the unit will be heard Wednesday or Thursday in the Federal Court.

The outfit includes about 150 Boston reservists, and is commanded by Lt. Col. Eugene Martiniz of 1 Washington Terr., Winthrop.

In private life Col. Martiniz is employed as a maintenance supervisor

254

for the Coast Guard at its Constitution Wharf base in Boston. He was wounded in World War II. The executive officer of the 513th is Maj. William R. Weiss Jr., of Lexington. The signal company is commanded by Capt. Ronald F. Garland of Holbrook.

At the court hearing on Thursday, Atty. Sherman contended that the men had not received their prescribed training for overseas duty.

He also alleged the Army had knowingly made "false entries in official records to reflect that the men did in fact receive the required training."

Sherman said the men were required to turn in forms stating they had received the training before they could get passes for home leave.

The 16 members of the unit named as plaintiffs in the suit, all from the Boston area, are:

John P. McAbee, Peter J. Bertolami, Donald Branneby, Robert M. Bruce, Robert O. Delaney, and his brother, William E.; Thomas O. Fata, William F. Freedman, Michael Gallahue, David P. Hickey, John Iaconelli, Andrew Mavinos, Francis J. Magri, John F. McKennedy, John F. Robinson and Donald A. Souliers.

513th Starts for Viet Today

October 15, 1968

By MILTON R. BENJAMIN
Herald Traveler, Washington Bureau Chief

WASHINGTON Army Secretary Stanley R. Resor yesterday flatly rejected charges by 92 Greater Boston reservists that they had not been adequately trained. The Pentagon said the unit was "fully qualified" for duty in Vietnam and would begin shipping out today.

Atty. Peter Sherman, counsel for the 92 members of the 513th Maintenance Battalion, planned to make a last-ditch legal effort this morning to block their deployment. He was scheduled to appear at 10 a.m. before Judge Simon E. Sobeloff in the U.S. Circuit Court of Appeals in Baltimore. Chief Judge Rozel Thomsen of the U.S. District Court in Maryland yesterday dismissed

Sherman's motion for a preliminary injunction which would have blocked the Army from sending the men to the war zone pending a full hearing. Thomsen ruled he did not have jurisdiction to intervene.

About 30 members of the 51-man unit were scheduled to ship out from Andrews Air Force Base, Maryland, today. The remainder of the 513th was scheduled to leave for Vietnam at 7:30 o'clock Wednesday morning. An advance party of 10 men from the unit left for Vietnam Oct. 3.

The 513th includes 150 reservists who trained at the Boston Army Base until they were activated May 13. They have been stationed at Fort Meade, Md., since May 20.

RESOR, in a letter to Sen. Edward M. Kennedy, said yesterday that a "careful and intensive review" had been made of the three principal charges brought by the men. The reservists had claimed that:

— They had not been trained in the job they were assigned to perform.

— They had not been trained in such required areas as rapid fire of the M-16 rifle.

— Unit training records had been falsified to indicate they had been fully trained.

Resor said the investigation carried out last week showed that "with two exceptions, every member of the unit who was scheduled for deployment was clearly qualified (in his assigned job) to the standards established by Army regulations." He said the other two were judged "adequately" qualified.

The Army secretary said that as far as training in such areas as use of the M 16 was concerned, "additional training sessions have been conducted for the past few days."

"THESE WILL BE completed prior to deployment and the result will be that each unit member who stated that he had not received adequate training will have received the necessary instruction."

Resor said that on the third allegation, "falsification of records" the deputy commander at Fort Meade had been assigned "to fully explore these charges."

"However," in view of the steps taken to ascertain the status of individual training and to provide any additional
training required, I see no reason why plans concerning deployment of the unit should be affected by the investigation," Resor said.

"I have been personally assured by officials at Fort Meade, including the battalion commander himself, that the battalion is adequately trained and fully qualified to perform its mission.

"THE COMMANDING general First Army, and the commanding general, Continental Army Command, have concluded that this unit is qualified for its mission and should be deployed as presently scheduled. I agree," Resor said.

Sherman, commenting on the Army's action, said he was "surprised at the casual and somewhat secretive approach to nearly 100 sworn affidavits making rather serious charges."

"My clients are not hippies or radicals or ardent war protestors," Sherman said. "They were not challenging the legality of the war or the call up; they feel that if they must go they ought to be prepared to defend themselves and to perform their mission."

Sherman said the Army appeared "more concerned about getting these men to Vietnam than getting to the bottom of their charges."

Regulars Ordered To Second Tour

October, 1968

WASHINGTON Second involuntary tours in Vietnam are coming up this year for about 18,000 soldiers and 6,000 Marines,

That's because the war has stretched out so long. The turnover of the usual one-year tour in Vietnam now reaches many who have been away from the war zone the planned two-year interval.

Up to now the number of non volunteers ordered a second time to Vietnam has amounted to a trickle. The exceptions have been those with skills in short supply, such as helicopter pilots.

The new turnabout will affect career servicemen for the most part, rather than draftees and one-term enlistees. Draftees serving two year hitches may not be returned to the war zone and it isn't practical to return those serving a normal three-year enlistment.

The Army plans to send back 4,950 officers mostly in the captain-major-lieutenant colonel bracket and 12,900 enlisted men, chiefly senior

non-commissioned officers, according to the Pentagon.

The Marines plan second tours for 1,000 officers and 5,000 enlisted men.

The Army and Marines provide the bulk of the 540,500 servicemen in Vietnam and the 50,000-a-month manpower turnover creates a problem of maintaining a flow of key officers and noncoms in Southeast Asia.

The Air Force is sending only about 150 noncommissioned officers back for second involuntary tours this year, those having been away longest going back first. A spokesman said the Air Force is now just reaching the point where it will be necessary to return some enlisted specialties for second tours.

The Navy said it does not expect to send any officers or enlisted men to Vietnam for second involuntary tours the rest of this year although last July about 230 Navy Seabees who had finished previous war tours earlier than 1966 were ordered back.

Top General Stepped In Salute Penalty Scrapped

Boston Globe 10/9/68
By MARTIN F. NOLAN
Globe Washington Bureau

WASHINGTON The commanding general of the 4th Infantry Division in Vietnam has stopped pusnishing non-saluters under his command by sending them to combat areas.

The Defense Department made the announcement here the day after Maj. Gen. Charles P. Stone defended his controversial policy.

Stone's order, promulgated a month ago, said that any G.I. cited for failure to salute would be transferred to combat areas in the Vietnamese countryside.

Stone issued the order to his 18,000 men Sept. 7th in the division daily bulletin, under the heading of "military courtesy." The order, which surprised many of the GIs, was revealed in the Boston Globe last Saturday.

The Pentagon announcement did not indicate whether Stone's shift in policy was his idea or that of his commander, Gen Creighton W. Abrams, head of U.S. military forces in Vietnam.

Abrams has reviewed the policy Monday in his Saigon headquarters while Stone was defending it at the 4th Division's base camp near Fleiku.

Stone, a 6-foot-5 general with a reputation for toughness, had said the order was necessary to maintain "responsiveness and alertness within the garrison."

Abrams, a cigar-chewing former tank commander with an equal reputation for toughness, apparently thought otherwise. An Army spokesman said in Washington Tuesday that the matter was considered "an internal problem" of Abrams' Saigon command.

Stone's about-face came in a routine publication in Tuesday's daily bulletin to the effect that Paragraph two of the Sept. 7th Division bulletin was hereby remanded.

One Pentagon source said there is no doubt that all the people involved will know what the new directive means. They're probably carrying a copy of the
original order in their wallets to show to their grandchildren"

Pentagon officials made clear that awarding combat assignments for non-saluting or other infractions was not standard Army policy.

"But that doesn't mean it hasn't happened before," one officer said.

One Pentagon official recalled another order of dubious technical legality a unit commander in Vietnam who offered a case of beer to the first man who shot a Viet Cong. The original saluting order said: "effective immediately, any person stationed in base camp who is cited for failure to salute will be immediately transferred to the forward area."

Stone went further and extended the order to the two-thirds of his men stationed outside the division's base camp near Pleiku: "an individual already stationed in a forward area, such as a brigade trains area, who is cited for failure to salute will be sent further forward. Unit commanders will indicate actions taken to comply with this directive."

A brigade trains area is a supply depot for infantry patrols scouting the Vietnamese jungle. "Further forward" would have meant that a miscreant G.I. would be taken from a Quarter-master unit and placed in a rifle patrol.

Since two-thirds of the men in these forward areas are outside the base camp, the division order applied to all 1,000 of Stone's men.

Normal military policy for failure to salute, even in a combat zone, usually means restricting a man to his barracks or some similar small penalty.

The Universal Code of Military Justice says nothing about such a policy as Stone ordered, although there was nothing illegal about the general's action.

Ted Pleads for Boston Reservists

October, 1968

By MILTON R. BENJAMIN
Herald Traveler Washington Bureau Chief. Copyright 1968 Boston Herald Traveler Corp.

WASHINGTON Sen. Edward M. Kennedy yesterday asked the Army to postpone temporarily shipment of the 513th Maintenance Battalion to Vietnam pending a "full investigation" after 67 more Greater Boston reservists charged they had not received all their mandatory training.

A pentagon spokesman informed the Herald Traveler shortly before Kennedy's action that the Army had investigated "as far as they're going to and as far as they are concerned, it's a closed case." The men are scheduled to be shipped out to Vietnam Saturday.

Kennedy, in a letter to Army Secretary Stanley R. Resor, asked him to "conduct a full and prompt investigation" of the reservists' claim the haven't been adequately trained and to "keep this unit available until an appropriate inquiry is satisfactorily completed.

"I don't question, nor do these men question, their obligation as reservists on active, duty," Kennedy said "They only question their preparedness to fulfill their reserve obligation."

An additional 67 members of the unit, who had been home in the Boston area on leave, signed affidavits yesterday on their return to Ft. Meade, Md., backing their 16 fellow reservists who filed suit last Thursday charging they had not received all their mandatory training.

A total of 83 of the 150 Greater Boston reservists in the 251-man unit have signed affidavits contending they are inadequately trained. More are expected to submit affidavits today.

Lt. Col. Eugene Martinez of Winthrop, commander of the battalion, said earlier that the 16 men who brought the suit didn't reflect the attitude of the unit and that the other men were "upset by what they've done."

In the suit filed in U.S. District Court in Baltimore, the men charged that Army records had been falsified to reflect training they claim they did not receive.

THEY ALSO charged that the Army wouldn't let them go home on leave before shipping out until they had turned in forms which states they had received all their mandatory training.

Kennedy, in his letter to Resor, said that "without regard to the legal issues involved it seems to me imperative in the public interest that the facts be ascertained.

"Therefore, I urge you to conduct a full and prompt investigation of these claims and to keep the unit available until an appropriate inquiry is satisfactorily completed," Kennedy said.

Rep. F. Bradford Morse asked Defense Secretary Clark M. Clifford Friday to conduct a "full investigation" of the charges.

The Army, without questioning any of the reservists who filed the suit, stated yesterday that "the charges are unfounded.

259

"The unit passed the Army training test Aug. 15 and 16 and received a satisfactory rating," a Pentagon spokesman said. "We have checked and as far as the Army is concerned, there is no foundation that there were irregularities in the training records. They (the men) have completed all required training. That's the end of it. Period."

AN ARMY spokesman said the investigation had been carried out over the weekend by officials at Ft. Meade, where the Boston Army Base reserve unit has been stationed since it was activated in May, and by officials of the First Army.

Kennedy, in his letter to Resor, noted that a member of his staff and the attorney for the men, Peter Sherman, had met with representatives of the Inspector General's office and the Army's office of Legislative liaison last Wednesday to discuss the allegations.

"In spite of assurances that there would be a full investigation, I am informed that two members of the advance party were among those involved and that they were deployed on schedule Oct. 3 without their contentions having been resolved," Kennedy said.

"I am further advised that two other members of the unit were packed and prepared to be substituted for these two had the court so ordered but that the two who claimed they had not been trained were sent away," Kennedy said.

Judge Roszel C. Thomsen chief federal judge in Maryland, turned down Sherman's request for a temporary restraining order last Thursday and the Army shipped out two of the 16 plaintiffs as part of an advance party two hours later.

THOMSEN, in rejecting Sherman's motion, ruled that they lacked jurisdiction in the case. Assistant U.S. Atty. Stephen D. Shawe filed papers in U.S. District Court yesterday asking Thomsen also to dismiss Sherman's request for a preliminary injunction barring the Army from shipping the rest of the unit to Vietnam Saturday.

Sherman said he would file his response Wednesday morning. A ruling probably will be handed down later in the day Wednesday.

The Supreme Court yesterday cancelled the reprieve from Vietnam service which Justice William O. Douglas had granted in recent weeks to men in five other reserve units.

The men in those five units had challenged the constitutionality of the reserve call up. The reservists in the 513th have not questioned this.

Shawe noted the distinction last Thursday when he said it was his understanding the plaintiffs in this case "are not contesting the validity of the reserve call up or the validity of any orders to ship any of them anywhere the army wants to ship them.

"WHAT THEY WANT to do is prevent the Army from sending them to Vietnam unless and until they are properly trained," Shawe said. Herald Traveler October, 1968

Sgt. John P. McAbee, one of the two shipped out in the advance party, said in sworn testimony, revealed yesterday that his specialty had been changed since his activation in May from Nike launcher control missile repairman to computer repairman, then to gas turbine generator repairman, and on Aug. 20 to

260

senior shoe repairman.

McAbee said he had "received no training in any of these specialties and therefore (AM) not capable of performing them." He said his sole duty since the reserve call up has been "in a clerical capacity."

Other members of the unit charged in their affidavits that they hadn't been trained in their military specialties, use of the M16 rifle, escape, survival, biological warfare and other mandatory areas. In the latest affidavits signed yesterday, Joseph M. Balfe attested that when it came time for training in rapid fire of the M16, "I was told by the company commander to stay in and do some more typing and that he would see that my records were taken care of."

Other reservists supported in their affidavits charges made earlier that officers had ordered clerks to falsify records to indicate that more men had attended mandatory classes than were actually present.

Reservists who submitted affidavits yesterday in support of the original 16 were;

Thomas A. Walsh, Kenneth F. Hanick, Paul M. Scola, Paul G. Uizzardi, Paul R. Cabral Sr., Edward J. Berlo, John E. White, Joseph M. Balfe, George H. Scholderer, James R. MacQuarrie, Edwin A. Scanion, Richard F. Bohane, Robert E. O'Hare, Bruce D. Williams. Also Arthur Dondero, Robert E. Reagan, Jr., James J. Manning, Anthony Albano, Richard K. Mims, Saul Needle, Robert J. Denekamp, Robert W. Burke, Roy C. Nash, Henry G. Clausen, James B. Mitchell, Robert M. Flaherty, Michael J. Livinston, Francis J. Voss Jr., Edward F. Hunt.

Also Henry F. Kelley, Joseph D. MacQuarrie, Michael J. Taplin, John S. Buckley, James A. Fontaine, Williams B. Wilder, Paul M. Bridges, Paul J. Monbouquette, Lawrence M. Mayion, Vincent J. Cosgrove Jr., Francis G.

O'Brien, George W. Turchinetz, Daniel B. Willis.

Also Kenneth C. Ravioli, Daniel J. August, James R., Lally, Leo F. Egan Jr., Robert H. Rapport, Kevin M. Sullivan, David M. Freedman, Thomas P. Ford Jr., Albert Toy, Glen E. Murphy, Ira M. Zigeleaum, Robert N. Strickland.

Also Lawrence Goldberg, Bradford E. Ferguson, Herbert W. Moiler, Charles E. Pazwad, Ralph J. Masciulli, Robert E. Campbell, Martin D. Cohen, John Walsh, Mortimer McGrath, David Howe Wood, Roger J. Toth, Frederick S. Prifty.

BOSTON HEARLD TRAVELER, TUESDAY, OCT. 15, 1968
'We're a Mess' Viet Bound Reservist
(Herald Traveler Washington Bureau)

WASHINGTON

"On paper we look fine," Pfc. William Freedman, of 6 West Terr. Salem, said as he sat slumped in his chair. "But in reality we're a mess."

Freedman, Pfc. Peter J. Bertolami, of 132 Wildwood Ave. Arlington, and Pfc. Ralph Masciulli, of 41 Sewall Street, Somerville, are members of the 513th Maintenance Division.

They will be leaving for Vietnam in 24 hours. Last night, they sat in a room and talked.

"We're a little bitter," Bertolami said. "We are disappointed the Army didn't take into account our claims."

THE THREE MEN, and 89 others from the Boston area, charged they hadn't been trained in the jobs they must do in Vietnam.

Masciulli, a Northeastern graduate, who was teaching at a technical school when his unit was called up to duty in May, is classified as field artillery repairman.

"I've never repaired a howitzer," he said. "I didn't even repair one in training. I haven't even seen a field artillery piece since August, I'm simply not qualified.

"If we've never operated or repaired something, I don't see how the Army thinks we can repair it under combat conditions."

BERTOLAMI, a Boston College graduate, was working for a publishing company five months ago. Now he's a requisition specialist.

"I've been doing nothing but detail work," Bertolami said. "I don't feel qualified in my job. I feel if we are going over there we should be qualified."

Freedman, an alumnus of Merrimack College, said that when Army investigators talked to him about his training, they told him:

"We're not concerned with the quality of your training. We just want to know if you attended the classes. That's all. You're not paid to think. You're paid $190 a month. We're paid $600 a month. We'll do the thinking. You just do your little job and shut up."

"I was a little disappointed in the outcome of the investigation," Bertolami said. "All three made a point of stating that they would be willing to go to Vietnam if they were properly trained.

"Naturally, I'm scared," Freeman said. "I'd feel much safer if we'd proven ourselves in the States."

The reservists 150 of the 250-man unit said several of the regulars in the outfit had told them they would rather not be going to Vietnam with the 513th.

"They feel we're not trained and they'd like to go with a regular Army unit which is trained," one said. "Frankly, I can't blame them."

'WE Want Training So We Won't Be SlaughterED'

2 Reservists Detail Army 'Negligence'
PETER WERWATH

BEVERLY "We want to be properly trained so we won't be slaughtered when we go over there."

That was one of the comments yesterday by Pfc. William J. Freedman, one of 16 men of Ft. Meade's 513th Maintenance Battalion who filed suit Thursday in an attempt to bar the Army from sending their unit to Vietnam text Saturday.

Freedman and nearly 100 other men of the one company, 215-man Reserve battalion that was called up in May, are home on leave this weekend.

A large group was on leave when the legal action was taken, and Freedman expects sizeable support from them when they return.

Pfc. James W. McLaughlin of Plymouth said the Army's negligence is "tantamount to premeditated murder."

He said the petitioners are supported by all the men in the unit. Some are afraid to speak out because they have jobs and wives and children waiting for them when they get home. They are afraid of reprisals for bucking the establishment.

"But when this comes to a head next week I think they'll be with us to a man."

McLaughlin has taken no part in the suit because he has filed papers as a conscientious objector and has been placed on administrative hold.

He said he is an "objective observer since I'm not caught up in the emotions of the thing I'm probably not going to Vietnam."

Both men claim they received inadequate or no training in the areas of survival chemical warfare, physical proficiency, and M-16 rifle training.

Freedman said many of the men were given occupational "slots" they were not trained for.

"Sixty of the kids were supposed to be retrained, and either this was not done or they were trained for positions other than those they were previously trained for.

"The material readiness and group status reports were falsified. They always said we were the best trained unit in the Army and we were ready to go anytime.

"IN FACT, after we arrived at Ft. Meade in Maryland, 40 per cent of the men were declared excess and transferred to other units, because their MOS (Military Occupational Specialty) slots didn't fit in."

Freedman said that when affidavits of the 16 petitioners were made public Wednesday Pfc. William Delaney and Sgt. John P. McAbee were immediately sent to their commanding officer, Col. Eugene Martinez.

"It came as a complete surprise to him," said McLaughlin. "He gave them a lecture on patriotism, threatened them with court marshall, refused them counsel, and then restricted them to the company area."

263

McAbee and Delaney were scheduled to arrive in Vietnam this morning. They tried in vain to get a restraining order from a U.S. District Court judge.

"McABEE was taken away Thursday for what they said was intensified training," said Freedman. "He was supposed to receive training for things he had missed. He was supposed to have had 48 hours of training inside of four hours and he didn't even receive half of it."

"Now he's classified as a shoe repairman and works as a training NCO. There's no such MOS."

A few reservists began to seek support from Rep. John McCormack and Sens. Edward Kennedy. In response to queries from the legislators, Col. Raymond Reid, Army liason officer for Congress, answered by quoting the material readiness and group status reports, which McLaughlin says "presented a picture that is untrue. "They were told that the morale was very high. In fact, morale has always been low. Few of the men were ever happy or accommodated," McLaughlin said.

Freedman and McLaughlin stated the reports said the group had the required number of vehicles. They claim it had far less.

They claim that M-16 training was a farce, since the scorers recorded the minimum requirements even if a man failed.

They claim only 40 men were present at a physical proficiency test, while the whole company of 251 men was supposed to be present.

They also claim that only 88 men were present at the required gas chamber test, and that the training NCO filled out fake test cards for those who didn't attend.

FREEMAN said the unit never performed an Army mission:

"They never gave us any vehicles to repair, for instance, to see if we were competent."

The two men said Sen. Kennedy's office is "very interested" in their plight. Freedman cited McAbee as an example of the MOS snafu.

"He was given the MOS of Nike missile launcher repairman since he was trained in school for that. Because we didn't have any NIKES, his MOS was changed to gas turbine generator repairman. He doesn't even know what one looks like.

GIs List Gripes About Readiness

Boston Globe, October, 1968

FORT MEADE, MD. PFC Martin V. Cohen of Revere, Mass., the United States Army and this vast military post have become a private nightmare.

Last May, Cohen, 26, married and the father of a baby son, was finishing his second year at Suffolk Law School when his Reserve unit, the 513th Maintenance Battalion, was activated for Vietnam duty. With 19 officers and 231 other enlisted men from Boston, he was shipped here to learn the duties that a combat support unit must provide for front-line troops.

Since that time, Cohen's company has had 10 different first sergeants, 100 replacements for "excess" personnel, one attempted suicide, one near mental breakdown, and almost no professional training.

Last week, Martin Cohen and 15 other enlisted men filed suit to prevent authorities from having them sent to Vietnam this Saturday.

"The whole thing has been falsified from the start," Cohen said Tuesday of their training. "The Army said it called us up because we were a good support unit. But the equipment records and the training records are false, our ability is false. We haven't even passed one inspection."

COPIED RECORDS

Cohen and his original group have produced records to this effect Army records they copied and signed, notarized affidavits. They have since been joined in their suit by 87 other men of the 513th and caused Sen. Edward Kennedy (D-Mass.) to demand a full investigation by the Army.

Their attorney, Peter Sherman of Washington, will appear in U.S. Court in Baltimore today to try to prevent dismissal of the suit by the government.

Last Thursday, Sherman said good-bye to two men of the 513th "advance party" who were shipped to Vietnam before he could get a restraining order. One of these was Robert G. Delaney, of 53 Custer st., Jamaica Plain, whose brother Bill has remained here under an Army regulation that prohibits more than one man in a family from going to Vietnam.

"Lt. Col. Martinez asked me why I cared now," Billy said. "It's not just my brother. We hope we can change the system."

Sp-4 Roy C. Nash, 26, of 32 Coolidge rd., Medford, is a Cornell graduate with a master's degree in accounting from Columbia University. He is considered a "reports clerk" with the 513th but he says he "has never typed an official report" in nearly five months.

"One officer admitted to me it would take us nine months after we got to Vietnam before we could perform our support mission," Nash said.

COLONEL'S VIEW

Frank Voss Jr., 25, of (44 Powder House Rd. extension Medford,) a Boston College engineering graduate serving as a mechanic chimed in "Lt. Col. Martinez admitted we had never been given a mission since we were activated."

Lt. Col. Martinez, who says the unit can "fix anything from typewriters to computers," told his company Tuesday, "I know you're not qualified in our military specialty (MOS) I know you have not received some "training but you will get it in Vietnam."

The men of the 513th, who say Martinez has called them "yellow rabble rousers," claim they have not even had training in first aid or use of the M-16 rifle.

"In some cases our work will be the difference between life and death for the men we support," said Sp-4 Mick Taplin, 21, of 39 Floral St., Newton Highlands, who is trained as a postal clerk.

Delaney added, "We can't function as a support unit because we're not trained to do any job."

Tuesday, they had a new company commander. Capt. Peter Roughan, whose name is pronounced, "Rowan," and the battalion is now known as "Roughan and Martinez' Laugh-In."

US Court to Rule On Reservist Plea

By BERTRAM G. WATERS
Globe Staff Reporter

BALTIMORE A Federal judge said today he would rule Monday on whether to hold hearings in the case of 92 Army reservists who seek a stay of shipment to Vietnam until they are fully trained.

Judge Rozell C. Thomsen said he would need time to study dozens of relevant Army regulations before deciding on the government's motion to dismiss a law suit brought by the 513th Maintenance Battalion men at nearby Fort Meade. This is largely a Boston-based group and all the complainants in the suit are from Greater Boston.

However, it was admitted by the Government attorney the Army will not move the men to Vietnam before next Wednesday and may delay even longer regardless of the judge's decision Monday.

The original shipment date was set for Oct. 12, Columbus Day.

During today's court session government attorneys introduced an affidavit from 1st Army-Maj. Gen. William Fondren which stated his intention to keep the 513th at Fort Meade until all training required by regulation is complete.

Such a promise would satisfy most of the men's complaints, and probably prevent a lengthy trial, according to their attorney. Peter R. Sherman of Washington.

Affidavits signed by the 92 men state they have not received training in everything from first aid to their military job specialties, and that records purporting to show that their training is complete are false.

Asst. U.S. Atty. Steven Shawe introduced evidence today that showed all but one of the 17 original plaintiffs had been interviewed in August and September by the Army and signed statements to the effect their training was complete. Some men since have claimed they were forced to sign such statements or be denied a final home leave before shipment to Vietnam.

A full-scale Army investigation into the matter was launched last week at the request of Sen. Edward M. Kennedy (D-Mass.). A final report on the investigation has been promised for next week.

Court Ruling Sends Reserves to Viet

AP October, 1968

WASHINGTON The Supreme Court yesterday turned down a challenge to President Johnson's mobilization of reservists and freed the Army to send 256 soldiers to Vietnam.

Eight justices joined in the action and gave not one word of explanation for their ruling.

The ninth, Justice William O. Douglas, dissented and said the Army had not lived up to its promise to the reservists. The Army, acting swiftly after learning of the court's ruling, announced immediately that five of the protesting units would be sent to Vietnam according to plan. 110 members of the 1002nd Composite unit of New York City, at Fort Lee, Va.; 80 members of the 1018th Composite Service Co. of Schenectady. N.Y., at Fort Lee; 43 members of the 74th Field Hospital from New York and New Jersey, at Fort Lee, and seven members of the 173rd Quartermaster Co. of Greenwood, Miss., also at Fort Lee.

"In light of the Supreme Court action vacating Justice Douglas' stays of movement in the cases involving certain mobilized reserve component units, the Department of the Army will begin deployment of these units according to plan," the announcement said.

Douglas, who had temporarily blocked the Army from sending the men to Vietnam, said the issue was not the power of Congress "but how legislation should be heard, in order, if possible, to avoid creating a 'credibility gap' between the people and their 'government.'"

The reservists lodged two major claims;

1. That in being called up for 24 months as units they were not given credit for active duty time some already had served as individuals and,

2. That they could be called up only in time of war or of national emergency declared by Congress.

Their appeals presented the first challenges to the 1966 law which authorized Johnson to mobilize the ready reserve for Vietnam action.

Until the law was enacted reserve units could be called to active duty only in time of war or of national emergency.

DOUGLAS had ordered the Army, in some instances at the last minute, not to send the men to Vietnam until the court could consider their pleas. The justices did so at a private conference following this opening day.

The Mississippi unit includes Pfc. Joe Don Looney, former University of Oklahoma backfield star who played professional football with the Baltimore Colts, Detroit Lions, Washington Redskins, and the New York Giants.

267

Endnotes

[1] Cpt. Leo R. Cass, Annual Historical Supplement of the Headquarters and Main Support Co., 513th Maint. Battalion, 17 Oct.1968—3 Oct.1969.

[2] Christian G. Appy, *Working Class War*; American Combat Soldiers and Vietnam (Chapel Hill; University of North Carolina Press, 1993), pp. 52—53.

[3] Christian G. Appy, *Working Class War*; American Combat Soldiers and Vietnam (Chapel Hill; University of North Carolina Press, 1993), p. 18.

[4] Appy, pp 24—27 and James William Gibson, *The Perfect War; Technowar in Vietnam* (Boston; Atlantic Monthly Press 1986), pp. 214—215.

[5] James Fallows, "*What Did You Do in the War Daddy?*" Vietnam Anthology and Guide to a television History, Stephen Cohen, ed. (New York; Alfred A Knopf, 1983), p. 384.

[6] Appy, p. 26. The rate of black deaths in Vietnam in 1965 was double their army participation rate, but this was brought down to normal proportions within three years because of the black soldier's struggle against racism.

[7] Lyndon B. Johnson, *The Vantage Point: Perspectives of the Presidency, 1963—1969* (New York, Chicago and San Francisco: Holt Rinehart and Winston, 1971), pp. 146—147.

[8] Ibid., p. 149.

[9] *Public Papers of the President of the United States. Lyndon B. Johnson, Containing the Public Messages, Speeches and Statements of the President, 1965, II* (Washington: GPO, 1966), p. 795.

[10] Lawrence S. Baskir and William A. Strauss, *Chance and Circumstance: The Draft and the War and the Vietnam Generation* (New York: Alfred A. Knopf, 1978), p. 50.

[11] Col. Donald C. Odegard, *Non-Mobilization and Mobilization in the Vietnam War,* (Draft Report of the Study Group)10 January 1980, (Carlisle Barracks, Penn.; Strategic Studies Institute, US Army War College), p. 44.

[12] General C. Westmoreland, *A Soldier Reports,* (Garden City, NY; Double

Day Co., Inc., 1976), pp. 193, 354.

[13] Robert McNamara, *In Retrospect*, (Random House, Inc., New York 1995). p.32.

[14] Cpt Leo R. Cass, *Annual Historical Supplement of the Headquarters and Main Support Co., 513th Maint. Battalion*, 17 Oct.1968—3 Oct.1969, p. 5

[15] Cpt Leo R. Cass, *Annual Historical Supplement of the Headquarters and Main Support Co., 513th Maint. Battalion*, 17 Oct. 1968—3 Oct. 1969, p. 3.

[16] Christian G. Appy, *Working Class War*; American Combat Soldiers and Vietnam (Chapel Hill; University of North Carolina Press, 1993), pp. 25—26

[17] Cincinnatus, *Self-Destruction, The Disintegration and Decay of the United States Armed Forces During the Vietnam Era*, (New York: W.W. Norton, 1981) p. 155.

[18] Cincinnatus, p. 145.

[19] Cincinnatus, pp. 147—148.

[20] Cincinnatus, pp. 157—159.

[21] Gibson, p. 116.

[22] Cpt. Leo R. Cass, *Annual Historical Supplement of the Headquarters and Main Support Co., 513th Maint. Battalion*, 17 Oct.1968—3 Oct.1969. p. 11.

[23] Cincinnatus, *Self-Destruction, The Disintegration and Decay of the United States Armed Forces During the Vietnam Era*, (New York: W. W. Norton, 1981), pp. 54—56.

[24] Cincinnatus, p. 55.

[25] Cincinnatus, p. 53.

[26] Leon Trotsky, *History of the Russian Revolution.*

[27] Appy, pp. 244—245.

[28] Cincinnatus, p. 156 and Richard Moser, *The New Winter Soldiers: GI and Veteran Dissent During the Vietnam Era Perspectives in the Sixties*, (New Brunswick: Rutgers, 1996), p. 44.

[29] Matthew Rinaldi, *"The Olive Drab Rebels: Military Organization During the Vietnam Era,"* Radical America, Vol. 8, No. 3.

[30] Gabriel and Savage, quoted in Appy, p.254.

[31] The Bond, September 22, 1969.

[32] Cortright, pp. 35 — 36.

[33] Cortright, p. 36 and Heini, p. 329.

[34] Moser, p. 47 and Cortright, pp. 37 — 38, 133.

[35] Rees, p. 152 and Cortright, pp. 37 — 38.

[36] Tom Wells, *The War Within: America's Battle over Vietnam,* (New York: Henry Hol,

1994), p. 474.

[37] Moser, p. 133 and Cortright, p. 35.

[38] Wells, p. 475.

[39] Leon Trotsky, *History of the Russian Revolution.*

[40] Colonel Robert D. Heini, Jr., "The Collapse of the Armed Forces," *Armed Forces Journal*, June 7, 1971, reprinted in Marvin Gettleman, et al., *Vietnam and America: A Documented History* (New York: Grove Press, 1955), p. 327.

[41] Eugene Linden, "Fragging and Other Withdrawal Symptoms," *Saturday Review*, January 8, 1972, p. 12.

[42] Cincinnatus, pp 51 — 52.

[43] Appy, p. 246 and Richard Moser, *The New Winter Soldiers: GI and Veteran Dissent During the Vietnam Era (Perspectives in the Sixties)* (New Brunswick: Rutgers, 1996), p. 44.

[44] Heini, p. 328.

[45] Terry Anderson, "The GI Movement and the Response from the Brass," in Melvin Small and William Hoover, eds., *Give Peace a Chance (Syracuse: Syracuse University, 1992)*, p. 105.

[46] Andy Stapp, *Up Against the Brass* (New York: Simon and Schuster, 1970),

p. 182 and Heini, pp. 328—329 and Appy, pp. 230—231.

[47] Vietnam GI, June 1969.

[48] Linden, p. 14.

[49] Wells, p. 474.

[50] Linden, pp. 12—13.

[51] David Cortright, *Soldiers in Revolt: The American Military Today* (Garden City, New York: Doubleday, 1975), p. 44 and Moser, p. 50.

[52] Cortright, p. 47 and Moser, p. 50.

[53] Quoted in Heini, p. 328.

[54] Linden, p. 15.

[55] Appy, p. 283

[56] James T. Currie and Richard B. Grossland; *Twice the Citizen,* U. S. Government Printing Office, Supt. of Documents Wash. DC 20402

[57] Sal Lopes. *The Wall* (New York: Collins Publishers, 1987) p. 95.

About the Author

Full Circle tells about an idealistic young man who leaves a small secure Italian neighborhood in the North End of Boston to serve a tour of duty in Vietnam.

Ralph Masciulli brings to life the anxiety in living one day at a time as he counts the days and wake-ups towards his final goal of going home. He relates the trauma going from an environment which as a young man everything was a big joke to a war environment where the smallest detail was important. In 1966 he joined a low priority Army Reserve Unit from Boston, the 513th Maintenance Battalion. Everyone wanted to join the 513th because it was a new unit and by the time it got up to speed the war would be over or so we thought.

Ralph attended St. Anthony's Grammar School and Christopher Columbus High School, both local parochial schools run by the Franciscans. After high school he graduated from Northeastern University where he received his BS, Masters Degree, and Certificate of Advanced Graduate Studies (CAGS). His career spanned thirty years in secondary and higher education, six years at MIT Lincoln Labs and three years at Wang Labs. He serves on the executive committee of the Institute of Electrical and Electronic Engineers (IEEE), Boston Chapter and is retired from The Benjamin Franklin Institute of Technology where he was a full professor and chairman of the Electronic and Computer Departments.

Ralph Masciulli is also the author of The Corner Boys, a collection of short stories about family, friends and traditions of Italians growing up in the North End of Boston.

Printed in the United States
by Baker & Taylor Publisher Services